The Least You Should Know About English

FORM B
Third Edition

The Least You Should Know About English

Basic Writing Skills

TERESA FERSTER GLAZIER

Western Illinois University

HOLT, RINEHART AND WINSTON

New York   Chicago   San Francisco   Philadelphia
Montreal   Toronto   London   Sydney
Tokyo   Mexico City   Rio de Janeiro   Madrid

This text is available in Form A, Form B, and Form C so that a different form may be used in various semesters. The three forms are essentially the same except that they have different exercises, writing assignments, and essays.

Library of Congress Cataloging in Publication Data

Glazier, Teresa Ferster.
    The least you should know about English.

    Includes index.
    1. English language—Rhetoric—Problems, exercises,
etc.   2. English language—Grammar—1950-   —Problems,
exercises, etc.   I. Title.
PE1413.G57   1986   808'.042   85–5440

ISBN 0-03-002607-5

CBS COLLEGE PUBLISHING
Holt, Rinehart and Winston
The Dryden Press
Saunders College Publishing

To the Instructor

This book is for students who need to review the rules of English composition and who may profit from a simplified approach. The main features of the book are these:

1. It's truly basic. Only the indisputable essentials of spelling, grammar, sentence structure, and punctuation are included because research has shown that putting too much emphasis on mechanics is not the way to help students learn to write.
2. It stresses writing. A writing section, EIGHT STEPS TO BETTER WRITING (pp. 200–38), provides writing assignments to be used along with the exercises. The section has been kept brief because students learn to write by *writing* rather than by reading pages and pages *about* writing. Even though the section is only 39 pages (compared to 198 for the first part of the text), students will undoubtedly spend more time on it than on all the rest of the book.
3. It uses little linguistic terminology. A conjunction is a connecting word; gerunds and present participles are *ing* words; a parenthetical constituent is an interrupter. Students work with words they know instead of learning a vocabulary they'll never use again.
4. It has abundant practice sentences and paragraphs—enough so that students learn to use the rules automatically and thus carry their new skills over into their writing.
5. It includes groups of thematically related, informative sentences on such topics as sled-dog racing, the College Football Hall of Fame, totem poles of the Northwest Coast Indians, the usefulness of spiders, Wisconsin's Rustic Roads Act, the litter on Mount Everest, controlling avalanches, Houdini's magic, the history of ice cream, underground cities, and the comeback of Mount Saint Helens . . . thus making the task of doing the exercises more interesting.
6. It provides perforated answer sheets at the back of the book so that the students can correct their own work, thus teaching themselves as they go.
7. It includes four essays to read and summarize. Students improve their reading by learning to spot main ideas and their writing by learning to write concise summaries.
8. It can be used as a self-tutoring text. Simple explanations, abundant exercises, and answers at the back of the book provide students with a writing lab in their own rooms.

9. It's an effective text for the "one-to-one conference" method of teaching because its simple, clear organization makes it easy for students to use on their own, thus keeping the conference hour free for discussing individual writing problems.

The instructor is provided with an enlarged packet of ditto master tests covering all parts of the text (four for each section). These tests are free upon adoption of the text and may be obtained through the local Holt representative or by writing to the English Editor, Holt, Rinehart and Winston, 383 Madison Avenue, New York, NY 10017.

Students who have previously been overwhelmed by the complexities of English should, through mastering simple rules and through writing and rewriting simple papers, gain enough competence to succeed in further composition courses.

TFG

Macomb, Illinois

Acknowledgments

To the reviewers of the previous editions of this text, as well as to the reviewers of this edition—Betty Pex of the College of San Mateo and Carol Croxton of the University of Southern Colorado—I am grateful for important suggestions. And once again I am indebted to Christopher Glazier, Kenneth Glazier, Jr., Gretchen Glazier Boyer, Teresa Edwards, and Liz Roth for writing some of the exercises and meticulously correcting my first drafts.

Contents

WHAT IS THE LEAST YOU SHOULD KNOW?

1. SPELLING

2. SENTENCE STRUCTURE

3. PUNCTUATION AND CAPITAL LETTERS

4. WRITING

What Is the Least You Should Know?

What **Is** the Least
You Should Know?

Most English textbooks try to teach you as much as they can. This one will teach you the least it can—and still help you learn to write acceptably. You won't have to bother with predicate nouns and subordinating conjunctions and participial phrases and demonstrative pronouns and all those terms you've been hearing about for years. You can get along without them if you'll learn thoroughly a few basic rules. You *do* have to know how to spell common words; you *do* have to recognize subjects and verbs to avoid writing fragments and run-together sentences; you *do* have to know a few rules of punctuation—but rules will be kept to a minimum.

Unless you know these few rules, though, you'll have difficulty communicating in writing. Take this sentence for example:

Let's eat grandfather before we go.

We assume the writer isn't a cannibal but merely failed to capitalize and put commas around the name of a person spoken to. If the sentence had read

Let's eat, Grandfather, before we go.

then no one would misunderstand. Or take this sentence:

The instructor flunked Mac and Chris and Ken passed.

Did Chris flunk or pass? There's no way of knowing unless the writer puts a comma either after *Mac* or after *Chris*. If the sentence reads

The instructor flunked Mac and Chris, and Ken passed.

we know Chris flunked, but if the sentence reads

The instructor flunked Mac, and Chris and Ken passed.

then we know Chris passed. Punctuation makes all the difference.

What you'll learn from this book is simply to make your writing so clear that no one will misunderstand it.

The English you'll learn to write is called standard English, and it may differ slightly from the English spoken in your community. All over the country, various dialects of English are spoken. In northern New England, for example, people leave the *r* off certain words and put an *r* on others. President Kennedy said *dollah* for *dollar*, *idear* for *idea*, and *Cubar* for *Cuba*. In black communities many people leave the *s* off some verbs and put an *s* on others, saying *he walk* and *they walks* instead of *he walks* and *they walk*.

But no matter what English dialect people *speak*, they all must *write* the same dialect—standard English. You can say, "Whacha doin? Cmon," and everybody will understand, but you can't *write* that way. If you want your readers to understand what you write, you'll have to write the way English-speaking people all over the world write—in standard English. Being able to write standard English is essential in college, and it probably will be an asset in your career.

It's important to master every rule as you come to it because many rules depend on the ones before. For example, unless you learn to pick out subjects and verbs, you'll have trouble with run-together sentences, with fragments, with subject-verb agreement, and with punctuation. The rules are brief and clear, and it won't be difficult to master all of them . . . *if you want to*. But you do have to want to!

Here's the way to master the least you should know:

1. Study the explanation of each rule carefully.
2. Do the first exercise (ten sentences). Then tear out the perforated answer sheet at the back of the book and correct your answers. If you miss even one answer, study the explanation again to find out why.
3. Do the second exercise and correct it. If you miss a single answer, go back once more and study the explanation. You must have missed something. Be tough on yourself. Don't just think, "Maybe I'll hit it right next time." Go back and master the rules, and *then* try the next exercise. It's important to correct each group of ten sentences before going on so that you'll discover your mistakes while you still have sentences to practice on.
4. You may be tempted to quit when you get several exercises perfect. Don't! Make yourself finish every exercise. It's not enough to *understand* a rule. You have to practice it. Just as understanding the strokes in swimming won't help unless you actually get into the pool and swim, so understanding a rule about writing isn't going to help unless you practice using it.
    If you're positive, however, after doing five exercises, that you've mastered the rules, take Exercise 6 as a test. If you miss even one answer, you must do all the rest of the exercises. But if you get

Exercise 6 perfect, then spend your time helping one of your friends. Teaching is one of the best ways of learning.

5. But rules and exercises are not the most important part of this book. The most important part begins on page 200—when you begin to write. The writing assignments, grouped together for convenience, are to be used along with the exercises.

Mastering these essentials will take time. Generally, college students are expected to spend two hours outside of class for each hour in class. You may need more. Undoubtedly, the more time you spend, the more your writing will improve.

Spelling

1   Spelling

Anyone can learn to spell. You can get rid of most of your spelling errors by the time you finish this book if you want to. It's just a matter of deciding you're going to do it. If you really intend to learn to spell, master the first seven parts of this section. They are

YOUR OWN LIST OF MISSPELLED WORDS
WORDS OFTEN CONFUSED
CONTRACTIONS
POSSESSIVES
WORDS THAT CAN BE BROKEN INTO PARTS
RULE FOR DOUBLING A FINAL CONSONANT
A LIST OF FREQUENTLY MISSPELLED WORDS

Master these seven parts, and you'll be a good speller.

YOUR OWN LIST OF MISSPELLED WORDS

On the inside back cover of this book write correctly all the misspelled words in the papers handed back to you. Review them until you're sure of them. That will take care of most of your errors.

WORDS OFTEN CONFUSED

By mastering the spelling of these often-confused words, you will take care of many of your spelling problems. Study the words carefully, with their examples, before you try the exercises.

a, an	Use *an* before a word that begins with a vowel sound (*a, e, i,* and *o,* plus *u* when it sounds like *uh*).

Use *an* before a word that begins with a vowel sound (*a, e, i,* and *o,* plus *u* when it sounds like *uh*).
    an apple, an essay, an icicle
    an heir, an honest man (silent *h*)
    an uproar, an umpire (the *u*'s sound like *uh*)
Use *a* before a word that begins with a consonant sound (all the sounds except the vowels, plus *u* or *eu* when they sound like *you*).
    a pencil, a hotel, a history book
    a union, a uniform, a unit (the *u*'s sound like *you*)
    a European trip (*Eu* sounds like *you*)

accept, except

Accept is a verb and means "to receive willingly." (See p. 55 for an explanation of verbs.)
    I *accept* your gift. (receive it willingly)
Except means "excluding" or "but."
    Everyone came *except* him. (but him)

advice, advise

Advise is a verb (pronounce the *s* like *z*).
    I *advise* you to go.
Use *advice* when it's not a verb.
    I don't need any *advice*.

affect, effect

Affect is a verb and means "to influence."
    The lack of rain *affected* the crops.
Effect means "result." If *a, an,* or *the* is in front of the word, then you'll know it isn't a verb and will use *effect*.
    The lack of rain had a harmful *effect* on the crops.

all ready, already If you can leave out the *all* and the sentence still makes sense, then *all ready* is the form to use. (In that form, *all* is a separate word and could be left out.)

I'm *all ready* to go. (*I'm ready to go* makes sense.)

Dinner is *all ready*. (*Dinner is ready* makes sense.)

But if you can't leave out the *all* and still have the sentence make sense, then use *already* (the form in which the *al* has to stay in the word).

I'm *already* late. (*I'm ready late* doesn't make sense.) ·

are, or, our

Are is a verb.

We *are* studying English.

Or is used between two possibilities, as "tea *or* coffee."

Take it *or* leave it.

Our shows we possess something.

Our class meets at eight.

brake, break

Brake means "to slow or stop motion." It's also the name of the device that slows or stops motion.

You *brake* to avoid an accident.

You slam on your *brakes*.

Break means "to shattter" or "to split." It's also the name of an interruption, as "a coffee break."

You *break* a dish or an engagement or a record.

You enjoy your Thanksgiving *break*.

choose, chose

I will *choose* a partner right now.

I *chose* a partner yesterday.

clothes, cloths

Her *clothes* were attractive.

We used soft *cloths* to polish the car.

coarse, course

Coarse describes texture, as *coarse* cloth.

Her suit was made of *coarse* material.

Course is used for all other meanings.

Of *course* I enjoyed that *course*.

complement, compliment

The one spelled with an *e* comple̲tes something or brings it to perfection.

A 30° angle is the *complement* of a 60° angle.

His blue tie *complements* his gray suit.

The one spelled with an *i* has to do with praise. Remember "*I* like compliments," and you'll remember to use the *i* spelling when you mean praise.

She gave him a *compliment*.

He *complimented* her on her well-written paper.

conscience, conscious	*Conscious* means "aware."
	    I was not *conscious* that it was raining.
	The extra *n* in *conscience* should remind you of NO, which is what your conscience often says to you.
	    My *conscience* told me not to cut class.

desert, dessert	*Dessert* is the sweet one, the one you like two help-ings of. So give it two helpings of *s*.
	    We had apple pie for *dessert*.
	The other one, *desert*, is used for all other meanings.
	    Don't *desert* me.
	    The camel moved slowly across the *desert*.

do, due	You *do* something.
	    I *do* the best I can.
	But a payment or an assignment is *due*; it is scheduled for a certain time.
	    My paper is *due* tomorrow.

does, dose	*Does* is a verb.
	    He *does* his work well. She *doesn't* care about cars.
	A *dose* is an amount of medicine.
	    That was a bitter *dose* of medicine.

feel, fill	*Feel* describes your feelings.
	    I *feel* ill.
	    I *feel* happy about that A.
	Fill is what you do to a cup.
	    Will you *fill* my cup again?

forth, fourth	The number *fourth* has four in it. (But note that *forty* does not. Remember the word *forty-fourth*.)
	    This is our *fourth* game.
	    That was our *forty-fourth* point.
	If you don't mean a number, use *forth*.
	    She walked back and *forth*.

have, of	*Have* is a verb. When you say *could have*, the *have* may sound like *of*, but it must not be written that way. Always write *could have, would have, should have, might have*.
	    I should *have* finished my work sooner.
	    Then I could *have* gone home.
	Use *of* only in a prepositional phrase (see p. 61).
	    I often think *of* him.

hear, here	The last three letters of *hear* spell "ear." You *hear* with your ear.

I can't *hear* you.

The other spelling *here* tells "where." Note that the three words indicating a place or pointing out something all have *here* in them: *here, there, where.*

Where are you? I'm right *here.*

it's, its	

It's is a contraction and always means "it is" or "it has."

It's too late now. (It is too late now.)

It's been a long time. (It has been a long time.)

Its is a possessive pronoun. (Possessive pronouns such as *its, yours, hers, ours, theirs, whose* are already possessive and never take an apostrophe. See p. 31.)

The committee gave *its* report.

knew, new	

Knew has to do with knowledge (both start with *k*).
New means "not old."

I *knew* I wanted a *new* job.

know, no	

Know has to do with knowledge (both start with *k*).
No means "not any."

I *know* she has *no* money left.

EXERCISES

Underline the correct word. Don't guess! If you aren't sure, turn back to the explanatory pages. When you've finished ten sentences, tear out the perforated answer sheet at the back of the book and correct your answers. Correct each group of ten sentences before continuing so that you'll catch your mistakes while you still have sentences to practice on.

☐EXERCISE 1

1. (Are Our) (knew new) apartment is (all ready already) to move into.
2. (It's Its) location is (a an) asset because (it's its) near a small lake.
3. I like to walk back and (forth fourth) along the lake.
4. Of (coarse course) I (feel fill) that exercise is important.
5. I (know no) it has a good (affect effect) on my health.
6. I (hear here) the schools in the district are excellent.
7. That's (a an) important factor for (are our) family.

8. And we can (choose chose) between public transportation and driving (are our) own car.
9. We've become (conscience conscious) of the money we spend on gas.
10. I (do due) think we're making a good move. We should (have of) made it sooner.

☐EXERCISE 2

1. For our (forth fourth) anniversary last year we (choose chose) (a an) Ozarks tour.
2. But this year (are our) plans (are our) for a trip to the Mojave (Desert Dessert).
3. Of (coarse course) we're working out (a an) itinerary.
4. I (hear here) (it's its) (a an) interesting trip.
5. I (know no) we're (all ready already) looking forward to it.
6. (It's Its) important to have cool (clothes cloths) for such a trip, and I'm going to (choose chose) a few (knew new) ones.
7. My wife (choose chose) a blue suit that (complements compliments) her blue eyes.
8. Of (coarse course) I gave her a (complement compliment) on her choice.
9. We're going to (accept except) the (advice advise) of friends and get (a an) early start every day.
10. Then we'll take a (brake break) in the middle of each afternoon.

☐EXERCISE 3

1. I should (have of) registered for this (coarse course) earlier.
2. (It's Its) bound to have (a an) (affect effect) on my writing.
3. Most of the material is (knew new) to me.
4. (Are Our) instructor has given me some (advice advise) that I intend to (accept except).
5. I'm going to (do due) all the exercises and of (coarse course) write all the papers.
6. I (know no) (it's its) going to be work, but I (accept except) the challenge.
7. I (hear here) this (coarse course) is basic for all other composition (coarses courses).
8. I'm glad I (choose chose) to take this one first, (are or) I might (have of) had difficulties.
9. My (conscience conscious) tells me I'd better put (forth fourth) considerable effort.
10. I've (all ready already) received a (complement compliment) on one of my papers.

☐ EXERCISE 4

1. I'm taking (a an) elementary (coarse course) in astronomy and (all ready already) have learned a lot.
2. Until now, I never (knew new) whether a point of light was a star (are or) a planet.
3. Now I (know no) that planets (are our) seen only in the path followed by the sun and moon.
4. I should (have of) taken this (coarse course) earlier, for it (does dose) add to the pleasure of looking at the night sky.
5. (It's Its) good to be able to recognize the constellations.
6. I used to (know no) only the Big Dipper.
7. Of (coarse course) I'm (conscience conscious) I have more to learn.
8. But I (do due) (know no) now how to find Cassiopeia and the Pleiades.
9. I'm going to (accept except) the (advice advise) of my professor and spend (a an) hour every evening locating constellations.
10. I won't (choose chose) astronomy as a major, but this study is having (a an) (affect effect) on my knowledge of the universe.

☐ EXERCISE 5

1. I've just read (a an) article stating that at death the average American has spent a total of seven years watching television.
2. Most people are not (conscience conscious) of how much they watch.
3. They don't really (choose chose) to watch TV; they simply snap the set on without thinking because they (are our) uncomfortable without it.
4. Instead of a freely chosen diversion, television has become (a an) addiction requiring a nightly fix, and many people suffer withdrawal symptoms if the set must be sent out for repair.
5. The article has had (a an) amazing (affect effect) on my thinking.
6. Of (coarse course) I (all ready already) (knew new) I was spending too much time watching TV, but I didn't (know no) it would eventually add up to seven years of my life.
7. Seven years (does dose) seem like a lot of time to spend watching other people live, and I think (it's its) time to (brake break) my TV habit.
8. I should (accept except) the (advice advise) of my (conscience conscious) to snap the set off and (do due) my own living.
9. I could be seeing friends, pursuing a hobby, (are or) doing any number of other interesting things.
10. In the end, I don't want to have spent seven years of my life watching others live when I could (have of) been living myself.

Source: Jeffrey Schrank, *Snap, Crackle, and Popular Taste.* New York: Dell Publishing Co., 1977.

☐EXERCISE 6

1. I received (a an) invitation last week that I'd like to (accept except).
2. My grandparents invited me to their (knew new) cottage near Fort Lauderdale for the (forth fourth) week in June.
3. Of (coarse course) I'd like to go, but I've (all ready already) taken a summer job.
4. I wouldn't (brake break) my contract, and I (know no) I can't get a week off.
5. It (does dose) seem a shame to spend the whole summer (hear here).
6. I've just the right (clothes cloths) too although I didn't (choose chose) them with that in mind.
7. I won't ask anyone's (advice advise) because I'd never (desert dessert) my job.
8. Nothing could persuade me (are or) have any (affect effect) on my decision.
9. I could (have of) had a great time, but I (feel fill) that I must obey my (conscience conscious).
10. I (do due) hope I can go to Fort Lauderdale at Christmas because (it's its) a place I want to see.

☐EXERCISE 7

1. (A An) Arab oil embargo was the immediate cause of (are our) 55-mph speed limit law.
2. That law had (it's its) tenth birthday in 1984.
3. (It's Its) been a hard law to enforce, but the government estimates that (it's its) saved between 2,000 and 4,000 lives a year.
4. Another (affect effect) has been to decrease by 90,000 the number of accidents causing severe head injuries.
5. And paralyzing spinal-cord injuries (do due) to excessive speeds have decreased by 60 to 70 percent.
6. Of (coarse course) some people (are our) unwilling to (accept except) government interference.
7. They (feel fill) that what they (do due) is their own business, and they simply (brake break) the law.
8. They're not concerned about the (affect effect) on others.
9. Some states have (all ready already) tried to change the law but have had (know no) success.
10. Uncle Sam refuses to give highway funds to any state that (does dose) not enforce the law.

□EXERCISE 8

1. You can't (choose chose) what happens to you, but you can (choose chose) how you react.
2. I (know no) I didn't react as I should (have of) when I failed that math test.
3. I should simply (have of) given a (complement compliment) to my friend who passed.
4. My (conscience conscious) bothers me now as I look back.
5. Of (coarse course) I had put (forth fourth) great effort in that (coarse course).
6. Therefore it was hard to (accept except) failure.
7. The hardest problem on the test concerned the (complement compliment) of an angle.
8. I (know no) now how to (do due) the problem, but of (coarse course) (it's its) too late.
9. I (hear here), however, that the test won't have a great (affect effect) on (are our) grades.
10. I've (all ready already) decided to make (a an) exceptional effort to pass the next test.

□EXERCISE 9

1. I never (knew new) anything about Nobel prizes (accept except) their name.
2. But last week I read (a an) article about them.
3. Alfred Nobel, the Swedish inventor of dynamite, left a fund to provide prizes for persons that Swedish educational institutes (choose chose).
4. The prizes go to those who the judges (feel fill) have conferred the greatest benefit on humanity.
5. The prizes are given in the fields of physics, chemistry, physiology (are or) medicine, literature, and peace.
6. They were first awarded in 1901 and have been given annually ever since (accept except) during the two world wars.
7. In 1968 (a an) economics prize was added by the central bank of Sweden.
8. (It's Its) often been the custom to divide a prize among two (are or) three winners.
9. And of (coarse course) sometimes a winner refuses to (accept except) a prize, as when Hitler forbade Germans to (accept except) a prize because the peace prize had been given to one of his enemies.
10. A Nobel prize, which in 1984 amounted to a diploma, a gold medal, and $181,000, is the greatest (complement compliment) anyone could receive.

□EXERCISE 10

1. For my history paper, I've been reading (a an) article about Demosthenes, an Athenian statesman who has been called the greatest orator of all time.
2. As a boy, he was clumsy and (conscience conscious) of a speech impediment.
3. He (knew new) that people couldn't understand him and that they laughed at him.
4. But he had a strong will and (choose chose) to (do due) something about his problem.
5. He went (forth fourth) to the seashore where no one could (hear here) him and practiced speaking with pebbles in his mouth.
6. The (affect effect) was amazing; he began to speak more distinctly.
7. Then with his (knew new) voice he shouted until he could (hear here) himself above the roar of the waves.
8. Years later his forceful speeches giving (advice advise) to his countrymen to resist King Philip of Macedon were called "philippics," a term that came to be applied to any bitter and powerful oratory.
9. And even today (a an) especially bitter speech or tirade is called a "philippic."
10. (It's Its) amazing that such (a an) unpromising youngster could (have of) become such a great orator.

JOURNAL WRITING

The surest way to learn these Words Often Confused is to use them immediately in your own writing. Therefore begin to keep a journal, writing each day at least three sentences that make use of some words or rules you have learned that day. If you write about things that interest you, then you'll be inclined to reread your journal occasionally and thus review what you've learned. You might write about your changing ideas, your relationship to a friend, your opinion about something that has happened, your goals . . . .

WRITING ASSIGNMENT

The writing assignments, grouped together for convenience at the back of the book, are to be used along with the exercises. Turn to page 200 for your first writing assignment, or follow your instructor's directions concerning the assignments.

WORDS OFTEN CONFUSED (continued)

Here are more words often confused. Study them carefully, with their examples, before attempting the exercises. When you've mastered all 40 of the word groups in these two sections, you'll have taken care of many of your spelling problems.

lead, led

The past form of the verb is *led.*
   She *led* the parade yesterday.
If you don't mean past time, use *lead,* which rhymes with *bead.* (Don't confuse it with the metal *lead,* which rhymes with *dead.*)
   She will *lead* the parade today.

loose, lose

Loose means "not tight." Note how *l o o s e* that word is. It has plenty of room for two *o*'s.
   My shoestring is *loose.*
The other one, *lose,* has room for only one *o.*
   They are going to *lose* that game.

moral, morale

Moral has to do with right and wrong.
   It was a *moral* question.
Morale means "the spirit of a group or an individual." Pronounce these two words correctly, and you won't confuse them—*móral, morále.*
   The *morale* of the team was excellent.

passed, past

Passed is a verb.
   He *passed* the house.
Use *past* when it's not a verb.
   He walked *past* the house. (It's the same as *He walked by the house,* so you know it isn't a verb.)
   He's coasting on his *past* reputation.
   In the *past* he had always *passed* his exams.

peace, piece

Remember "piece of pie." The one meaning "a *piece* of something" always begins with *pie.*
   I gave him a *piece* of my mind.
The other one, *peace,* is the opposite of war.
   They signed the *peace* treaty.

personal, personnel

Pronounce these two correctly, and you won't confuse them—*pérsonal, personnél.*
   He had a *personal* interest in the election.
Personnel means "a group of workers."
   She was in charge of *personnel* at the factory.

principal, principle	*Principal* means "main." Both words have *a* in them: 　　　princip**a**l 　　　　m**a**in The *principal* of the school spoke. (main teacher) The *principal* problem is financial. (main problem) He lost both *principal* and interest. (main amount of money) A *principle* is a "rule." Both words end in *le*: 　　　princip**le** 　　　　ru**le** He lived by his *principles*. (rules) I object to the *principle* of the thing. (rule)
quiet, quite	Pronounce these two correctly, and you won't misspell them. *Quiet* rhymes with *diet*. 　　Be *quiet*. *Quite* rhymes with *bite*. 　　The book is *quite* interesting.
right, write	*Right* means "correct" or "proper." 　　I got ten answers *right*. *Write* is what you do with a pen. 　　I'm going to *write* my paper now.
than, then	*Than* compares two things. 　　I'd rather have this *than* that. 　　The movie was better *than* I had expected. *Then* tells when (*then* and *when* rhyme, and both have *e* in them). 　　*Then* he started home.
their, there, they're	*Their* is a possessive pronoun (see p. 31). 　　*Their* house is painted pink. *There* points out something. (Remember the three words indicating a place or pointing out something all have *here* in them: *here, there, where*.) 　　*There* is where I left it. 　　*There* were clouds in the sky. *They're* is a contraction and always means "they are." 　　*They're* happy now. (They are happy now.)
threw, through	*Threw* means "to throw something" in past time. 　　He *threw* the ball. I *threw* away my chance. If you don't mean "to throw something," use *through*. 　　I walked *through* the door. 　　She's *through* with her work.

to, too, two

Two is a number.
  I have *two* brothers.
Too means "more than enough" or "also."
  The lesson was *too* difficult and *too* long. (more than enough)
  I found it boring *too*. (also)
Use *to* for all other meanings.
  He likes *to* snorkel. He's going *to* the beach.

weather, whether

Weather refers to atmospheric conditions.
  This *weather* is too hot for me.
Whether means "if."
  I don't know *whether* I'll go.
  Whether I'll go depends on the *weather*.

were, where

Were is a verb.
  We *were* miles from home.
Where refers to a place. (Remember the three words indicating a place or pointing out something all have *here* in them: *here, there, where*.)
  Where is he? There he is.
  Where are you? Here I am.

who's, whose

Who's is a contraction and always means "who is" or "who has."
  Who's there? (Who is there?)
  Who's been eating my pizza? (Who has been . . . .)
Whose is a possessive pronoun. (Possessive pronouns such as *whose, its, yours, hers, ours, theirs* are already possessive and never take an apostrophe. See p. 31.)
  Whose book is this?

woman, women

Remember that the word is just *man* or *men* with *wo* in front of it.
  wo man . . . *woman* . . . one woman
  wo men . . . *women* . . . two women

you're, your

You're is a contraction and always means "you are."
  You're very welcome. (You are very welcome.)
Your is a possessive pronoun.
  Your toast is ready.

EXERCISES

Underline the correct word. When you've finished ten sentences, tear out the answer sheet at the back of the book and correct your answers. WATCH OUT! Don't do more than ten sentences at a time, or you won't be teaching yourself while you still have sentences to practice on.

☐EXERCISE 1

1. I (hear here) that you got (a an) unusually big promotion last week.
2. Of (coarse course) I'm sure you must (have of) earned it.
3. A promotion was (do due) for someone who (does dose) so much for the company.
4. The management was (quiet quite) (right write) to advance you.
5. I wonder (weather whether) you'll be happy in your (knew new) role.
6. Are you glad (you're your) changing departments, (are or) will you miss your old friends?
7. (Who's Whose) the (woman women) taking your old job?
8. I hope she's as good with the (personal personnel) as you were.
9. The (moral morale) of the department was good when you (lead led) the way.
10. I hope (their there) won't be (to too two) many changes from the way things were done in the (passed past).

☐EXERCISE 2

1. I was hiking along a road when a (peace piece) of (loose lose) gravel got into my shoe.
2. (It's Its) surprising what an (affect effect) one little pebble can have.
3. I got it out and (threw through) it away, but my foot still hurts (were where) the pebble was.
4. This is great (weather whether) for hiking, and I'm going again this afternoon (our or) tomorrow.
5. (You're Your) (right write) about exercise being essential.
6. I (passed past) my physical exam with (quiet quite) a good record.
7. My (principal principle) goal now is to (loose lose) about ten pounds.
8. (Than Then) I'll be just the (right write) weight for my height.
9. But (there they're) is always (to too two) much good food around (are our) house.
10. (It's Its) easier to exercise (than then) to diet.

□EXERCISE 3

1. Last summer I visited (a an) interesting (knew new) aquarium.
2. (It's Its) the Monterey Bay Aquarium in California, and (it's its) the largest indoor aquarium on the West Coast.
3. (A An) unusual aspect of it is (it's its) regional focus.
4. The exhibits of more (than then) 300 species of plants and animals show what's under the water along the central California coast.
5. Most spectacular is a giant kelp forest, which is like a magnificent cathedral when looked at (threw through) the glass walls.
6. If (you're your) a nondiver, you can now see for the first time what a forest of giant kelp is really like.
7. (It's Its) (quiet quite) (a an) amazing view (threw through) this tallest aquarium tank in the country.
8. Of (coarse course) I stroked a starfish in the hands-on tide pool and also looked (threw through) a free telescope at some pelicans.
9. (Than Then) I walked (passed past) the tank (were where) little sea otters were diving and playing.
10. I never (knew new) before that the annual food bill for one sea otter is $10,000.

□EXERCISE 4

1. In the (passed past) I thought I didn't like music, but now I (know no) I do.
2. I thought I had to do (too two) much practicing when I was young, but now I (choose chose) practicing over most other activities.
3. I enjoy all the (knew new) things I'm learning (threw through) being in the orchestra.
4. I don't (know no) (weather whether) I'm much good or not, but I (loose lose) myself in my music.
5. My (principal principle) interest, of (coarse course), is my horn, but (their there they're) are other instruments I like (to too two).
6. (It's Its) good to (hear here) others play.
7. Once I (lead led) the orchestra during a practice session and found it (quiet quite) exciting, but of (coarse course) I didn't (lead led) it during a performance.
8. I'll practice hard on any (peace piece) and (accept except) my instructor's (advice advise).
9. Maybe I'll be able to (right write) music someday; at least I get (complements compliments) on my attempts now.
10. I've (all ready already) decided to (choose chose) music as my career.

☐EXERCISE 5

1. I never (knew new) much before about the origin of the Olympic Games.
2. Now I (know no) (there they're) named for athletic contests held in ancient Greece (threw through) many centuries.
3. (It's Its) probable that they began in 776 B.C. in the valley of Olympia.
4. After that, they were held every four years, and that (lead led) to measuring time by the four-year interval between the games—(a an) Olympiad.
5. At first the only event was a race the length of the stadium, but later (a an) additional event was the pentathlon, which consisted of running, wrestling, leaping, throwing the discus, and hurling the javelin.
6. As the years (passed past), boxing and chariot racing were added.
7. (Than Then) the games lasted for five days.
8. (Their There) was no greater honor for any Greek (than then) to (accept except) the simple branch of wild olive given to a winner.
9. The winners were praised in poetry and song, and (their there) strength and beauty were preserved in statues.
10. In A.D. 394 the games were abolished, but in 1896 the first modern Olympic Games (were where) held in a (knew new) marble stadium constructed in Athens for the purpose.

☐EXERCISE 6

1. I was (quiet quite) surprised to learn that the United States sent (a an) Olympic team to the first modern Olympic Games in Athens in 1896.
2. The games had not been held for the (passed past) 1,500 years.
3. The ten U.S. contestants met in New York but found that (their there) boat fare was going to be higher (than then) they had expected.
4. Finally they got enough money and set (forth fourth) on a German steamship for the 12-day trip to Naples.
5. Of (coarse course) (there they're) was (know no) room on deck to practice (their there) broad and high jumps or pole vaults or 100-meter dashes.
6. From Naples (their there) was a train ride to Brindisi, (were where) they took a steamer to Patras in Greece.
7. (Than Then) they had a ten-hour train ride across Greece to Athens.
8. When they arrived, they (were where) glad they had 12 days to get in shape.
9. But they hadn't been given the (right write) date and had to perform the next morning.
10. They didn't (know no) (who's whose) fault the misunderstanding was, but even so they won 9 of the 12 track events.

□EXERCISE 7

1. I've been reading (a an) anthology of American poetry in my literature (coarse course).
2. I'm (quiet quite) familiar with Frost and Sandburg and never (loose lose) interest in them.
3. But now I'm learning some (knew new) names like Millay and Lindsay; (their there they're) interesting (to too two).
4. I've (all ready already) read most of the poets; some are easier to read (than then) others.
5. I like to (choose chose) favorite poems and (right write) them in my journal, (were where) I can refer to them easily.
6. (It's Its) good to (know no) (are our) poetic heritage and the (principal principle) poets of the (passed past).
7. I'm (quiet quite) sure I like the older poetry better (than then) the modern.
8. I'm (conscience conscious), of (coarse course), that I haven't studied as much modern poetry.
9. (It's Its) just my (personal personnel) preference.
10. (Who's Whose) your favorite poet, (are or) do you have one?

□EXERCISE 8

1. In western Europe in the (passed past) few years, the frog and toad population has been declining.
2. The (principal principle) reason was that the frogs and toads had difficulty migrating from (their there) winter habitats to breeding sites in lakes and ponds.
3. They had to cross busy roads (were where) as many as 80 percent (were where) killed by passing vehicles.
4. (Than Then) a few years ago (quiet quite) (a an) unusual thing happened.
5. Conservationists (choose chose) to form volunteer "toad patrols."
6. The patrols were (lead led) to the places (were where) frogs and toads crossed busy roads.
7. (Their There) the patrols trapped the amphibians in plastic pails and carried them safely across the road.
8. Today patrols in Scandinavia, the Netherlands, Switzerland, and West Germany (are our) trapping thousands of traveling toads during a three-week period each year and carrying them across the pavements.
9. (All ready Already) (there they're) is (a an) increase in the frog and toad population.
10. (It's Its) hoped that these efforts will have a long-term (affect effect).

Source: *National Wildlife*, Aug.–Sept. 1983.

☐EXERCISE 9

1. The (principal principle) goal of the Nature Conservancy, a national nonprofit organization, is to conserve natural resources.
2. The Conservancy is (quiet quite) concerned about what has happened in the (passed past).
3. (Threw Through) carelessness, vast natural areas have (all ready already) been lost.
4. The Conservancy is trying to get laws (passed past) to protect (are our) most important natural habitats.
5. (Their There They're) buying tracts of land (were where) (their there they're) are endangered plants (or our) animals.
6. (Than Then) they turn the land over to other organizations to manage.
7. They work (threw through) local groups and the federal government (to too) save all they can.
8. Every (peace piece) of timberland or (desert dessert) that they can save will be of value in the future.
9. They have (lead led) the way in preserving the habitat along the Mississippi (were where) bald eagles stay in the winter.
10. (Threw Through) (their there they're) efforts, people are coming to (know no) more about conservation and are taking a (personal personnel) interest in it.

☐EXERCISE 10

1. (It's Its) (to too two) early to (know no) the results of the election.
2. (Are Our) candidate may (loose lose) because of the poor turnout.
3. (It's Its) bad (weather whether) for election day.
4. (Are Our) candidate is a person of sound (principals principles).
5. I (know no) her high (moral morale) standards would never let her (accept except) a bribe.
6. She has had (a an) excellent voting record in the (passed past).
7. Some (woman women) are planning a victory celebration.
8. They aren't sure (weather whether) they'll have enough help.
9. They went (threw through) the membership list and (choose chose) some members to phone.
10. (Were Where) are all the (woman women) who offered to help?

JOURNAL WRITING

In your journal write several sentences using words you may formerly have had trouble with.

Proofreading Exercise

See if you can correct all six errors in this student paper before checking with the answers at the back of the book.

I LEARNED TO PAINT

Yesterday I learned to paint. Oh, I had painted before, and I thought I new how. But that was before yesterday.

Yesterday a friend whose a professional painter helped me paint my apartment. First of all, we spent hours filling all the cracks and removing all the hooks and nails and outlet covers. We washed the kitchen walls to get off any grease, and we lightly sanded one wall that was rough. Of coarse we had all ready moved all the furniture away from the walls. We didn't even open the paint cans until the day was half over. Than we used paintbrushes to paint all the corners and edges that a roller wouldn't get to. Finally, in the very last hour of are long day, we used the rollers to paint the walls. That part of the job went quickly, and the whole place looked great when we had finished.

I learned a lot yesterday. I learned that when you want to paint a room, you don't simply start painting.

CONTRACTIONS

Two words condensed into one are called a contraction.

is not	isn't
you have	you've

The letter or letters that are left out are replaced with an apostrophe. For example, if the two words *do not* are condensed into one, an apostrophe is put where the *o* is left out.

do not	don't

Note how the apostrophe goes in the exact place where the letter or letters are left out in these contractions:

I am	I'm
I have	I've
I shall, I will	I'll
I would	I'd
you are	you're
you have	you've
you will	you'll
she is, she has	she's
he is, he has	he's
it is, it has	it's
we are	we're
we have	we've
we will, we shall	we'll
they are	they're
they have	they've
are not	aren't
cannot	can't
do not	don't
does not	doesn't
have not	haven't
let us	let's
who is, who has	who's
where is	where's

One contraction does not follow this rule:

will not	won't

In all other contractions that you're likely to use, the apostrophe goes exactly where the letter or letters are left out. Note especially *it's, they're, who's,* and *you're.* Use them when you mean two words. (See p. 31 for the possessive forms—*its, their, whose,* and *your*—which don't take an apostrophe.)

EXERCISES

Put an apostrophe in each contraction where a letter or letters have been left out. When you finish ten sentences, tear out the perforated answer sheet at the back of the book and correct your answers. Be sure to correct each group of ten sentences before going on so you'll catch your mistakes while you still have sentences to practice on.

☐EXERCISE 1

1. Wheres Ramón? Whats happened to him?
2. Hes entered in the broad jump, and hes not here.
3. Hes coming. Everybodys here now.
4. Lets go to the other end of the field.
5. Theres a better view from this side.
6. Whos keeping score, and whos the timekeeper?
7. Its only a practice meet, but its important.
8. The coach's speech wasnt long, but its been an inspiration to us.
9. I heard hes leaving. I hope its not true.
10. Im sure its not true, or hed have told us.

☐EXERCISE 2

1. Were studying contractions, and Im finally getting the hang of them.
2. Well, that shouldnt be hard.
3. It isnt if I just remember to put the apostrophe where the letter or letters have been left out.
4. Thats the idea.
5. Im now sure of the difference between its and it's.
6. Yes, thats important.
7. In our class everybodys trying to pass all the daily tests.
8. Itd have been good if youd learned these rules long ago.
9. Were all aware of that, but its not too late yet.
10. Thats right. Its never too late.

☐EXERCISE 3

1. Weve quit using some old grammatical forms that have gone out of date.
2. Why bother about them when theyre no longer essential?
3. Its no use to fight a battle thats going to be lost anyway.
4. Its more important to concentrate on rules that are essential.
5. Its also important for me to read good writing if Im going to learn to write.

6. Im told that if I read more, Ill find my writing improving.
7. Ill not only increase my vocabulary, but Ill see how ideas are presented.
8. Its interesting to see how a magazine article develops a thesis statement.
9. Its good to watch for sentence variety too.
10. Maybe it wont be long until Ill be writing more easily.

□EXERCISE 4

1. Ive heard that laughing out loud is an indication of mental health.
2. Wont smiling do, or doesnt that count?
3. No, its laughing aloud thats the indicator.
4. Well, my dad must be in good mental health; hes always chuckling.
5. And its supposed to be good for your physical health too.
6. Thats reasonable; a good belly laugh is relaxing.
7. Ive been thinking that Ive never heard our history prof laugh.
8. Thats right. I havent either.
9. Lets make a project of seeing whether we can make him laugh.
10. Ill bet we cant, but Im willing to try.

□EXERCISE 5

1. Its necessary to have a dictionary if youre going to improve your vocabulary.
2. If youll learn some word roots, youll find your vocabulary growing.
3. Dont try to look up every new word.
4. Its better to look up only those words youre vaguely familiar with.
5. Look up words youve wondered about.
6. Theyre the ones youll learn most readily.
7. If youll keep a list of new words, that will help.
8. Its important also to use the new words youve learned.
9. Use a word three times, and its yours.
10. Its true that a good vocabulary and academic success usually go together.

□EXERCISE 6

1. I havent eaten since morning, and Im hungry.
2. Ill get lunch now if youll give me a hand this afternoon.
3. Just tell me what youd like me to do.
4. Lets plant our garden this afternoon if it doesnt rain.
5. Dont you think its a lot of work for what well get out of it?
6. Wouldnt you enjoy homegrown vegetables?
7. I dont think its going to save us much money.

8. Thats not the point; its the fresh vegetables that are important.
9. Well, if youd like to try growing things, Im willing.
10. Great. Ive bought all the seeds, and heres a hoe.

□EXERCISE 7

1. Im trying to decide on a major.
2. Its a decision thats going to affect my entire life.
3. I dont want to get into a field that just brings in money.
4. If Im going to work, Ive got to like the job Im doing.
5. Its got to be fun, or I dont want it.
6. I dont think theres much difference between work and play.
7. If youve found the right job, its as much fun as play.
8. Ive known people who say their jobs are fun.
9. Thats what Im looking for.
10. And thats why its so important that I choose the right major.

□EXERCISE 8

1. Weve had icy streets ever since weve been back from our vacation.
2. Its no fun to walk in this weather; Im staying inside.
3. But Im going skiing this weekend if weve had snow by then.
4. Youre welcome to come too if youd like to.
5. But I suppose youll be working on your term paper.
6. Youll have yours finished before Ive written my first sentence.
7. Im writing a paper about children and TV.
8. Its not only watching violence thats harmful to children.
9. Its the fact that when theyre watching TV, theyre doing nothing else.
10. Theyre missing a chance to play games, to be creative, to draw a picture, or to hit a baseball instead of watching someone else do it.

□EXERCISE 9

1. Theres something comfortable about clothes youve worn for years.
2. I have a coat thats been with me for a long time, and I wouldnt feel comfortable without it.
3. Its getting a little worn at the elbows, and some day itll have to go, but a new one wont be the same.
4. Its a part of me, and Im afraid my friends wouldnt recognize me in any other coat.
5. Its too bad its wearing out, but maybe with a couple of elbow patches itll last one more year.
6. Ive been so busy decorating our house that I havent had time for much else.

7. Ive given the living room a first coat of paint, and now its ready for the second.
8. Ive never done any painting before, and Im enjoying it.
9. Its satisfying to see the house look its best for a change.
10. Whether Ive saved much money is anybody's guess.

☐EXERCISE 10

1. Why dont evergreen trees lose their needles the way deciduous trees lose their leaves?
2. Actually they do lose them; they just dont lose them all at once.
3. When they lose their needles, theyre constantly replacing them with new ones.
4. Its true, though, that evergreen needles do last a long time.
5. Ive just learned that bristlecone pine needles last 30 years before theyre ready to fall.
6. Evergreen needles are tough and lasting whereas other leaves arent.
7. Ive learned something else thats interesting about leaves.
8. A tree may lose its leaves in the autumn in one climate and be evergreen in another climate.
9. Thats true of the red maple.
10. A red maple in New England loses all its leaves in the autumn, but a red maple in Florida doesnt lose them all at once.

JOURNAL WRITING

Doing exercises helps you learn a rule, but even more helpful is using the rule in writing. In your journal write some sentences using contractions. You might write about your reaction to the week's news. Or choose your own subject.

WRITING ASSIGNMENT

From now on, along with doing the exercises, you will be expected to follow your instructor's directions concerning the writing assignments, which begin on page 200.

POSSESSIVES

The trick in writing possessives is to ask yourself the question, "Who does it belong to?" (Modern usage has made *who* acceptable when it comes first in a sentence, but some people still say "*Whom* does it belong to?" or even "*To whom* does it belong?") If the answer to your question ends in *s*, simply add an apostrophe after the *s*. If it doesn't end in *s*, then add an apostrophe and *s*.

one boys bike	Who does it belong to?	boy	Add *'s*	boy's bike
two boys bikes	Who do they belong to?	boys	Add *'*	boys' bikes
the mans hat	Who does it belong to?	man	Add *'s*	man's hat
the mens hats	Who do they belong to?	men	Add *'s*	men's hats
childrens game	Who does it belong to?	children	Add *'s*	children's game
one girls coat	Who does it belong to?	girl	Add *'s*	girl's coat
two girls coats	Who do they belong to?	girls	Add *'*	girls' coats

This trick will always work, but you must ask the question every time. And remember that the key word is *belong*. Who does it *belong* to? If you ask the question another way, you may get an answer that won't help you. Also, if you just look at a word without asking the question, you may think the name of the owner ends in an *s* when it really doesn't.

TO MAKE A POSSESSIVE
Ask "Who (or what) does it belong to?"
If the answer ends in *s*, add an apostrophe.
If it doesn't end in *s*, add an apostrophe and *s*.

Cover the right-hand column and see if you can write the following possessives correctly. Ask the question each time.

the womans dress _____	woman's
the womens ideas _____	women's
Stephens apartment _____	Stephen's
James apartment _____	James'
the Browns house _____	the Browns'
Mr. Browns house _____	Mr. Brown's

(Sometimes you may see a variation of this rule. *James' book* may be written *James's book*. That is correct too, but the best way is to stick to the simple rule. You can't be wrong if you follow it.)

In such expressions as *a day's work* or *Saturday's game*, you may ask how the work can belong to the day or the game can belong to Saturday. Those are simply possessive forms that have been in our language for a long time. And when you think about it, the work really does belong to the day (not the night), and the game does belong to Saturday (not Friday).

A word of warning! Don't assume that because a word ends in *s* it is necessarily a possessive. Make sure the word actually possesses something before you add an apostrophe.

A few words, called possessive pronouns, are already possessive and don't need an apostrophe added to them. Memorize this list:

my, mine	its
your, yours	our, ours
his	their, theirs
her, hers	whose

Note particularly *its, their, whose,* and *your.* They are already possessive and don't take an apostrophe. (They sound just like the contractions *it's, they're, who's,* and *you're,* which stand for two words and of course have to have an apostrophe.)

As a practice exercise, cover the right-hand column below with a sheet of paper, and on it write the correct form (contraction or possessive). If you miss any, go back and review the explanations.

(It) raining.	It's
(You) car needs washing.	Your
(Who) to blame?	Who's
(They) planning to come.	They're
The cat drank (it) milk.	its
(Who) been sitting here?	Who's
The wind lost (it) force.	its
(Who) going with me?	Who's
My book has lost (it) cover.	its
(It) all I can do.	It's
(You) right.	You're
(They) garden has many trees.	Their
(It) sunny today.	It's
(Who) car shall we take?	Whose
The club lost (it) leader.	its

Here's one more practice exercise. Cover the right-hand column with a sheet of paper, and on it write the possessives.

1. My sisters spent the summer at my grandparents home.

grandparents'. (You didn't add an apostrophe to *sisters*, did you? The sisters don't possess anything.)

2. Students grades depend on their term papers.

Students' (Who do the grades belong to?)

3. My friends spent an evening at Charles house.

Charles' (Who does the house belong to?)

4. Charles was invited to my mothers apartment.

mother's (Charles doesn't possess anything in this sentence.)

5. Sarahs job is less challenging than yours.

Sarah's (*Yours* is a posessive pronoun and doesn't take an apostrophe.)

6. Last nights game was exciting.

night's (The game belonged to last night.)

7. The Morgans apartment has been redecorated.

Morgans' (Who does the apartment belong to?)

8. The Morgans like their apartment.

(No apostrophe in this sentence. *Their* is a possessive pronoun telling who the apartment belongs to.)

9. The girls team beat the womens team.

girls', women's (Did you ask who each team belongs to?)

10. The girls enjoy playing on their team.

(No apostrophe. *Their* is a possessive pronoun telling who the team belongs to. The girls don't possess anything in this sentence.)

11. The two instructors gave the same test.

(No apostrophe. The sentence merely tells what the instructors did.)

12. The two instructors tests were the same.

instructors' (Who did the tests belong to?)

13. The sign above the gate said "The Hansons."

Hansons (meaning the Hansons live there) or Hansons' (meaning it's the Hansons' house).

EXERCISES

Put the apostrophe in each possessive. WATCH OUT! **First,** make sure the word really possesses something; not every word that ends in *s* is a possessive. **Second,** remember that possessive pronouns don't take an apostrophe. **Third,** remember that even though a word seems to end in *s*, you can't tell where the apostrophe goes until you ask the question, "Who (or what) does it belong to?" In the first sentence, for example, "Who does the car belong to?" "Everybody." Therefore you'll write *everybody's.*

☐EXERCISE 1

1. Is everybodys car available this morning?
2. Jennifers car is parked across the street.
3. Whose car is in the driveway?
4. It's probably either Jeromes or Allens.
5. And Andys motorbike is in the driveway too.
6. We're all planning a days trip to Turkey Run State Park.
7. Everybodys interest in the park is different.
8. Andys only aim is to ride on the bridle trail.
9. And Ashleys plan is to take a guided nature tour.
10. Some peoples interest is mainly in the famous homecooked dinner at the Lodge.

☐EXERCISE 2

1. Orchestras from all over the city are competing in the music contest.
2. I think the judges will like Rays interpretation of Mozart.
3. I know Rogers trumpet solo will be excellent.
4. Rogers picture was in the paper last night; Guys was in last week.
5. Tchaikovskys Fourth Symphony is my favorite.
6. Its theme keeps running through my head.
7. Lisas talent in singing should help her get a scholarship.
8. Victor can't get a scholarship because his fathers income is too high.
9. Last nights program was interesting, and todays should be good too.
10. Tonights concert will be the final performance.

☐EXERCISE 3

1. The instructor read everyones paper aloud.
2. One persons paper was on law enforcement; another persons was on making shortbread.
3. We enjoyed hearing all the students papers read.
4. And Dereks confidence was boosted by the instructors remarks.
5. Finally each students paper will be revised.

6. Rewriting ones paper is a good learning experience.
7. My typewriter should have its ribbon changed.
8. After that, I'll type my paper in its final form.
9. Our class is reading one of Charles Dickens novels.
10. We're reading some of Carl Sandburgs poetry too.

☐EXERCISE 4

1. My little brothers only request for Christmas was a computer.
2. We agreed to get him one, but everybodys reason for doing so was different.
3. My moms idea was that it might help him with his math.
4. My sisters reason was that it would make him learn to type.
5. My dads idea was that it would keep him away from the video arcades.
6. I suppose my little brothers reason for wanting one was that he saw computers at all his friends houses.
7. When he unwrapped the computer Christmas morning, everybodys excitement was high.
8. With my dads help he got it hooked up and started to play a math game.
9. But before long my brothers interest began to wane.
10. Will he eventually make good use of the computer? It's anybodys guess.

☐EXERCISE 5

1. Ivans ability in juggling is quite a social asset.
2. He performed magic tricks for our daughters birthday party.
3. The childrens delight was obvious.
4. The success of the party was due mainly to Ivans skill.
5. The afternoons final excitement was a trip to the zoo.
6. We spent most of our time at the monkeys cages.
7. The monkeys seemed to enjoy watching us as much as we did them.
8. A bear stood on its hind legs.
9. And a bear cub was being nuzzled by its mother.
10. The most beautiful spot in the zoo is the aviary with its birds and trees and flowers.

☐EXERCISE 6

1. Carolines hobby is flower arranging.
2. She took a semesters course in Japanese flower arranging last spring.
3. And now she has given a demonstration at the Womens Club.
4. Some of Carolines arrangements have even taken prizes at fairs.
5. She finds the flowers for her arrangements in her parents garden.

6. Her sister Barbaras hobby is pottery making.
7. She's been making pottery for two years now.
8. The two girls hobbies go nicely together.
9. Barbs low pottery vases are perfect for her sisters Japanese arrangements.
10. Both girls spend hours on their hobbies.

☐EXERCISE 7

1. Last week a few of my friends and I went to see one of Ohios famous museums—the College Football Hall of Fame, not far from Cincinnati.
2. There we saw more than 500 photographs of famous players and coaches.
3. And the Time Tunnel text and pictures trace the evolution of football.
4. The Greeks game of *harpastum* is supposed to have been the beginning of football.
5. The ancient game included throwing, kicking, running with a ball, and even tackling.
6. Later, soccer and rugby were forerunners of todays game.
7. We saw Knute Rocknes statue and heard a recording of one of his famous speeches.
8. The next day we went to Ohios other football museum—the Pro Football Hall of Fame in Canton.
9. Among the prized exhibits is Joe Namaths football uniform.
10. And we listened to a recorded account of Tom Dempseys record-breaking 63-yard field goal.

☐EXERCISE 8

1. My brothers ambition is to be a mountain climber.
2. So he was delighted at our familys decision to drive to Grand Teton National Park.
3. His first days program there included a training class in the School of Mountaineering.
4. A beginners training includes learning safety precautions and proper climbing techniques.
5. My brothers excitement was unbounded as he made a practice climb on a small peak.
6. Meantime the rest of the familys enjoyment was mainly in following the self-guiding trails and taking photographs.
7. Some of my dads photographs were worth framing.
8. My sisters favorite trail was the Jenny Lake Nature Trail.
9. Our weeks stay was not long enough to see all we wanted to see.
10. But my brothers longing to climb a really tall peak was satisfied.

☐EXERCISE 9

1. One of Japans oldest customs is now losing favor.
2. A Japanese childs ability to eat with chopsticks was once taken for granted.
3. Now almost half the elementary school children in Japan have failed to learn one of Japans most distinctive customs.
4. A child used to be taught to use chopsticks at home, but now the parents preference is often for knives and forks.
5. Many of the countrys artistic customs are disappearing.
6. Peoples dress has been westernized.
7. Both womens and mens clothes follow western trends, and the kimono is less often seen.
8. Childrens clothes are almost always western.
9. Womens taste in decorating their houses is straying from the artistic Japanese style.
10. Even Japans beautiful tea ceremony is no longer a daily occurrence.

☐EXERCISE 10

1. Dr. Jones is head of the Geography Department.
2. Dr. Jones office is in Hansen Hall, but he's seldom there.
3. He's usually off somewhere conducting one of the departments field trips.
4. Part of a students course load is made up of field trips.
5. A students preparation for each trip consists of reading books and listening to lectures.
6. Dr. Jones lectures are especially interesting.
7. Last Sundays trip to the Wisconsin Dells taught us something about the geology of the area.
8. In the spring we'll take a weeks trip to the Rockies.
9. And in the summer we're going to the East Coast for two weeks.
10. I've learned a lot from the departments excellent field trip program.

JOURNAL WRITING

In your journal write some sentences using the possessive forms of the names of the members of your family or the names of your friends.

WRITING ASSIGNMENT

As you continue with the exercises, continue also with the writing assignments in the latter part of the book.

Review of Contractions and Possessives

Add the necessary apostrophes. Try to get these exercises perfect. Don't excuse an error by saying, "Oh, that was just a careless mistake." A mistake is a mistake. Be tough on yourself!

☐EXERCISE 1

1. Therell be more snow tonight, Im afraid.
2. Lorens car doesnt have snow tires, and hes going to need them.
3. Hed better buy some, or hell be in trouble on those hills.
4. The Womens Club had a guest speaker at its annual luncheon.
5. The ladies enjoyed the speakers wit and the chairpersons jokes.
6. Most childrens TV programs do everything for the child.
7. A childs day should have time for spontaneous play.
8. "Mr. Rogers Neighborhood" is an excellent childrens program.
9. Its good for children who get too much criticism.
10. Its theme is that everyone is an important person.
11. Mr. Rogers message is that each person is acceptable and unique.
12. Its a psychiatric theory thats good for adults too.
13. The Reeds garden looks as if a gardener cared for it.
14. Its the result of Mr. Reeds hours of work.
15. I can see Mrs. Reeds hand in it too of course.

☐EXERCISE 2

Theres a little lake with steep rocky sides and crystal clear water that you can see down into forever. Some say its bottomless, but everyone agrees its deep.

Theres one spot where a big tree grows over the lake, and someones tied a rope to one of its branches to swing on. Its a great sensation, I discovered, to swing out over the water and then let go. I think everyone gets an urge to yell as loud as possible to enhance an awkward dive. Its a great feeling to cast off from the high rocks holding onto the rope as it swings out over the water. Just before the farthest point of the ropes travel is the best place to let go and drop into the water. Those with initiative try flips and twists as they dive, but however its done, its a great sensation. Some say its for kids, but I hope I never grow too old to have fun at it.

Proofreading Exercise

In this paragraph are errors from all the material you have studied. Can you correct the four errors before checking with the answers at the back of the book? The errors are in the first five lines.

SUGAR RAY LEONARD

People find it hard to believe that Sugar Ray Leonard, the boxing champion, grew up in poverty. They think that anyone who speaks as well as he does must of come from at least a middle-class home. But Leonards parents were poor. He was one of seven children and didnt go beyond high school. He was eager to succeed, however, and his ambition lead him to work on language skills. "I used to practice reading from a magazine before a mirror," he says, "so I could learn good grammar and enunciation and get out of the slang of the streets—from the *dis* and *dats* and *Wha's happenin', man*. I knew if I was going to be more than just a fighter, I'd have to learn the language."

WORDS THAT CAN BE BROKEN INTO PARTS

Breaking words into their parts will often help you spell them correctly. Each of the following words is made up of two shorter words:

book keeper . . . bookkeeper   room mate . . . roommate
over run   . . . overrun   tail light   . . . taillight
over rate   . . . overrate   with hold   . . . withhold

Becoming aware of prefixes such as *dis, inter, mis*, and *un* is also helpful. Then when you add a word to the prefix, the spelling will be correct:

dis appear   disappear   mis spell   misspell
dis appoint   disappoint   mis step   misstep
dis approve   disapprove   un natural   unnatural
dis satisfied   dissatisfied   un necessary   unnecessary
dis service   disservice   un nerve   unnerve
inter racial   interracial   un noticed   unnoticed
inter related   interrelated

Note that no letters are dropped, either from the prefix or from the word added to it.

Have someone dictate the above list for you to write and then mark any words you miss. Memorize the correct spellings by noting how each word is made up of a prefix and a word.

RULE FOR DOUBLING A FINAL CONSONANT

Most spelling rules have so many exceptions that they aren't much help. But here's one that has almost no exceptions and is really worth learning.

Double a final consonant when adding an ending that begins with a vowel (such as *ing*, *ed*, *er*) if all three of the following are true:

1. **the word ends in a single consonant,**
2. **the final consonant is preceded by a single vowel (the vowels are a, e, i, o, u),**
3. **and the accent is on the last syllable (or the word has only one syllable).**

We'll try the rule on the following words to which we'll add *ing*, *ed*, or *er*.

begin   1. It ends in a single consonant—*n*,
2. preceded by a single vowel—*i*,
3. and the accent is on the last syllable—*be gin'*.
Therefore we double the final consonant and write *beginning, beginner*.

stop   1. It ends in a single consonant—*p*,
2. preceded by a single vowel—*o*,
3. and the accent is on the last syllable (there is only one).
Therefore we double the final consonant and write *stopping, stopped, stopper*.

motor   1. It ends in a single consonant—*r*,
2. preceded by a single vowel—*o*,
3. but the accent isn't on the last syllable. It's on the first—*mo' tor*.
Therefore we don't double the final consonant. We write *motoring, motored*.

sleep   1. It ends in a single consonant—*p*,
2. but it isn't preceded by a single vowel. There are two *e*'s.
Therefore we don't double the final consonant. We write *sleeping, sleeper*.

kick   1. It doesn't end in a single consonant. There are two—*c* and *k*.
Therefore we don't double the final consonant. We write *kicking, kicked, kicker*.

Note that *qu* is treated as a consonant because *q* is almost never written without *u*. Think of it as *kw*. In words like *equip* and *quit*, the *qu* acts as a consonant. Therefore *quit* does end in a single consonant preceded by a single vowel, and the final consonant is doubled—*quitting*.

Also note that *bus* may be written either *bussing* or *busing*. The latter is more common.

EXERCISES

Add *ing* to these words. Correct each group of ten by using the perforated answer sheet at the back of the book.

☐EXERCISE 1

1. put
2. control
3. admit
4. mop
5. plan

6. hop
7. jump
8. knit
9. mark
10. creep

☐EXERCISE 2

1. return
2. swim
3. sing
4. benefit
5. loaf

6. nail
7. omit
8. occur
9. shop
10. interrupt

☐EXERCISE 3

1. begin
2. spell
3. prefer
4. interpret
5. hunt

6. excel
7. wrap
8. stop
9. wed
10. scream

☐EXERCISE 4

1. feel
2. murmur
3. turn
4. weed
5. subtract

6. stream
7. expel
8. miss
9. get
10. stab

☐EXERCISE 5

1. forget
2. misspell
3. fit
4. plant
5. pin

6. trust
7. sip
8. flop
9. reap
10. fight

Progress Test

This test covers everything you've studied so far. One sentence in each pair is correct. The other is incorrect. Read both sentences carefully before you decide. Then write the letter of the correct sentence in the blank.

_____ 1. A. It dosen't matter whether he phones me or not.
　　　　　　B. His opinion won't have any effect on my decision.

_____ 2. A. I'm planning a week's vacation in the spring.
　　　　　　B. The hostess past the piece of pie to me.

_____ 3. A. It's regretable that our team lost.
　　　　　　B. The seal was flopping about in the water.

_____ 4. A. The Larson's apartment is too small for such a crowd.
　　　　　　B. My father's job is his principal interest.

_____ 5. A. I omitted the fourth question on my test.
　　　　　　B. Of coarse I know what you're intending to do.

_____ 6. A. His work sounds more interesting than yours.
　　　　　　B. I'm quiet sure I'm right about that problem.

_____ 7. A. I've all ready learned quite a bit in this course.
　　　　　　B. An honest opinion is all I'm asking for.

_____ 8. A. You should of seen all the new clothes she bought.
　　　　　　B. Diana's conscience won't let her cheat.

_____ 9. A. It's quite an honor to be invited.
　　　　　　B. I hear the womens' athletic club is looking for new members.

_____ 10. A. Its a good idea to cut out desserts if you want to lose weight.
　　　　　　B. The Kellys have invited us over for the evening.

_____ 11. A. She's the most studious person I've ever known.
　　　　　　B. My puppy flunked it's obedience test.

_____ 12. A. Your going to be quite cold in those clothes.
　　　　　　B. This weather is too cold to suit me.

_____ 13. A. Who's car is that in the Jacobsons' driveway?
　　　　　　B. Won't he be through with his new job soon?

_____ 14. A. I don't intend to lose my temper.
　　　　　　B. Elizabeths' report was excellent.

_____ 15. A. When he was captain, he lead the team to victory.
　　　　　　B. My instructor's advice was good.

A LIST OF FREQUENTLY MISSPELLED WORDS

Have someone dictate this list of commonly misspelled words to you and mark the ones you miss. Then memorize the correct spellings, working on ten words each week.

Pronounce these words correctly, and you won't misspell them: *athlete, athletics, nuclear.* And be sure to pronounce every syllable in these words: *environment, government, mathematics, probably, studying.* Also try to think up memory devices to help you remember correct spellings. For example, you *labor* in a *laboratory*; the two *l*'s in *parallel* are parallel; and the *r* separates the two *a*'s in *separate.*

1. absence	33. disastrous	65. humorous
2. across	34. discipline	66. immediately
3. actually	35. discussed	67. independent
4. a lot	36. disease	68. intelligence
5. amateur	37. divide	69. interest
6. among	38. dying	70. interfere
7. analyze	39. eighth	71. involved
8. appearance	40. eligible	72. knowledge
9. appreciate	41. eliminate	73. laboratory
10. argument	42. embarrassed	74. leisure
11. athlete	43. environment	75. length
12. athletics	44. especially	76. library
13. awkward	45. etc.	77. likely
14. becoming	46. exaggerate	78. lying
15. beginning	47. excellent	79. marriage
16. belief	48. exercise	80. mathematics
17. benefit	49. existence	81. meant
18. buried	50. experience	82. medicine
19. business	51. explanation	83. necessary
20. certain	52. extremely	84. neither
21. college	53. familiar	85. ninety
22. coming	54. February	86. ninth
23. committee	55. finally	87. nuclear
24. competition	56. foreign	88. occasionally
25. complete	57. government	89. opinion
26. consider	58. grammar	90. opportunity
27. criticism	59. grateful	91. parallel
28. decision	60. guarantee	92. particular
29. definitely	61. guard	93. persuade
30. dependent	62. guidance	94. physically
31. development	63. height	95. planned
32. difference	64. hoping	96. pleasant

97. possible
98. practical
99. preferred
100. prejudice
101. privilege
102. probably
103. professor
104. prove
105. psychology
106. pursue
107. receipt
108. receive
109. recommend
110. reference
111. relieve
112. religious
113. repetition
114. rhythm

115. ridiculous
116. sacrifice
117. safety
118. scene
119. schedule
120. secretary
121. senior
122. sense
123. separate
124. severely
125. shining
126. significant
127. similar
128. sincerely
129. sophomore
130. speech
131. straight
132. studying

133. succeed
134. success
135. suggest
136. surprise
137. thoroughly
138. though
139. tragedy
140. tried
141. tries
142. truly
143. unfortunately
144. until
145. unusual
146. using
147. usually
148. Wednesday
149. writing
150. written

USING YOUR DICTIONARY

By working through the following 13 exercises, you'll become familiar with what you can find in an up-to-date desk dictionary.

1. PRONUNCIATION

Look up the word *irreparable* and copy the pronunciation here.

Now under each letter with a pronunciation mark over it, write the key word having the same mark. You'll find the key words at the bottom of one of the two dictionary pages open before you. Note especially that the upside-down *e* (ə) always has the sound of *uh* like the *a* in *ago* or *about*. Remember that sound because it's found in many words.

Next, pronounce the key words you have written, and then slowly pronounce *irreparable*, giving each syllable the same sound as its key word.

Finally note which syllable has the heavy accent mark. (In most dictionaries the accent mark points to the stressed syllable, but in one dictionary it is in front of the stressed syllable.) The stressed syllable is *rep*. Now say the word, letting the full force of your voice fall on that syllable.

When more than one pronunciation is given, the first is more common. If the complete pronunciation of a word isn't given, look at the word above it to find the pronunciation.

Look up the pronunciation of these words, using the key words at the bottom of the dictionary page to help you pronounce each syllable. Then note which syllable has the heavy accent mark, and say the word aloud.

neophyte   indefatigable   indictment   cowardice

2. DEFINITIONS

The dictionary may give a number of meanings for a word. Read through all the meanings for each italicized word and then write a definition appropriate to the sentence.

1. His book was published *posthumously*. _____

   _____

2. He spent more time on his *avocation* than on his job. _____

   _____

3. She had always felt an *antipathy* toward cats. _____

   _____

4. You'd have to be pretty *credulous* to believe that story. _____

   _____

5. The drizzle turned into a *veritable* downpour. _____

   _____

3. SPELLING

By making yourself look up each word you aren't sure how to spell, you'll soon become a better speller. When two spellings are given in the dictionary, the first one (or the one with the definition) is the more common.

Underline the more common spelling of each of these words.

theater, theatre   travelog, travelogue

plough, plow   donut, doughnut

4. COMPOUND WORDS

If you want to find out whether two words are written separately, written with a hyphen between them, or written as one word, consult your dictionary. For example:

> half sister   is written as two words
> brother-in-law   is hyphenated
> stepson   is written as one word

Write each of the following correctly.

teddy bear _____   counter clockwise _____

dining room _____   out moded _____

self conscious _____   non cooperative _____

5. CAPITALIZATION

If a word is capitalized in the dictionary, that means it should always be capitalized. If it isn't capitalized in the dictionary, then it may or may not be capitalized, depending on how it's used (see p. 186). For example:

Indian   is always capitalized

college   is capitalized or not, according to how it's used
> She's attending college.
> She's attending St. Petersburg Junior College.

Write these words as they are given in the dictionary (with or without a capital) to show whether they must always be capitalized or not.

Government _____   Mother _____

God _____   English _____

Dragonfly _____   Republican _____

6. USAGE

Because a word is in the dictionary is no indication that it is in standard use. The following designations indicate whether a word is used today and where and by whom.

obsolete	now gone out of use
archaic	not now used in ordinary language but retained in some Biblical, literary, and legal expressions
colloquial informal	used in informal conversation but not in formal writing
dialectal regional	used in some localities but not everywhere
slang	popular but nonstandard expression
nonstandard substandard	not used by educated people

Look up each italicized word and write the designation that indicates its usage. Dictionaries differ. One may list a word as slang whereas another will call it colloquial. And still another may give no designation, thus indicating that that particular dictionary considers the word in standard use.

1. From the grocery she brought home a *poke* of potatoes. _____

2. *Methinks* he *doth* protest too much. _____

3. I'm going *irregardless* of the cost. _____

4. He didn't have the *know-how* to handle that job. _____

5. She was *light-complected.* _____

6. I got the *brush-off* from the boss. _____

7. Getting a promotion shouldn't make him *high-hat* his friends. _____

8. She *hath* no faults who *hath* the art to hide them. _____

7. DERIVATIONS

The derivations or stories behind words will often help you remember the current meanings. For example, if you heard that a doctor had given a patient a placebo and you consulted your dictionary, you would find that *placebo* originally was a Latin word meaning "I shall please." Knowing the derivation is a help in remembering the present-day definition— "a harmless, unmedicated substance given merely to please the patient."

Look up the derivation of each of these words. You'll find it in square brackets either just before or just after the definition.

gymnasium _____

circus _____

dandelion _____

pandemic _____

July _____

8. SYNONYMS

Sometimes at the end of a definition, a group of synonyms is given. For example, at the end of the definition of *beautiful*, you'll find several synonyms. And if you look up *handsome* or *pretty*, you'll be referred to the synonyms under *beautiful*.

List the synonyms for the italicized words.

1. The *old* mansion is being turned into a boys' club. _____

_____

2. His actions *puzzle* me. _____

_____

3. Her *anger* was gradually building. _____

_____

9. ABBREVIATIONS

Find the meaning of the following abbreviations.

mm _____   e.g. _____

loc. cit. _____   RCMP _____

10. NAMES OF PEOPLE

The names of people will be found either in the main part of your dictionary or in a separate biographical section at the back.

Identify the following.

Paul Gauguin _____

Kamehameha I _____

Jacob Grimm _____

Luther Burbank _____

11. NAMES OF PLACES

The names of places will be found either in the main part of your dictionary or in a separate gazetteer section in the back.

Identify the following.

Mackinac Island _____

James Bay _____

Petrified Forest _____

Kilauea _____

12. FOREIGN WORDS AND PHRASES

Give the language and the meaning of the italicized expressions.

1. I got tired of his saying *Gesundheit* each time I sneezed. _____

_____

2. We learned about the new ruling only after it was already a *fait accompli.*

_____

3. I felt *de trop* at that party. _____

4. They were acting *in loco parentis.* _____

13. MISCELLANEOUS INFORMATION

Find these miscellaneous bits of information in your dictionary.

1. How long is the Mississippi River? _____

2. How many pounds are in a kilogram? _____

3. What is the meaning of the British term *gaol?* _____

4. What is the plural of son-in-law? _____

5. What is the capital of Saudi Arabia? _____

6. When did Mahatma Gandhi die? _____

7. What is the population of Tacoma, Washington? _____

8. What is another name for Ursa Minor? _____

9. What are the names of the Great Lakes? _____

_____

10. What is Parkinson's Law? _____

_____

2

Sentence Structure

2   Sentence Structure

The most common errors in freshman writing are fragments and run-together sentences. Here are some fragments:

> Having given the best years of his life to his farm
> Although we had food enough for only one day
> The most that I possibly could do
> Because I had tried very hard

They don't make complete statements. They leave the reader wanting something more.

Here are some run-together sentences:

> The snow was packed the skiing was great.
> We missed Kathy she was too busy to come.
> We'll go again next Friday maybe she can come then.
> On the way home it rained the pavement was slippery.

Unlike fragments, they make complete statements, but the trouble is they make *two* complete statements, which shouldn't be run together into one sentence without punctuation. The reader has to go back to see where there should have been a pause.

Both fragments and run-together sentences bother the reader. Not until you can get rid of them will your writing be clear and easy to read. Unfortunately there is no quick, easy way to learn to avoid them. You have to learn a little about sentence structure—mainly how to find the subject and the verb in a sentence so that you can tell whether it really is a sentence.

FINDING SUBJECTS AND VERBS

When you write a sentence, you write about *something* or *someone*. That's the subject. Then you write what the subject *does* or *is*. That's the verb.

Birds fly.

The word *Birds* is the something you are writing about. It's the subject, and we'll underline it once. *Fly* tells what the subject does. It shows the action in the sentence. It's the verb, and we'll underline it twice. Because the verb often shows action, it's easier to spot than the subject. Therefore always look for it first. For example, in the sentence

Michael drives his car to the campus every day.

which word shows the action? Drives. It's the verb. Underline it twice. Now ask yourself who or what drives. Michael. It's the subject. Underline it once.

Study the following sentences until you understand how to pick out subjects and verbs.

Last night hail dented the top of my car. (Which word shows the action? Dented. It's the verb. Underline it twice. Who or what dented? Hail. It's the subject. Underline it once.)
Yesterday Kent jogged five kilometers. (Which word shows the action? Jogged. And who or what jogged? Kent.)
This year my sister works at Hardee's. (Which word shows the action? Works. Who or what works? Sister.)

Often the verb doesn't show action but merely tells what the subject *is* or *was*. Learn to spot such verbs (*is, are, was, were, seems, appears . . . .*)

Dan is my friend. (First spot the verb is. Then ask who or what is. Dan is.)
That guy in the red shirt is our team captain. (First spot the verb is. Then ask who or what is. Guy is.)

Allison seems happy these days. (First spot the verb <u>seems</u>. Then ask who or what seems. <u>Allison</u> <u>seems</u>.)

He appears tired. (First spot the verb <u>appears</u>. Then ask who or what appears. <u>He</u> <u>appears</u>.)

Sometimes the subject comes after the verb.

In the middle of the street stood the lost puppy. (Who or what stood? <u>Puppy</u> <u>stood</u>.)

Where is the meeting? (Who or what is? <u>Meeting</u> <u>is</u>.)

There was a big crowd at the game. (Who or what was? <u>Crowd</u> <u>was</u>.)

There were not enough seats for everyone. (Who or what were? <u>Seats</u> <u>were</u>.)

Here are your skates. (Who or what are? <u>Skates</u> <u>are</u>.)

Note that *there* and *here* (as in the last three sentences) are never subjects. They simply point out something.

In commands, the subject often is not expressed. It is *you* (understood).

Keep calm. (<u>You</u> <u>keep</u> calm.)

Shut the door. (<u>You</u> <u>shut</u> the door.)

As you pick out subjects in the following exercises, you may wonder whether, for example, you should say the subject is *dunes* or *sand dunes*. It makes no difference so long as you get the main subject, *dunes*, right. In the answers at the back of the book, usually—but not always—the single word is used. Don't waste your time worrying about whether to include an extra word with the subject. Just make sure you get the main subject right.

EXERCISES

Underline the subject once and the verb twice. Find the verb first, and then ask **Who** or **What.** When you've finished ten sentences, compare your answers carefully with those on the perforated answer sheet.

☐EXERCISE 1

1. During spring vacation I visited the Dunes State Park in Indiana.
2. That trip was a great experience.
3. The sand dunes shift constantly.
4. Beyond the dunes was the lake.
5. I watched the white froths of foam on the slate and silver water.
6. I walked along the smooth beach for miles.
7. Far out I saw a boat with vacationers.
8. Their voices broke the silence.
9. At night the dunes are spectacular in the moonlight.
10. And the stars seem quite close.

☐EXERCISE 2

1. Our sun is five billion years old.
2. The invisible "black holes" in space were once huge stars.
3. A "black hole" is simply the remnant of a collapsed star.
4. The star's top-heavy gravity crushed it to the size of a golf ball.
5. Then gravity crushed it further to "nothing."
6. Thus it "disappeared."
7. It became a "black hole."
8. It is ten billion light-years to the farthest quasar.
9. There are 100 billion galaxies in the universe.
10. Try to imagine such numbers.

☐EXERCISE 3

1. The names of the days of the week have interesting origins.
2. Monday is the moon's day.
3. Tuesday is the day of Tiu, the Anglo-Saxon god of war.
4. Wednesday is the day of Woden, chief god in Germanic mythology.
5. Thursday is the day of Thor, god of thunder in Scandinavian myths.
6. Friday is the day of Frigga, wife of Woden and goddess of love.
7. Saturn gave his name to Saturday.
8. And the sun's day is Sunday.
9. Most people say these names without thinking of their origins.
10. Think sometimes of their early meanings.

☐EXERCISE 4

1. Last summer I went to the Calgary Stampede.
2. There is limited parking space at the Stampede grounds.
3. But buses from all over the city bring people there.
4. The chuck wagon races are the most exciting part of the Stampede.
5. It takes a driver and two outriders for each chuck wagon.
6. At the starting sign, the outriders toss the camp stove on the wagon.
7. Then they jump aboard.
8. And the wagon starts at a frightening speed.
9. Sometimes there are serious accidents.
10. It is a dangerous but exciting sport.

☐EXERCISE 5

1. Litter is everywhere.
2. Even the world's highest mountain has rubbish.
3. Mount Everest base camp at 17,000 feet is full of litter.
4. Climbers leave debris of all sorts.
5. They leave pots, plates, plastic bags, cooking gas, and oxygen bottles.
6. They even leave tents.
7. But now Nepal hopes to end the problem.
8. A new rule requires ten extra porters on each expedition.
9. Their job is to haul away the litter.
10. Thus each expedition now plans to leave the world's highest mountain clean and beautiful.

☐EXERCISE 6

1. Scientists wanted to study the emperor penguin.
2. It is the largest of all penguins.
3. But Antarctica is a cold place to study it.
4. Temperatures go as low as $-126°$F.
5. So the scientists brought some penguin eggs to San Diego.
6. They finally succeeded in hatching an emperor penguin chick.
7. A large stuffed Snoopy dog became the young chick's "mother."
8. In the wild, emperor penguin chicks nestle on the feet of their mother.
9. So the newly hatched chick nestled on the feet of the Snoopy dog.
10. And now scientists have an emperor penguin for long-term study.

☐EXERCISE 7

1. On summer evenings nighthawks swoop through the air.
2. They become active just before dark.
3. Then they fly above houses and treetops.

4. The nighthawk emits a nasal "Peent" cry.
5. It has a large froglike mouth from ear to ear.
6. During flight the nighthawk opens its mouth.
7. It catches insects in its open mouth.
8. In cities the nighthawks nest on flat-topped buildings.
9. They sit lengthwise on limbs but diagonally on wires.
10. Listen for nighthawks sometime just before dusk.

□EXERCISE 8

1. Dog sleds are no longer the principal means of transportation in the North.
2. But sled-dog racing is increasingly popular.
3. From New Hampshire to Alaska, sled-dog races are annual events.
4. Sled-dog racers call themselves "mushers."
5. Their Alaskan husky dogs, weighing 45 to 50 pounds, have astonishing power.
6. They love to run and to pull sleds over miles of snow.
7. Many dogs run 20 miles per hour.
8. At night they stay outdoors in temperatures of −50°F.
9. Day by day the mushers prepare their dogs for the All-Alaska Sweepstakes.
10. It is a grueling 408-mile round trip out of Nome.

□EXERCISE 9

1. There are seven presidential libraries in the United States.
2. Each library also contains a museum.
3. The exhibits include historic documents and possessions of the president.
4. Gerald Ford is the only president with two libraries.
5. One is on the University of Michigan campus at Ann Arbor.
6. The other is in Grand Rapids, Ford's hometown.
7. The latter offers a 20-minute film on Ford's life.
8. The John F. Kennedy Library overlooks the Boston Harbor.
9. It draws the biggest crowds of all the libraries.
10. In 1980 half a million people visited it.

□EXERCISE 10

1. The Lyndon B. Johnson Library in Austin, Texas, has 36 million pages of documents.
2. The Harry S. Truman Library in Independence, Missouri, contains Truman's White House piano.

3. The Dwight D. Eisenhower Center in Abilene, Kansas, illustrates Ike's military and political years.
4. Eisenhower's boyhood home is on the grounds of the center.
5. The Herbert Hoover Library in West Branch, Iowa, is the least visited of all the libraries.
6. The reason is its remoteness from major population centers.
7. The Franklin D. Roosevelt Library in Hyde Park, New York, celebrated the 100th anniversary of FDR's birth in 1982.
8. It contains his collection of naval and other maritime souvenirs.
9. The American people are proud of these libraries.
10. Visit one of them sometime.

WRITING ASSIGNMENT

As you continue the exercises, you are expected to continue the writing assignments from the latter part of the book.

SUBJECTS NOT IN PREPOSITIONAL PHRASES

A prepositional phrase is simply a preposition and the name of someone or something. We don't use many grammatical terms in this book, and the only reason we're mentioning prepositional phrases is to get them out of the way. They're a bother in analyzing sentences. For example, you might have difficulty finding the subject and verb in a long sentence like this:

> During the first week of his vacation, one of the fellows drove to the North Woods in his new car.

But if you cross out all the prepositional phrases like this:

> ~~During the first week~~ of his vacation, one ~~of the fellows~~ drove ~~to the North Woods~~ ~~in his new car.~~

then you have only two words left—the subject and the verb. And even in short sentences like the following, you might pick the wrong word as the subject if you didn't cross out the prepositional phrases first.

> One ~~of my friends~~ lives ~~in Monroeville.~~
> Most ~~of the team~~ went ~~on the trip.~~

The subject is never in a prepositional phrase. Read this list several times to learn to recognize prepositional phrases.

about the desk	**in** the desk
above the desk	**inside** the desk
across the desk	**into** the desk
after vacation	**like** the desk
against the desk	**near** the desk
along the street	**of** the desk
among the desks	**off** the desk
around the desk	**on** the desk
at the desk	**outside** the desk
before vacation	**over** the desk
behind the desk	**past** the desk
below the desk	**since** vacation
beneath the desk	**through** the desk
beside the desk	**to** the desk
between the desks	**toward** the desk
beyond the desk	**under** the desk
by the desk	**until** vacation
down the street	**up** the street
during vacation	**upon** the desk
except the desk	**with** the desk
for the desk	**within** the desk
from the desk	**without** the desk

EXERCISES

Cross out the prepositional phrases. Then underline the subject once and the verb twice. Correct each group of ten sentences before going on.

☐EXERCISE 1

1. One of the most interesting places on our trip was the Japanese garden in the East-West Center in Honolulu.
2. We followed a bamboo-shaded path through the garden.
3. Clumps of ferns bordered the path.
4. Near the path flowed a little stream.
5. In small pools beside the stream were orange and black and white tropical fish.
6. Here and there were Japanese stone lanterns.
7. At the top of the garden was a small waterfall.
8. Stone slab steps beside the waterfall led to a Japanese teahouse.
9. An atmosphere of peace enveloped the garden.
10. Some of the best things in life are still free.

☐EXERCISE 2

1. Behind our house is a row of tall poplar trees.
2. In the front are some blue spruces.
3. In the summer dozens of birds nest in our trees.
4. Among the noisiest are the jays.
5. In winter many birds visit our feeder for grain and seeds.
6. Of them all, the magpies are the most colorful.
7. From branch to branch hop small gray squirrels.
8. During the holidays bird lovers flock to woods and marshes and meadows for the National Audubon Society's Christmas bird count.
9. Most of the participants are experienced bird-watchers.
10. The results of the bird count are important for conservation purposes.

☐EXERCISE 3

1. The largest island in the world is Greenland.
2. New Guinea in the Pacific is the second largest.
3. Both of these islands contain unexplored regions.
4. The interior of Greenland is under an ice cap.
5. In New Guinea a rugged interior discourages travel.

6. Some of the primitive people in New Guinea still use stone tools.
7. Their small thatched houses often stand on poles above the swampy ground.
8. Villages sometimes communicate by the beat of drums.
9. Many of the people have little knowledge of our civilization.
10. Some of the tribes never go outside their own valleys.

□EXERCISE 4

1. One of the greatest magicians of all time was Houdini.
2. After his birth in Budapest in 1874, his family moved to New York City.
3. From the age of 14, he practiced magic tricks.
4. At the age of 17, he became a professional magician.
5. One of his tricks was his Metamorphosis Trick.
6. The meaning of *metamorphosis* is "change."
7. In this trick he escaped, with his hands bound, from a locked trunk.
8. Then Houdini's brother, with hands also bound, appeared in the trunk.
9. On another occasion 40,000 people watched Houdini's daring handcuffed jump from a Pittsburgh bridge.
10. In about three minutes he freed himself under water.

□EXERCISE 5

1. One of the most scenic places in the United States is the 49th state.
2. At the beginning of last summer I flew to Anchorage in Alaska.
3. From there I took a number of backpacking trips.
4. Alaska has 8,000 miles of scenic highways.
5. Within its vastness, everything is big.
6. For example, the Malaspina Glacier is 1,700 square miles in area.
7. And one of the longest navigable rivers in the world is the Yukon.
8. The 20,320-foot Mount McKinley is the tallest peak in North America.
9. Snow perpetually covers the upper two-thirds of the mountain.
10. Mount McKinley is in Denali National Park.

□EXERCISE 6

1. Tobogganing over hard-packed snow is an exciting sport.
2. The Indians were the first to use toboggans.
3. They probably transported things on them.
4. A modern toboggan carries 12 people.

5. A steersman in the rear trails a foot in the snow to guide the toboggan.
6. In the Far North snowshoeing is popular.
7. Snowshoes for traveling in the woods are only two feet long.
8. But Alaskan snowshoes for racing are seven feet long.
9. The first to use snowshoes were the Indians.
10. They probably tied branches of a fir tree to their feet.

Underline the subject once and the verb twice. If you aren't sure, cross out the prepositional phrases first.

☐EXERCISE 7

1. In Rochester, Minnesota, the Municipal Power Plant cools its steam turbines with river water.
2. That warm water then flows into small Silver Lake.
3. During the entire winter the warm water keeps most of the lake free of ice.
4. Some years ago Canada geese discovered this haven of warm water.
5. Now in the first week of September the first geese arrive from Canada.
6. Ten thousand spend the winter on Silver Lake.
7. With their long black necks and white cheeks, they are striking birds.
8. With a wingspan of seven feet, some weigh as much as 20 pounds.
9. With no fear, they come to visitors on the shore for handouts of bread or grain.
10. In late March or early April, they return to their nesting grounds in the lake region of Manitoba.

☐EXERCISE 8

1. The longest national paved road in the world is the Trans-Canada Highway.
2. Canada completed the highway in 1962.
3. About 4,860 miles long, it goes from the Pacific to the Atlantic.
4. At its beginning in Victoria, B.C., is a monument.
5. Through vast forests, over rugged terrain, along lakes, across wide plains, and past capital cities, the highway spans the country.
6. With some 500 bridges and a few automobile ferries, the road crosses rivers and straits.

7. Along the highway about every 50 miles are parks for resting or picnicking.
8. About every 100 to 150 miles are parks for camping.
9. Near the highway are a number of national parks.
10. At the maritime city of St. John's in New Brunswick, the highway comes to its end.

☐EXERCISE 9

1. Last spring I drove with a friend to Pinnacles National Monument near Salinas in California.
2. Neither of us had any mountain climbing experience.
3. Therefore we did no steep climbing.
4. But both of us enjoyed the sight of the rock climbers with their alpine apparatus.
5. Then we hiked the trail to the top of Juniper Canyon.
6. From there we had a view of the entire park and much of the valley.
7. After that we explored the cave at Bear Gulch.
8. With our flashlights we walked through the passageways and under enormous boulders.
9. The trip to Pinnacles was unquestionably one of our best.
10. Both of us hope to go there sometime again.

☐EXERCISE 10

1. With the shortage of jobs today, one field is still without enough applicants.
2. For the job openings in machine tool shops, there are not enough skilled blue-collar workers.
3. Americans today forget the dignity and importance of skilled blue-collar work.
4. Like the stonecutters of medieval Europe, the tool-and-die workers of today are skilled artisans.
5. They make the drills, lathes, presses, and other machines for manufacturing firms.
6. Such jobs often require many years of training in a vocational school.
7. But with 31,000 new openings for skilled machinists annually there are only 2,300 qualified applicants a year.
8. The prestige of white-collar jobs lures young people from careers as trained artisans.
9. Also the low pay for the necessary four years of apprenticeship training discourages them.
10. Such jobs, however, rank seventh in the United States in lifetime earnings.

MORE ABOUT VERBS AND SUBJECTS

Sometimes the verb is more than one word. Here are a few of the many forms of the verb *drive*:

I drive	I will be driving	I may drive
I am driving	I will have been driving	I could drive
I have driven	I will have driven	I might drive
I have been driving	I am driven	I should drive
I drove	I was driven	I would drive
I was driving	I have been driven	I must drive
I had driven	I had been driven	I could have driven
I had been driving	I will be driven	I might have driven
I will drive	I can drive	I should have driven

Note that words like the following are never part of the verb even though they may be in the middle of the verb:

already	even	never	only
also	ever	not	really
always	finally	now	sometimes
before	just	often	usually

Heather <u>had</u> never <u>driven</u> a car before. <u>She</u> <u>had</u> always <u>taken</u> the bus.

Two verb forms—*driving* and *to drive*—look like verbs, but neither can ever be the verb of a sentence. No *ing* word by itself can ever be the verb of a sentence; it must have a helping verb in front of it.

Lester driving his new car (not a sentence because there is no proper verb)

<u>Lester</u> <u>was</u> <u>driving</u> his new car. (a sentence)

And no verb with *to* in front of it can ever be the verb of a sentence.

To drive mountain roads (not a sentence because there is no proper verb and no subject)

<u>I</u> <u>like</u> to drive mountain roads. (a sentence)

These two forms, *driving* and *to drive*, may be used as subjects, or they may have other uses in the sentence.

<u>Driving</u> <u>is</u> expensive. <u>To drive</u> <u>is</u> expensive. <u>I</u> <u>like</u> to drive.

But neither of them can ever be the verb of a sentence.

Not only may a verb be composed of more than one word, but also there may be more than one verb in a sentence:

Pablo <u>read</u> the text and <u>did</u> the exercises.

Also there may be more than one subject.

Pablo and Rita <u>read</u> the text and <u>did</u> the exercises.

EXERCISES

Underline the subject once and the verb twice. Be sure to include all parts of the verb. Also watch for more than one subject and more than one verb. It's a good idea to cross out the prepositional phrases first.

☐**EXERCISE 1**

1. At the beginning of the year I could not concentrate.
2. Every few minutes during a lecture my mind would wander.
3. Then I began to yank my mind back each time.
4. Thus I became conscious of my problem and soon began to improve.
5. After a few weeks I was concentrating better.
6. Now I can sit through a lecture and keep my mind on it.
7. My mind wanders scarcely at all.
8. And surprisingly I am finding the lectures more interesting.
9. I should have been concentrating better at the beginning of the term.
10. Learning to concentrate has been one of my best achievements.

☐**EXERCISE 2**

1. The wind tore the needles from the white pine and scattered them around the yard.
2. The sleet and snow obliterated the view of the road.
3. I shoveled the walks but did not tackle the driveway.
4. A downy woodpecker was hammering at a tree in search of insects.
5. Hugh went to the woods and cut a spruce for a Christmas tree.
6. He removed the bottom branches and put the tree in a stand.
7. The children unpacked the decorations and put them on the tree.
8. The decorations had been used for three generations.
9. Some of the tinsel-framed pictures had been made 60 years before.
10. Everyone was in a good mood and had a good time.

□EXERCISE 3

1. Just for fun browse through the *Guiness Book of World Records* sometime.
2. There you will find some amazing facts.
3. One person in 1958 weighed 1,069 pounds.
4. So don't be discouraged about your weight.
5. The best-selling record of all time is "White Christmas" by Irving Berlin.
6. And the best-selling album is "Saturday Night Fever."
7. The first auto race was from Paris to Bordeaux and back in 1895 with a speed of 15.01 miles per hour.
8. The highest speed for bicycle riding today is 58.64 miles per hour.
9. The most translated poem is "If" by Rudyard Kipling.
10. It has appeared in 27 languages.

□EXERCISE 4

1. Seals spend most of their time in the water but are descended from land animals.
2. They have warm blood, breathe air, and bear living young on land.
3. A seal can close its eyes and ears in diving and can hold enough air in its lungs to stay underwater for several minutes.
4. It uses its flippers for swimming but also uses them like legs to pull itself along on the ground.
5. Conservationists have fought to protect seals and have to some extent succeeded.
6. Conservationists are also working for laws to provide for cleaner air and water.
7. In the past the saying was "clean as driven snow."
8. But today the saying must be changed to "dirty as driven snow."
9. Car exhausts and factories are pouring poisonous lead into the air.
10. And the poisonous lead is being absorbed by the snow.

□EXERCISE 5

1. Cities of the future may look different from those of today.
2. In some cities skyscrapers are going underground.
3. At the University of Minnesota, for example, the Engineering Building goes 110 feet beneath the campus and is only 20 feet above ground.
4. Five floors for the labs and offices have been excavated from glacial rock and limestone.
5. And above ground is the equipment for lighting and heating.

6. One advantage of underground buildings is the conservation of energy.
7. Minnesota's climate varies during the year by about 130°F. but remains about 50°F. all year round below ground.
8. Most of the underground space is lighted by natural light.
9. Reflective lenses on the roof beam sunlight down to the lowest levels.
10. And occupants find the buildings light and airy.

□EXERCISE 6

1. Lincoln was born in a crude log cabin near Hodgenville, Kentucky.
2. The cabin was chinked with clay and had only one room 18 by 16 feet and only one window and one door.
3. Today the cabin has been placed inside an impressive six-columned Grecian-style temple.
4. At 21, Lincoln moved to New Salem, Illinois, and spent six years there.
5. He worked as a rail-splitter, clerk, surveyor, and postmaster and studied law by candlelight.
6. From New Salem, Lincoln was first elected to the Illinois General Assembly.
7. Today New Salem has been reconstructed faithfully to portray that old town.
8. Visitors can ramble through homes, shops, a school, a gristmill, a sawmill, and the Rutledge Tavern.
9. The buildings have all been reproduced and furnished like those of 1830.
10. Visitors can also take a trip on the Sangamon River in a steamship like the one of Lincoln's day.

□EXERCISE 7

1. In my reading I have been learning a lot of miscellaneous facts.
2. For example, a giraffe's tongue may be as long as one and a half feet.
3. And badgers can run backward or forward equally fast.
4. In a pencil dot there are more atoms than the number of people on earth.
5. The estimated life span of Neanderthal man was 29 years.
6. The brightest star in the sky is Sirius in the constellation Canis Major.
7. There are at least 750,000 words in the English language.
8. The earliest form of perfume was incense.
9. But later the Egyptians extracted scent from flower petals and then rubbed the fragrant oil on their bodies.
10. A perfume jar in King Tutankhamen's tomb was still faintly fragrant after more than 3,000 years.

□EXERCISE 8

1. For the first time, scientists have made a map of the ocean floor.
2. A satellite sent them measurements of the height of the ocean surfaces.
3. The ocean surfaces are not the same level everywhere.
4. Within a distance of 30 miles eastward from Japan, for example, the ocean surface level drops 60 feet.
5. The surface level reflects the ocean floor level beneath.
6. The ocean surface is higher over underwater mountains and lower over underwater trenches.
7. Gravity causes this difference.
8. Thus scientists could map the ocean floor by measuring the distance between the satellite and the ocean surfaces.
9. The resulting ocean floor map shows hills and valleys.
10. And it reveals mountains as tall as Mount Everest and trenches six times deeper than the Grand Canyon.

□EXERCISE 9

1. Shoes have had a long history.
2. In ancient times people covered their feet with bark, leaves, or animal skins and held the materials in place with thongs.
3. Sandals of papyrus leaves have been found in Egyptian tombs of 2000 B.C.
4. During the Renaissance, people of high rank wore shoes with long toes and sometimes tied the toes up to their knees with small chains.
5. The highest-ranking persons wore shoes with the longest toes.
6. Some shoes were two and a half feet from heel to toe.
7. In 1324, Edward II originated shoe sizes, with a third of an inch between sizes.
8. Some Venetian ladies imitated Oriental styles and wore shoes with soles of blocks of wood.
9. Until the middle of the nineteenth century all shoes were made by hand.
10. And not until the time of the Civil War were shoes made differently for right and left feet.

□EXERCISE 10

1. I have been reading about the origin of the names of some common products.
2. Many products, of course, were named after their producers.

3. Bird's Eye products, for example, were named for the frozen food pioneer, Clarence Birdseye.
4. But the names of some other products have interesting stories behind them.
5. The Chevrolet was named for the famed race driver of the early 1900s, Louis Chevrolet.
6. Maxwell House coffee was first served in the Maxwell House hotel in Nashville, Tennessee, and took its name from the hotel.
7. And on a visit there, Teddy Roosevelt asked for a second cup and called the coffee "good to the last drop."
8. The buses between Duluth and Hibbing, Minnesota, were painted gray because of the dusty roads.
9. A hotel owner along the way likened them to running greyhound dogs.
10. And from that remark the Greyhound buses of today got their name.

JOURNAL WRITING

From your most recent paper, copy three sentences, and underline the subject and verb in each.

WRITING ASSIGNMENT

As you get back your writing assignments, are you keeping a list of your misspelled words on the inside back cover of this book?

CORRECTING RUN-TOGETHER SENTENCES

Any group of words having a subject and verb is a clause. The clause may be independent (able to stand alone) or dependent (unable to stand alone). Every sentence you have worked with so far has been an independent clause because it has been able to stand alone. It has made a complete statement.

If two independent clauses are written together with no punctuation or with merely a comma, they are called a run-together sentence. (Some textbooks call them a run-on sentence, a comma splice, or a comma fault.) Here are some examples.

> She mowed the lawn he prepared the lunch.
> She mowed the lawn, he prepared the lunch.
> I like camping therefore I enjoyed the trip.
> I like camping, therefore I enjoyed the trip.

Run-together sentences can be corrected in one of three ways:

1. Make the two independent clauses into two sentences.

> She mowed the lawn. He prepared the lunch.
> I like camping. Therefore I enjoyed the trip.

2. Separate the two independent clauses with a semicolon.

> She mowed the lawn; he prepared the lunch.
> I like camping; therefore I enjoyed the trip.
> I wrote a rough draft of my paper; then I revised it.
> I revised it once more; finally it was finished.

When a connecting word such as

also	however	otherwise
consequently	likewise	then
finally	moreover	therefore
furthermore	nevertheless	thus

comes between two independent clauses, that word must have a semicolon before it. It may also have a comma after it, especially if there seems to be a pause between the word and the rest of the clause.

> I like camping; however, I was too busy to go.
> I had work to do; furthermore, I was short of cash.
> She likes canvassing; also, she considers it a duty.
> The voter turnout was small; nevertheless, our candidate won.

The semicolon before the connecting word is required. The comma after it is a matter of choice.

3. Connect the two independent clauses with a comma and one of the following words:

and	or	so
but	nor	
for	yet	

She mowed the lawn, and he prepared the lunch.
I like camping, but I was too busy to go.
I helped with the canvass, for it was my duty.
We'd better hurry, or we'll never finish.
I've never tried scuba diving, nor do I want to.

But be sure there are two independent clauses. The first sentence below has two independent clauses. The second sentence is merely one independent clause with two verbs, and therefore no comma should be used.

She jogged two kilometers, and then she had breakfast.
She jogged two kilometers and then had breakfast.

THE THREE WAYS TO PUNCTUATE INDEPENDENT CLAUSES
He went to his room. He needed to study.
He went to his room; he needed to study.
He went to his room, for he needed to study.

Learn these three ways, and you'll avoid run-together sentences.

You may wonder when to use a period and capital letter and when to use a semicolon between two independent clauses. In general, use a period and capital letter. Only if the clauses are closely related in meaning should you use a semicolon.

EXERCISES

In each independent clause underline the subject once and the verb twice. Then be ready to give a reason for the punctuation.

☐EXERCISE 1

1. It takes weeks for a monarch butterfly to develop; its development is called metamorphosis.
2. Butterfly eggs are laid on milkweed leaves. From the eggs little caterpillars emerge.
3. The caterpillars eat milkweed leaves, but in turn the caterpillars may be eaten by birds.
4. A caterpillar sheds its skin several times during its growth; each time the skin is slightly larger.
5. Finally the caterpillar is full-grown, and it sheds its skin a final time.
6. Now it has turned into a beautiful chrysalis or sack. The chrysalis is jade green dotted with gold.
7. For several weeks the chrysalis is quiet. Changes are occurring within it.
8. Then finally it cracks open, and an adult monarch butterfly with soft limp wings emerges.
9. Soon the wings dry and harden. Then the monarch flies away.
10. It goes to find a mate and to start another generation

Most—but not all—of the following sentences are run-together. If the sentence is run-together, separate the two clauses with the correct punctuation —comma, semicolon, or period with a capital letter. In general, use the period with a capital letter rather than the semicolon. But either way is correct. Thus your answers may differ from those at the back of the book.

☐EXERCISE 2

1. I never liked math I always slept through class.
2. Then I suddenly woke up I had failed my midterm.
3. I went to see my professor and he confirmed my fears.
4. I had only one chance I had to do well on the final.
5. In other words, in four weeks I had to learn an entire semester's work I got busy.
6. I worked hours and hours and hours I hardly slept at all.

7. But I walked into that final confident and began doing each problem in a frenzy.
8. It took a week to get the grades during that week I slept.
9. Then the report came and I opened it.
10. I had not only passed but had got a good mark I must have aced that final.

☐EXERCISE 3

1. My high school adviser was close to me she was almost my best friend.
2. She was busy but she always made time for me.
3. Sometimes she would just listen occasionally she would give advice.
4. At first I wasn't interested in her suggestion about a career then I changed my mind.
5. It is going to take time but eventually I should get a good position.
6. I hope to finish college in three more years then I'll apply for a job.
7. In education we need a balance between receiving and sending.
8. Reading is receiving writing is sending.
9. Writing is hard work but it's satisfying.
10. It's not much fun to write but it's fun to have written.

☐EXERCISE 4

1. The first man to reach the North Pole alone was Naomi Uemura he planted the Japanese flag at the pole on May 1, 1978.
2. Uemura was then at the top of the world every direction was south.
3. His sledge had been pulled across the frozen Arctic by his 17 huskies it took 57 days to travel 477 miles.
4. Sometimes temperatures dropped as low as −68°F. and blizzards slowed him down.
5. He wore modern thermal underwear but the rest of his clothing was Eskimo gear.
6. One morning he was awakened by the barking of his dogs and he saw a giant white polar bear coming toward his tent.
7. Uemura was frightened and decided to play dead in his sleeping bag.
8. The bear destroyed the tent and ate the food supply then he poked the sleeping bag and turned it over.
9. Uemura lay still in the bag and finally the bear wandered off.
10. The next morning the bear returned and Uemura shot him at a range of 55 yards.

☐EXERCISE 5

1. In June the big brown bears of Alaska have a feast it is spawning time for the salmon.

2. Usually the brown bears are solitary wanderers but in June they come together by the dozens for a feast of sockeye salmon.
3. The salmon swim up the rivers by the thousands and leap out of the water to get to their spawning grounds farther up the rivers.
4. The brown bears have been hibernating for six months and are gaunt and hungry.
5. All the brown bears fish but they fish in different ways.
6. Some snatch a leaping salmon in midair some sit down in the middle of a river and pin the salmon to the bottom with their paws.
7. Others walk along the bank and then belly flop into the river on top of their prey.
8. To survive the coming winter the bears must put on huge quantities of fat a bear may eat a dozen of the five- to ten-pound fish in one day.
9. A mature bear may weigh more than 1,200 pounds but a newborn cub weighs less than two pounds.
10. A cub has a great appetite and feeding her cub can be a full-time job for a mother.

☐EXERCISE 6

1. The lake is silent no trout break the surface of the water.
2. No tree frogs chirp no loons are heard.
3. Because of acid rain hundreds of lakes across the country are silent researchers found the acidic content of fog near Los Angeles greater than that of vinegar.
4. Buildings and monuments are being corroded farmers are concerned about their crops.
5. Furthermore, acid rain has hurt the relations between Canada and the United States Canada blames the United States for half of the acid rain endangering its countryside.
6. Automobile exhausts are partly to blame the main culprit, however, is industrial smokestack emissions.
7. These emissions are responsible for most of the sulfur dioxide in the atmosphere the sulfur dioxide reacts in the sunlight with water vapor to become acid rain.
8. Environmentalists are now taking a stronger stand they are recommending more stringent pollution controls.
9. A "scrubbing" technique can remove as much as 90 percent of the sulfur dioxide from smokestack emissions the coal-burning utilities, therefore, will have to "scrub" their emissions.
10. The technique, however, is expensive industries naturally are not rushing to adopt it.

☐EXERCISE 7

1. Creating is always more satisfying than acquiring making a table is more fun than buying one.
2. My brother made an elegant coffee table from an old door and two cardboard cartons it just took a little imagination and some work.
3. He enameled the cartons and the center panel of the door white and the rest of the door he enameled black.
4. The result was striking it was the main attraction in his living room.
5. Another rewarding activity is refinishing it's particularly satisfying to refinish a family heirloom.
6. Each piece needs special treatment and it's important to know your woods.
7. An electric sander can be used for a badly marred piece but the final sanding must be done by hand.
8. You will have to remove the old finish from that cupboard or the new finish will never be right.
9. Strip the cupboard of old wax and varnish then apply a mixture of boiled linseed oil and turpentine and finally finish the piece with clear varnish.
10. It will take work but you can often turn a cast-off piece into a prized family possession.

☐EXERCISE 8

1. The first step toward success is to learn to work work is more important than luck.
2. A certain amount of tension is good for one unstring the lyre and the harmony is gone.
3. Henry Ford said, "Old men are always advising young men to save money that is bad advice don't save every nickel invest in yourself I never saved a dollar until I was forty years old."
4. A politician is worried about the next election a statesman is worried about the next generation.
5. Happiness comes from sharing experiences it does not come from owning things.
6. George Bernard Shaw wrote four novels in the first nine years of his writing career none was accepted by a publisher.
7. Always behave like a duck keep calm and unruffled on the surface but paddle like the devil underneath.
8. He is always ready to criticize yet he himself cannot tolerate criticism.
9. Some of his statements are thought-provoking others are just provoking.
10. The world's most valuable painting is the *Mona Lisa* in the Louvre it was assessed for insurance purposes at $100,000,000.

☐**EXERCISE 9**

1. The once desolate Demilitarized Zone (DMZ) between North and South Korea is still not inhabited by people but perhaps for that very reason it has become a haven for birds and animals.
2. The zone stretches for 151 miles between North and South Korea it is 2.5 miles wide.
3. After the war the zone was a land of bomb craters and shell holes but now nature has taken over.
4. Observation planes still patrol it and the sights in innumerable guns sweep it constantly.
5. But abandoned fields have turned into marshes for waterfowl and thickets provide a home for Asian river deer.
6. In the mountainous parts, lynx and tigers roam pheasants wander across abandoned roads.
7. The zone is one of the few places in the world unharmed by pesticides and herbicides thus wildlife can flourish.
8. The most spectacular inhabitant of the zone is the Manchurian crane, a striking white, black, and red bird with a wingspan of eight feet and with an elaborate mating ritual including wing flapping, bows, and leaps into the air.
9. Once there were hundreds of these cranes but now only a few flocks remain three of the flocks winter in the DMZ.
10. The crane is the symbol of the South Korean airline and also is something of a national symbol.

JOURNAL WRITING

Write three sentences to illustrate the three ways of punctuating two independent clauses in a sentence. Master this section before you go on. It will take care of many of your punctuation errors.

WRITING ASSIGNMENT

Continue with your writing assignments. Have someone dictate to you your list of spelling words on the inside back cover. Can you spell them all correctly now?

CORRECTING FRAGMENTS

There are two kinds of clauses: independent (which we have just finished studying) and dependent. A dependent clause has a subject and a verb just like an independent clause, but it can't stand alone because it begins with a dependent word (or words) such as

after	since	whereas
although	so that	wherever
as	than	whether
as if	that	which
because	though	whichever
before	unless	while
even if	until	who
even though	what	whom
ever since	whatever	whose
how	when	why
if	whenever	
in order that	where	

Whenever a clause begins with one of the above dependent words (unless it's a question, which would never give you any trouble), it is dependent. If we take an independent clause such as

We finished the game.

and put one of the dependent words in front of it, it becomes dependent:

After we finished the game
Although we finished the game
As we finished the game
Before we finished the game
Since we finished the game
That we finished the game
When we finished the game
While we finished the game

As you read the clause, you can hear that it doesn't make a complete statement. It leaves the reader expecting something more. Therefore it can no longer stand alone. It's a fragment and must not be punctuated as a sentence. To correct such a fragment, simply add an independent clause:

After we finished the game, we went to the clubhouse.
We went to the clubhouse after we finished the game.
We were happy that we finished the game early.
While we finished the game, the others waited.

In other words **EVERY SENTENCE MUST HAVE AT LEAST ONE INDEPENDENT CLAUSE.**

Note in the examples that when a dependent clause comes at the beginning of a sentence, it is followed by a comma. Often the comma prevents misreading, as in the following sentence:

When the instructor entered, the room became quiet.

Without a comma after *entered*, the reader would read *When the instructor entered the room* before realizing that that was not what the author meant. The comma prevents misreading. Sometimes if the dependent clause is short and there is no danger of misreading, the comma is omitted, but it's safer simply to follow the rule that a dependent clause at the beginning of a sentence is followed by a comma.

You'll learn more about the punctuation of dependent clauses on pages 173–78, but right now just remember the above rule.

Note that sometimes the dependent word is the subject of the dependent clause:

I finished the cookies <u>that were</u> left.

Sometimes the dependent clause is in the middle of the independent clause:

The cookies <u>that were left</u> didn't last long.

And sometimes the dependent clause is the subject of the entire sentence:

<u>What I was doing was</u> important.

Also note that sometimes the *that* of a dependent clause is omitted:

This is the house <u>that Jack built.</u>
This is the house <u>Jack built.</u>
I thought <u>that you liked math.</u>
I thought <u>you liked math.</u>

And finally the word *that* doesn't always introduce a dependent clause. It may be a pronoun (That is my book) or a describing word (I like that book).

EXERCISES

Underline the subject once and the verb twice in both the independent and the dependent clauses. Then put a broken line under the dependent clause.

☐**EXERCISE 1**

1. You have to practice until using the rules of writing becomes automatic.

2. When you know a few rules, writing becomes easier.

3. The only difference between an independent and a dependent clause is that the dependent clause begins with a dependent word.

4. If you know the dependent words, you'll have no trouble.

5. If you don't, you may not punctuate your sentences correctly.

6. A comma is required when a dependent clause comes first in a sentence.

7. When a dependent clause comes first in a sentence, a comma often prevents misreading.

8. When you have done a few sentences, the rule becomes easy.

9. It will help you when you are punctuating your papers.

10. When you punctuate correctly, your reader can read with ease.

Underline each dependent clause with a broken line.

☐**EXERCISE 2**

1. There's a clean-up crew out there that is working day and night.
2. It is cleaning the forest floor of debris, which amounts to about 3,000 pounds of dead plants and animals per acre every year.
3. First the debris is attacked by microorganisms, which may number ten billion in just 60 cubic inches of forest soil.
4. Then fungi and mushrooms soften the debris still more until it can be eaten by earthworms and insects.

5. As these creatures pass the debris through their digestive systems, the digested material returns vital minerals to the soil.
6. In a single acre in one year, earthworms digest some ten tons of debris and soil, which then nourish new plants and animals.
7. Charles Darwin said that without earthworms all vegetation would perish.
8. This recycling process, which involves billions of organisms, is relatively rapid.
9. Although pine needles may take three or four years to be turned into soil, red and yellow autumn leaves take only two.
10. Without this clean-up crew that recycles the forest floor, soil would not be replenished, and plants would cease to grow.

Source: *National Wildlife*, April–May 1983.

□EXERCISE 3

1. In Boettcher Hall in Denver, which is the first "surround" music hall in the country, the orchestra performs in the center of the hall, and the audience is seated all around it.
2. While most seats are within 65 feet of the stage, no seat is farther than 85 feet away.
3. The hall, which opened in 1978 to raves from the public and from music and architecture critics, will do much for the Denver Symphony.
4. Other cities that have "surround" music halls are Mexico City and Berlin.
5. The city that has the most telephones per capita is Washington, D.C.
6. It has more phones than it has people.
7. It has 158.6 phones per 100 persons whereas the national average is 77 phones per 100 persons.
8. I'm taking a course in astronomy that has opened my eyes to the universe.
9. I've learned that the light from one galaxy started to come to us 100 million years ago when dinosaurs were on earth, but it is reaching us only now.
10. And some matter in the universe is so dense that one teaspoonful of it would weigh as much as 200 million elephants.

If the clause is independent and therefore a sentence, put a period after it. If the clause is dependent and therefore a fragment, add an independent clause either before or after it to make it into a sentence. Remember that if the dependent clause comes first, it should have a comma after it.

☐EXERCISE 4

1. Whenever you are ready to leave

2. Fragments must not be punctuated as sentences

3. On the horizon the moon was just coming up

4. Because I tried harder and harder and finally succeeded

5. That she was a loving and trusting person

6. If I would study more and spend more time writing my papers

7. After I had played tennis for two hours without stopping

8. Although I had never been in Woodland Hills before

9. Wherever I went on those streets

10. While I enjoyed the view

☐EXERCISE 5

1. Where we camped last year

2. While she sat in the shade and drank lemonade

3. Don't try to stop me

4. Because I know she will understand

5. After I came home and took a long shower

6. Because most of my nervousness is caused by drinking too much coffee

7. As I become more and more sure of myself

8. I enjoy hang gliding

9. Before I took this course and learned a few rules

10. The cost of living in an apartment isn't really so great

On pages 72–73 you learned three ways of correcting run-together sentences. Now that you are aware of dependent clauses, you may use a fourth way. In the following run-together sentence

We had driven 400 miles we stopped for the night.

you can make one of the two independent clauses into a dependent clause by putting a dependent word in front of it, as in the following examples:

Since we had driven 400 miles, we stopped for the night.
We stopped for the night after we had driven 400 miles.
When we've driven 400 miles, we usually stop for the night.

This fourth way of correcting a run-together sentence is often the best because it puts the more important of the two ideas in the independent clause and thus makes it stand out.

Correct the following run-together sentences by making one of the clauses dependent. In some sentences you will want to put the dependent clause first; in others you may want to put it last or in the middle of the sentence. Since various words can be used to start a dependent clause, your answers may differ from those suggested at the back of the book.

☐EXERCISE 6

1. Yesterday we went to the zoo I hadn't been there for ages.

2. We went first to the sea lion tank I wanted to feed the sea lions.

3. They ignored the fish that we threw to them they had been fed too many fish.

4. They were named sea lions long ago someone thought they roared like lions.

5. They are really seals and are related to fur seals they lack the valuable coats of the fur seals.

6. In another part of the zoo small whales performed tricks they can be trained just like seals.

7. Next we saw a sable antelope she had a one-day-old baby.

8. She prodded the baby with her knee she wanted to make it walk.

9. She was persistent finally she made it take a couple of steps.

10. I always learn a lot at the zoo I should go more often.

☐EXERCISE 7

1. I've often said "busy as a beaver" I really knew nothing about beavers.

2. Now I know a little I've just read an article about them.

3. A beaver's four front teeth are constantly growing the beaver wears them down by gnawing trees to make dams.

4. A beaver's teeth are sharp a beaver can cut down a small willow in only a few minutes.

5. The tree suddenly begins to totter then the beaver dashes for safety.

6. Finally all is quiet again then the beaver returns to work.

7. A family of beavers work hard they can fell a thousand trees in a year.

8. A beaver has a flat tail he uses it in many ways.

9. He stands up to gnaw a tree his tail serves as a prop.

10. He slaps his tail against the water his tail sounds an alarm.

☐EXERCISE 8

1. One Christmas I got a new hockey stick I was about eleven.

2. I thought I could play better with a new stick therefore I was inspired.

3. We played with a tennis ball on the street we called it street hockey.

4. The goalie wore a baseball glove on one hand he wielded a hockey stick with the other.

5. We hit that tennis ball hard he tried to keep us from shooting it past him.

6. It got really cold in the winter then we flooded the backyard.

7. Finally the ice became solid my brother and I put on our skates.

8. We played with a real puck we pretended we were stars of the Maple Leafs.

9. The whole neighborhood gathered at our "rink" we felt like real pros.

10. Those were exciting games they left some great memories.

□EXERCISE 9

1. Most of the trash in the United States is burned or buried or dumped only a fraction of it is recycled.

2. Newsprint can be recycled many times it's a billion dollar business.

3. At the World Trade Center in New York, not even a memo is wasted each day's wastepaper is sold to paper brokers.

4. Aluminum is the most treasured trash reprocessing aluminum takes only 5 percent of the energy needed to smelt new metal.

5. The United States now recycles about 32 percent of its aluminum that is twice as much as was recycled 12 years ago.

6. But we don't recycle as much garbage as we should we lag behind other countries in turning refuse into a resource.

7. It isn't surprising that Japan is a leader among nations in recycling one Tokyo suburb recycles 90 percent of its garbage.

8. The rest of the suburb's garbage is burned for energy the suburb managers sometimes complain that there isn't enough garbage.

9. The United States needs to catch up with the other countries a valuable resource is being wasted.

10. Individual communities can act the national government also needs to pass laws to encourage recycling.

MORE ABOUT FRAGMENTS

We have seen that a dependent clause alone is a fragment. Any group of words that does not have a subject and verb is also a fragment.

> Spent too much time on video games (no subject)
> Julio wondering about his girlfriend (no proper verb. Although *ing* words look like verbs, no *ing* word by itself can ever be the verb of a sentence. It must have a helping verb in front of it.)
> Walking along the busy street (no subject and no proper verb)
> The letter that I had been expecting (no verb for an independent clause)

To change these fragments into sentences, we must give each a subject and an adequate verb:

> He spent too much time on video games. (We added a subject.)
> Julio was wondering about his girlfriend. (We put a helping verb in front of the *ing* word to make a proper verb.)
> Walking along the busy street, he met an old friend. (We added an independent clause.)
> The letter that I had been expecting finally came. (We added a verb to make an independent clause.)

Sometimes you can simply tack a fragment onto the sentence before or after it.

> Wondering why he hadn't phoned me. I finally phoned him.
> Wondering why he hadn't phoned me, I finally phoned him.

Or you can change a word or two in the fragment and make it into a sentence.

> Wondering why he hadn't phoned me.
> I wondered why he hadn't phoned me.

Are fragments ever permissible? Increasingly, fragments are being used in advertising and in other kinds of writing. In Exercises 4 through 8 you'll find advertisements that make use of fragments effectively to give a dramatic pause between individual parts of a sentence. But such fragments are used by writers who know what they're doing. The fragments are used intentionally, never in error. Until you're an experienced writer, stick with complete sentences. Especially in college writing, fragments should not be used.

EXERCISES

Put a period after each sentence. Make each fragment into a sentence either by adding an independent clause before or after it or by changing some words in it. Sometimes changing just one word will change a fragment into a sentence.

☐EXERCISE 1

1. Thinking we had missed the turn several miles back

2. Leaving me standing there holding the bag

3. Not just kids my own age but younger and older people too

4. Never believing anyone would come to my rescue

5. Whether we won or lost

6. Going to meetings that served no purpose

7. He decided to take charge of his life

8. Doing only the things that he wanted to do

9. Confidence that was built up after each win

10. If he were someone whom I could sit down and talk to

☐EXERCISE 2

1. Learning to say no has been difficult for me

2. Writing a clear thesis statement and backing it up with reasons

3. She looked in shop windows at the many things that she did not want

4. Begin at the beginning

5. If you do things for others without being asked

6. Something that will take years of experience to learn

7. Make your own decisions instead of letting someone else make them

8. Making a summary is excellent training in writing clearly

9. Writing a journal is good training too

10. Constantly striving to improve my writing

☐**EXERCICE 3**

1. My decision to look up all the words I don't know

2. Keep calm

3. Something that I had always wanted to do

4. While I still have time to finish my paper

5. Make out a study schedule

6. Which is what I should have done long ago

7. That the Mounties always get their man

8. Making the most of every opportunity

9. That the Nile is the longest river in the world

10. Making that decision changed my life

In the following excerpts from advertisements, the writers have chosen to use fragments. Although the fragments are effective in the ads, they wouldn't be acceptable in formal writing. On a separate sheet rewrite each ad, turning it into acceptable college writing.

☐**EXERCICE 4**

Come to Canada. The Endless Surprise. Around the corner. Down the road. Just over the hill. Wherever you turn, your Canadian vacation is a medley of fascinating histories and colourful cultures. Where honoured customs live on amid the modern. Old-world beside the cosmopolitan. And where your pleasure and comfort is always our first concern.

—Canada

☐EXERCISE 5

Spring and summer are full of big events. Like graduations and picnics. Maybe a June wedding. There's always a birthday to celebrate. Or, the big Fourth of July softball game.

To capture all your big events, get plenty of Polaroid 600 High Speed or Time-Zero Supercolor film.

—Polaroid

☐EXERCISE 6

Y is for you. You secretaries. We've spent the last 50 years making typing easier. For you. And our typewriters smarter. For you. And sturdier. For you. And you? Well, you didn't forget us. When asked which make of typewriter you prefer, you said IBM. Thank you.

—IBM

☐EXERCISE 7

Who cares? Who cares about smoggy skies and polluted lakes. About empty cans and trash littering our countryside. About plants and trees dying in our forests. And animals too. Who cares? Woodsy Owl, the Nation's new battler for a clean environment cares. And so should you. Join Woodsy in the fight against pollution. GIVE A HOOT! DON'T POLLUTE.

—American Automobile Association

☐EXERCISE 8

Close your eyes. Now have someone read this to you.

You are blind. A student. Facing four years of college. With about thirty-two textbooks to read. Plus fifty supplemental texts. How are you going to manage?

With Recording for the Blind. Since 1951, we've helped over 53,000 blind, perceptually and physically handicapped students get through school. By sending them recordings of the books they need to read. Free.

Recording for the Blind is nonprofit, and supported by volunteers and contributions from people like you who can imagine what it's like to be blind.

—Recording for the Blind, Inc.

Review of Run-together Sentences and Fragments

**SIX SENTENCES THAT SHOW HOW TO
PUNCTUATE CLAUSES**

I gave a party. Everybody came. I gave a party; everybody came.	(two independent clauses)
I gave a party; moreover, everybody came.	(two independent clauses connected by a word such as *also, consequently, finally, furthermore, however, likewise, moreover, nevertheless, otherwise, therefore, then, thus*)
I gave a party, and everybody came.	(two independent clauses connected by *and, but, for, or, nor, yet, so*)
When I gave a party, everybody came.	(dependent clause at beginning of sentence)
Everybody came when I gave a party.	(dependent clause at end of sentence) The dependent words are *after, although, as, as if, because, before, even if, even though, ever since, how, if, in order that, since, so that, than, that, though, unless, until, what, whatever, when, whenever, where, whereas, wherever, whether, which, whichever, while, who, whom, whose, why*

If you remember these six sentences and understand the rules for their punctuation, most of your punctuation problems will be taken care of. It is essential that you learn the italicized words in the above table. If your instructor reads some of the words, be ready to tell which ones come between independent clauses and which ones introduce dependent clauses.

Put periods and capital letters in these selections so that there will be no run-together sentences or fragments.

1. Robert Frost is undoubtedly the most beloved American poet people who are indifferent to most poetry can often quote "Birches" or "Stopping by Woods on a Snowy Evening" he writes about the country-side and the country people of Vermont and about his own choice to take the road less traveled by.

2. There's a place set deep in the woods of northern Minnesota that is very special to me every time I go there I'm surrounded with feelings of serenity the quietness of the area is something that I don't find any-where else there's an occasional cry of a hawk circling up above, and sometimes I hear chipmunks scurrying around in the leaves on the ground these noises always make me feel closer to nature I some-times wish that I could be as free as that hawk or as carefree as that chipmunk.

3. I began wrestling seriously in my freshman year the wrestling coach was walking around and talking to the kids playing football he was looking for recruits for the upcoming wrestling season several of my friends had decided that they would go out for the team I decided wrestling would be a good way to keep busy through the winter look-ing back over my wrestling years, I feel it was good for me I learned that through hard work I could accomplish my goals my career in wrestling is something that I can take pride in.

Here are the first four paragraphs of Martin Luther King, Jr.'s speech "I Have a Dream," given to 200,000 people gathered in front of the Lincoln Memorial in Washington on August 28, 1963. As King spoke, the audience could see the huge statue of Lincoln in the background.

The four paragraphs are printed here without the periods and capital letters that separate the sentences. Read the speech aloud and put in the periods and capital letters. (King does not use semicolons. And where you might expect a comma, he often begins a new sentence with *So* or *But*.) Correct your work by the original speech at the back of the book.

"I Have a Dream . . ."
Martin Luther King, Jr.

Five score years ago, a great American, in whose symbolic shadow we stand, signed the Emancipation Proclamation this momentous decree came as a great beacon light of hope to millions of Negro slaves who had been seared in the flames of withering injustice it came as a joyous daybreak to end the long night of captivity

But one hundred years later, we must face the tragic fact that the Negro is still not free one hundred years later, the life of the Negro is still sadly crippled by the manacles of segregation and the chains of discrimination one hundred years later, the Negro lives on a lonely island of poverty in the midst of a vast ocean of material prosperity one hundred years later, the Negro is still languished in the corners of American society and finds himself an exile in his own land so we have come here today to dramatize an appalling condition

In a sense we have come to our nation's Capital to cash a check when the architects of our republic wrote the magnificent words of the Constitution and the Declaration of Independence, they were signing a promissory note to which every American was to fall heir this note was a promise that all men would be guaranteed the unalienable rights of life, liberty, and the pursuit of happiness

It is obvious today that America has defaulted on this promissory note insofar as her citizens of color are concerned instead of honoring this sacred obligation, America has given the Negro people a bad check, a check which has come back marked "insufficient funds" but we refuse to believe that the bank of justice is bankrupt we refuse to believe that there are insufficient funds in the great vaults of opportunity of this nation so we have come to cash this check—a check that will give us upon demand the riches of freedom and the security of justice we have also come to this hallowed spot to remind America of the fierce urgency of now this is no time to engage in the luxury of cooling off or to take the tranquilizing drug of gradualism now is the time to make real the promises of Democracy now is the time to rise from the dark and desolate valley of segregation to the sunlit path of racial justice now is the time to open the doors of opportunity to all of God's children now is the time to lift our nation from the quicksands of racial injustice to the solid rock of brotherhood

Proofreading Exercise

Can you find all five errors in this student paper? They are errors in words often confused, contractions, and the punctuation of sentences. You're on your own now. No answer is provided at the back of the book for this exercise.

SONGS MY MOTHER TAUGHT ME

Thunderous applause filled the auditorium. A restraining hand was placed in mine as I squirmed with childish pride. Then the woman on the platform began her last number, "Songs My Mother Taught Me" by Anton Dvořák.

Tears of joy filled my eyes. Again their was applause and the audience slowly filed out. I overheard many complimentary remarks that evening about the soloist and after every one I resolved to do what she had done. I would fill the hearts of an audience with joy and sorrow, hope and faith. This I resolved as I listened to the first program I had ever heard my mother sing.

I couldnt express my feelings then, for I was to young. Now I have realized a part of that determination but only a part. I hope someday to do as she did that day long ago and sing to a large audience the "Songs *My* Mother Taught Me."

USING STANDARD ENGLISH VERBS

This chapter and the next are for those who need practice in using standard English verbs. Many of us grew up speaking a dialect other than standard English, whether it was in a farm community where people said *I ain't* and *he don't* and *they was* or in a black community where people said *I be* and *it do* and *they has*. Such dialects are powerful and colorful in their place, but in college and in the business and professional world, the use of standard English is essential. Frequently, though, after students have learned to speak and write standard English, they go back to their home communities and are able to slip back into their community dialects while they are there. Thus they have really become bilingual, able to use two languages—or at least two dialects.

The following tables compare four verbs in one of the community dialects with the same four verbs in standard English. Memorize the standard English forms of these important verbs. Most verbs have endings like the first verb *walk*. The other three verbs are irregular and are important because they are used not only as main verbs but also as helping verbs. We'll be using them as helping verbs in the next chapter.

Don't go on to the exercises until you have memorized the forms of these standard English verbs.

REGULAR VERB: WALK

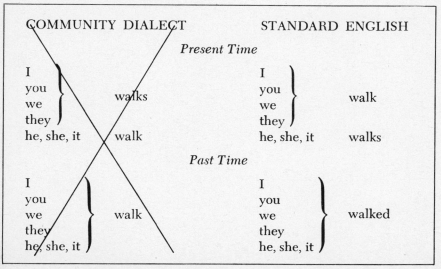

IRREGULAR VERB: HAVE

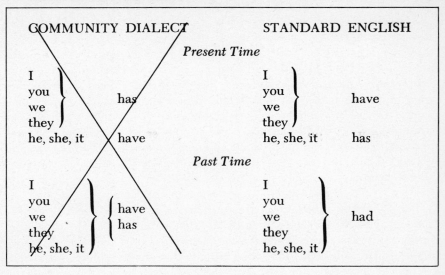

IRREGULAR VERB: BE

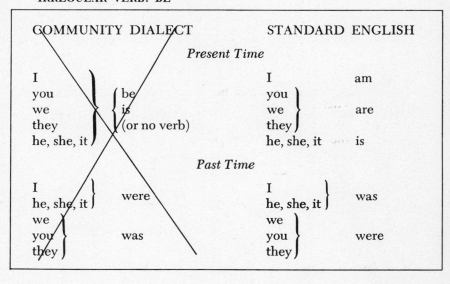

IRREGULAR VERB: DO

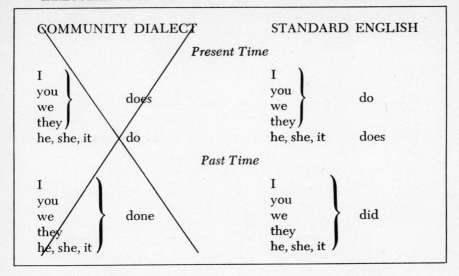

Sometimes students have difficulty with the correct endings of verbs because they don't hear the words correctly. As you listen to your instructor or to TV, note carefully the *s* sound and the *ed* sound at the end of words. Occasionally the *ed* is not clearly pronounced, as in *He asked me to go*, but most of the time you can hear it if you listen.

Try reading the following sentences aloud, making sure that you say every sound.

1. He walks to work and takes the bus home.
2. He likes his work and finds it challenging.
3. She never asks for any help.
4. She hopes they reversed the charge.
5. We walked a long way before we stopped.
6. He learned all he hoped he would from the course.
7. She decided to rest before she started to work.
8. We supposed no one was interested in our plan.

Now read some other sentences aloud from this text, making sure that you sound all the *s*'s and *ed*'s. Listening to others and reading aloud will help you use the correct verb endings automatically.

A good way to learn to speak standard English is to make a pact with a friend that you will both speak only standard English when you are together. By correcting each other, you'll soon find yourselves speaking easily.

EXERCISES

Underline the standard English verb form. All the verbs follow the pattern of the regular verb *walk* except the three irregular verbs *have*, *be*, and *do*. Keep referring to the tables if you're not sure which form to use. Correct your answers for each exercise before going on to the next.

☐EXERCISE 1

1. Yesterday when I (walk walked) to class, I (happen happened) to see Tony.
2. Tony (doesn't don't) know what he (want wants) to be.
3. Last year he (drop dropped) out of college, but this fall he (return returned).
4. He (do does) better now in all his courses.
5. He (ask asked) me to listen to the history paper he had written.
6. He read it to me, and that (help helped) him catch some errors.
7. We (finish finished) class early, and afterward I (talk talked) to the instructor.
8. We (discuss discussed) my term paper, and her comments (help helped) me.
9. She said that she (enjoy enjoyed) reading my paper.
10. I (work worked) hard on that paper. All the students (work works) hard in that class.

☐EXERCISE 2

1. Later that afternoon Tony (ask asked) me to go out for a coke.
2. It (please pleased) me that he (ask asked) me.
3. We (walk walked) down to the Sweet Shop and (order ordered) coke and pizza.
4. Tony (like likes) pizza now, but last year he always (order ordered) chili.
5. We (was were) at the Sweet Shop until six o'clock.
6. Then I (had has) to go home because I (need needed) to study.
7. I always (do does) all my homework.
8. I (has have) to work because I (want wants) an A in that course.
9. I (did done) all my homework last night before I (watch watched) TV.
10. When I (work works) hard, I (am be) satisfied.

☐EXERCISE 3

1. One day last month I (happen happened) to witness a car accident.
2. A police officer (walk walked) up to me and (ask asked) my name.

3. He (suppose supposed) I would be a witness.
4. I (learn learned) that the trial might take several days.
5. I (ask asked) if I could be excused.
6. He said no and (walk walked) away.
7. Therefore I (had have) my first day in court last week.
8. It (was were) an interesting experience.
9. I (am be) glad that I had to go.
10. I (learn learned) a lot that day.

□EXERCISE 4

1. André and I (jog jogged) all the way to the cafeteria yesterday.
2. We (was were) out of breath when we (arrive arrived) there.
3. André and I both (like likes) to ski.
4. We (want wanted) to go skiing last weekend, but it (was were) too warm.
5. Since it (be is) snowing today, we (hope hopes) to go tomorrow.
6. We (prefer prefers) downhill to cross-country.
7. There (be is) a fine ski slope only five miles from here.
8. We (plan plans) to have a full day of skiing.
9. Then we (intend intends) to come home in time for dinner.
10. After that if we (are is) not too tired, we (expect expects) to study.

□EXERCISE 5

1. I suddenly (has have) become aware of solar energy devices.
2. The apartment building where we (live lives) now (has have) solar panels on the roof.
3. Even though the government (has have) cut funds for solar energy research, sun-powered projects (are is) appearing all over the country.
4. Many new housing starts (include includes) solar energy features.
5. Sears (sell sells) solar hot water heaters in a number of cities.
6. Many low-income housing projects (draw draws) energy from rooftop solar collectors.
7. Private industry also now (has have) decided that solar energy (be is) a good investment.
8. A meat-packing plant in Wisconsin (has have) the world's largest sun-powered industrial system, which (save saves) the company $200,000 a year.
9. And one of the world's largest oil companies (has have) a solar power plant that (provide provides) electricity for 6,400 customers.
10. Some members of Congress (think thinks) the government should give more help to the young industry.

In these sentences cross out the community dialect words and write the standard English ones above.

☐EXERCISE 6

1. I attend a music camp last summer.

2. I plays the drums now, but I play the trombone last year.

3. I expects to go to the camp again this coming summer.

4. We work hard there last summer, and we learn a lot.

5. It be fun to work with so many other musicians last summer.

6. Yesterday I practice six hours. I likes to practice.

7. I enjoys playing in a band too.

8. I plans to major in music and wants to be a professional musician.

9. I hopes eventually to make my living that way.

10. If I changes my mind, I still has a good hobby for all my life.

☐EXERCISE 7

1. Most people thinks of wasps merely as insects that gives sharp stings.

2. But wasps is often helpful.

3. They destroys harmful caterpillars, and they stings only when they be frightened.

4. Unlike bees, most wasps dies at the beginning of winter.

5. Only a few queen wasps sleeps through the winter.

6. Then in the spring they lays eggs to start a new generation.

7. One difference between humans and other primates be in the use of tools.

8. Nonhumans uses tools only in rudimentary ways.

9. And they never passes their information about tools to the next generation.

10. But humans stores information about tools and passes it on from generation to generation.

STANDARD ENGLISH VERBS (compound forms and irregular verbs)

In the last chapter you studied the present and past forms of the regular verb *walk*. Other forms of regular verbs may be used with helping verbs. Here is a table showing all the forms of some regular verbs and the various helping verbs they are used with.

REGULAR VERBS

BASE FORM	PRESENT	PAST	PAST PARTICIPLE	*ING* FORM
(Use after *can, may, shall, will, could, might, should, would, must, do, does, did*.)			(Use after *have, has, had*. Or use after some form of *be* to describe the subject or to make a passive verb.)	(Use after some form of *be*.)
ask	ask (*s*)	asked	asked	asking
dance	dance (*s*)	danced	danced	dancing
decide	decide (*s*)	decided	decided	deciding
enjoy	enjoy (*s*)	enjoyed	enjoyed	enjoying
finish	finish (*es*)	finished	finished	finishing
happen	happen (*s*)	happened	happened	happening
learn	learn (*s*)	learned	learned	learning
like	like (*s*)	liked	liked	liking
need	need (*s*)	needed	needed	needing
open	open (*s*)	opened	opened	opening
start	start (*s*)	started	started	starting
suppose	suppose (*s*)	supposed	supposed	supposing
walk	walk (*s*)	walked	walked	walking
want	want (*s*)	wanted	wanted	wanting

Sometimes a past participle is used after some form of the verb *be* (or verbs that take the place of *be* like *appear, seem, look, feel, get, act, become*) to describe the subject.

He is satisfied.
He was confused.
He has been disappointed.
He appeared pleased. (He was pleased.)
He seems interested. (He is interested.)
He looked surprised. (He was surprised.)
He feels frightened. (He is frightened.)
He gets bored easily. (He is bored easily.)
He acts concerned. (He is concerned.)

Usually these past participles are called describing words that describe the subject rather than being called part of the verb of the sentence. What you call them doesn't matter. The only important thing is to be sure you use the correct form of the past participle (*ed* for regular verbs).

Sometimes the subject of the sentence neither *does* nor *is* anything. It just stays there passive in the sentence and is acted upon.

The lesson was studied by the children.

The subject is *lesson*. It doesn't do anything. It is passive. It is acted upon by the children. Thus we say that *was studied* is a passive verb. All you really need to remember is that whenever a form of *be* is used with a past participle, you must be sure to use the correct past participle form (*ed* for regular verbs).

Note that when there are several helping verbs, it is the last one that determines which form of the main verb should be used: she *should* finish soon; she should *have* finished yesterday.

When do you write *ask, use, finish, suppose*? And when do you write *asked, used, finished, supposed*? Here's a rule that will help you decide.

Write asked, used, finished, supposed

1. when it's past time:

> She asked for help last week.
> I used to skate last year.
> I finished my work early yesterday.
> When I saw you, I supposed you were busy.

2. when some form of be or have comes before the word:

> He has asked me to go with him.
> I am used to working late.
> I have finished my lunch now.
> I am supposed to be there at one.

IRREGULAR VERBS

All the verbs in the table on page 101 are regular. That is, they are all formed in the same way—with an *ed* ending on the past form and on the past participle. But many verbs are irregular. Their past and past participle forms change spelling instead of just adding an *ed*. Here is a table of some irregular verbs. (The present and the *ing* forms are not usually given in a list of principal parts because they are formed easily from the base form and cause no trouble.) Refer to this list when you aren't sure which verb form to use. Memorize all the forms you don't know.

BASE FORM	PAST	PAST PARTICIPLE
be	was, were	been
become	became	become
begin	began	begun
break	broke	broken
bring	brought	brought
buy	bought	bought
build	built	built
catch	caught	caught
choose	chose	chosen
come	came	come
cost	cost	cost
do	did	done
draw	drew	drawn
drink	drank	drunk
drive	drove	driven
eat	ate	eaten
fall	fell	fallen
feel	felt	felt
fight	fought	fought
find	found	found
fit	fitted *or* fit	fitted *or* fit
forget	forgot	forgotten *or* forgot
forgive	forgave	forgiven
freeze	froze	frozen
get	got	got *or* gotten
give	gave	given
go	went	gone
grow	grew	grown
have	had	had
hear	heard	heard
hold	held	held

BASE FORM	PAST	PAST PARTICIPLE
hurt	hurt	hurt
keep	kept	kept
know	knew	known
lay (to place)	laid	laid
lead	led	led
leave	left	left
lie (to rest)	lay	lain
lose	lost	lost
make	made	made
meet	met	met
pay	paid	paid
read (pronounced "reed")	read (pronounced "red")	read (pronounced "red")
ride	rode	ridden
ring	rang	rung
rise	rose	risen
run	ran	run
say	said	said
see	saw	seen
sell	sold	sold
shake	shook	shaken
shine (to give light)	shone	shone
shine (to polish)	shined	shined
sing	sang	sung
sleep	slept	slept
speak	spoke	spoken
spend	spent	spent
stand	stood	stood
steal	stole	stolen
strike	struck	struck
swim	swam	swum
swing	swung	swung
take	took	taken
teach	taught	taught
tear	tore	torn
tell	told	told
think	thought	thought
throw	threw	thrown
wear	wore	worn
win	won	won
write	wrote	written

EXERCISES

Write the correct form of each verb. Refer to the tables and explanations on the previous pages if you aren't sure which form to use after a certain helping verb. Do no more than ten sentences at a time before checking your answers.

☐EXERCISE 1

1. (like, meet) I have always __liked__ train trips because I have __met__ such interesting people.

2. (meet, build) Yesterday I __met__ a man who designs model airplanes and even __builds__ them.

3. (suppose) His models are __suppose__ to be the top of the line.

4. (meet, teach) On another trip I __met__ a girl who has __taught__ handicapped children for three years.

5. (devote, teach) She seemed __devoted__ to her work and loves all the children she has __taught__.

6. (give) Another person whom I met __gives__ flute lessons now and has __given__ flute lessons for many years.

7. (become, design) Then last week I __became__ acquainted with an engineer who __designed__ bridges.

8. (concern) She is __concerned__ about not damaging the environment.

9. (catch) I have __caught__ the morning train to Jacksonville every weekend this spring.

10. (suppose, surprise) I was __suppose__ to meet my cousin at the train station yesterday, but I was __surprised__ to find my uncle there too.

☐EXERCISE 2

1. (intend, be) One of my friends __intends__ now to go into law enforcement, and another of my friends __is__ majoring in business.

2. (plan, do) But another friend __plans__ to drop out of college soon because he __does__ not like studying.

3. (attend) Two of my friends _____attends_____ Shelby State Community College now.

4. (have) One of them _____Have_____ a job on weekends as well.

5. (wonder, do) I _____Wonder_____ if he _____does_____ not find that difficult.

6. (say, do) He _____Said_____, however, that it _____does_____ not bother him.

7. (intend, hope) He _____intends_____ to transfer to a four-year college in the fall and _____hopes_____ to graduate in two more years.

8. (be) Where _____Were_____ you last night? All of us _____were_____ at the lecture except you.

9. (miss, be) It did not matter to me that you _____missed_____ it, but we _____were_____ all expecting you.

10. (be, have) The lecture _____was_____ one of the best I _____have_____ ever heard.

☐EXERCISE 3

1. (have) Last year I _____had_____ a good relationship with my counselor.

2. (wish, have) I _____wish_____ that I _____had_____ the same counselor this year.

3. (know, make) My counselor last year _____knew_____ how to listen, and he always _____made_____ time for me.

4. (understand) He _____understood_____ the importance of listening.

5. (offer, make) He would seldom _____offer_____ advice or _____make_____ judgments.

6. (solve, talk) But I could often _____solve_____ my problems just by _____talking_____ to him about them.

7. (be) Sometimes a person with little training can _____be_____ a good counselor.

8. (be) The most important quality for a counselor _____is_____ the ability to listen.

9. (use) Now I _____use_____ that counselor's technique.

10. (have, spend) When my small son _____has_____ a problem, I _____spend_____ plenty of time listening.

Cross out the community dialect expressions and write the standard English ones above.

☐EXERCISE 4

1. I have already ~~went~~ *gone* to the store three times this morning.

2. She ~~done~~ *did* the best she could for him, and he ~~appreciate~~ it.

3. I ~~drunk~~ *drank* Pepsi at the party last night, but I have always ~~drank~~ *drunk* Diet-Pepsi before.

4. She ~~ask~~ *asked* him for his opinion yesterday, and he ~~give~~ *gave* it to her.

5. Then she mad at him because he ~~say~~ *said* unkind things.

6. The room was ~~fill~~ *filled* with people all talking at once.

7. I ~~seen~~ *saw* him at the carnival, but he never ~~seen~~ *saw* me.

8. We ~~was~~ *were* hoping you'd go with us if you ~~wasn't~~ *weren't* too busy.

9. Yesterday he ~~run~~ *ran* in the 100-meter race, but he has always ~~ran~~ *run* in the 200-meter before.

10. I ~~knowed~~ *knew* you ~~was~~ *were* going to win that race.

Avoiding Dialect Expressions

Although verbs cause the most trouble for those who have grown up speaking a dialect other than standard English, certain other expressions, more common in speech than in writing, should be avoided. Some (such as *he don't* and *you was*) are discussed elsewhere in the book. A few others are listed here.

DIALECT	STANDARD ENGLISH
anywheres, nowheres, somewheres	anywhere, nowhere, somewhere
anyways	anyway
hisself, theirselves	himself, themselves
this here book, that there book, those there books	this book, that book, those books
them books	those books
he did good, she sang good	he did well, she sang well
my brother he plays ball	my brother plays ball
haven't none, haven't got none haven't no, haven't got no haven't never haven't nothing wasn't no wasn't never (These are called double negatives.)	have none, haven't any have no, haven't any have never, haven't ever have nothing, haven't anything was no, wasn't any was never, wasn't ever
ain't	am not, isn't, aren't, hasn't, haven't

Cross out the community dialect expressions and write the standard English ones above.

□EXERCISE 5

1. I'd like to go, but I haven't no time.

2. I haven't done none of my homework for tomorrow.

3. This here book is hard to read, and anyways it's not interesting.

4. My friend he did good on last week's test.

5. He should be proud because that test hard.

6. Did you read all them books we was suppose to read?

7. I never read none of them.

8. I watch TV too long last night and didn't do no reading.

9. Now I've decide to spend the evening studying.

10. I want to pass that there test tomorrow.

☐EXERCISE 6

1. We're planning to take a trip somewheres this summer.

2. But we ain't decided yet where we'll go.

3. My brother he want to go fishing in Wisconsin.

4. But I wasn't never much interested in fishing.

5. Besides I don't want to go anywheres we been before.

6. Anyways we have lots of time to decide.

7. I want to get one of them atlases and see where the state parks is.

8. I'd like to go to one of them if it ain't too far.

9. I never been to none of the state parks in our state.

10. But I'll probably let my brother suit hisself about where we go.

JOURNAL WRITING

Write three sentences using verbs you have missed in the exercises or in your papers.

Proofreading Exercise

See if you can find all ten errors in this student composition before checking with the answers at the back of the book. You'll find errors in words confused, contractions, possessives, and the punctuation of independent and dependent clauses.

A DOLPHIN LESSON

The stuff I'm learning in college doesnt have much to do with life—or so I thought. I learn about the Napoleonic Wars. I study Freuds theory of the id. I learn to do statistical analysis. I read Sandburg's poems. But then I go out to have pizza with my friends and we talk only about parties.

But last week something clicked.

Out at Marine World I saw some Atlantic bottle-nosed dolphins put on a show. With their sleek gray bodies, front flippers, and strong tails, they looked beautiful and friendly as they repeatedly surfaced and than dived again into the water. Their performance was astounding. They "walked" on there tails on the surface of the water, turned nose over tail in the air, jumped three times their body length in the air, spun in the air, jumped threw hoops, and jumped over a rope stretched high across the pool. They performed faultlessly. Every minute was exciting.

But the best part came at the end when the trainer told how she trains them. It takes her six months to teach a dolphin to do an air spin and a year or more to get it ready for show business. She said she uses affection training and operant conditioning. Operant conditioning! I had just been reading in my psychology coarse about B. F. Skinner's theory of operant conditioning—the theory that animals or children or adults can be trained by giving them rewards for good behavior.

And hear I was seeing the theory in practice! The trainer said, "When they do something we like, we give them something they like." When a dolphin does what the trainer wants she gives it an affectionate pat and a small fish. If it doesn't do what she wants, she ignores it or sometimes even gives it a tiny bop on the snout.

So here was my psychology course being used in real life. Maybe more of the things Im learning in college relate to reality. I'll have to see.

Progress Test

This test covers everything you have studied so far. One sentence in each pair is correct. The other is incorrect. Read both sentences carefully before you decide. Then write the letter of the correct sentence in the blank.

_B_ 1. A. I've joined the bowling league it's fun.
      B. His principal interest these days is swimming.

_B_ 2. A. Working all that time and getting nothing for it.
      B. Doesn't he make quite a bit of money too?

_B_ 3. A. I have chose this field because I like nursing.
      B. His car broke down, and he spent the night in the desert.

_A_ 4. A. Whether I win or lose isn't important.
      B. You're new clothes are better than any you've had in the past.

_A_ 5. A. She doesn't want to lose her self-confidence.
      B. When my brother arrived, he ask me to phone you.

_A_ 6. A. He was suppose to plan the trip for the two teams.
      B. I chose this course because I knew I needed it.

_A_ 7. A. When you can't spell, you're in trouble.
      B. Our car wouldn't start, we were left stranded.

_B_ 8. A. She did good on her comprehensive test.
      B. I worked for hours; then I finally finished.

_A_ 9. A. She chose warm clothes for her trip.
      B. We was sure that woman was your mother.

_B_ 10. A. Never having been in a track meet before.
       B. The puppy wouldn't eat its food.

_A_ 11. A. If at first you don't succeed, try again.
       B. When she came in the door, I knew what had happen.

_B_ 12. A. Working steadily, he soon finished painting the room.
       B. He studies best the night before a exam.

_B_ 13. A. I jumped in my car and was off to the races.
       B. I enjoyed competing however I didn't win any prize.

_B_ 14. A. It don't make any difference to me whether you come or not.
       B. I'm not sure who's to blame.

_B_ 15. A. They was standing in the rain for an hour.
       B. Finally the bus came, and they got in.

MAKING SUBJECTS, VERBS, AND PRONOUNS AGREE

All parts of a sentence should agree. In general if the subject is singular, the verb should be singular; if the subject is plural, the verb should be plural.

Each of the girls has her own bank account.

Both of the girls have their own bank accounts.

Brian and Loretta have a good friendship.

She and her sister were at the rally.

There were 50 people in the classroom.

Many of my friends are in that class.

The following words are singular and take a singular verb:

(*one* words)	(*body* words)	
anyone	anybody	each
everyone	everybody	either
no one	nobody	neither
one	somebody	
someone		

One of my friends is from Mexico.

Everybody in the class has to give a report.

Either of the candidates is acceptable.

The following "group" words take a singular verb if you are thinking of the group as a whole, but they take a plural verb if you are thinking of the individuals in the group:

audience	family	kind
band	flock	lot
class	group	number
committee	heap	none
crowd	herd	public
dozen	jury	team

The jury is ready. . . . . The jury are still arguing.
The team is on the field. . . . . The team are suiting up.
A dozen rolls is plenty. . . . . . A dozen are planning to go.
My family is behind me. . . . My family are all scattered.

Here are some subject-verb pairs you can *always* be sure of. No exceptions!

you were	(*never* you was)
we were	(*never* we was)
they were	(*never* they was)
he doesn't	(*never* he don't)
she doesn't	(*never* she don't)
it doesn't	(*never* it don't)

Not only should subject and verb agree, but a pronoun also should agree with the word it refers to. If the word referred to is singular, the pronoun should be singular; if that word is plural, the pronoun should be plural.

Each of the boys has *his* own room.

The pronoun *his* refers to the singular subject *Each* and therefore is singular.

Both of the boys have *their* own rooms.

The pronoun *their* refers to the plural subject *Both* and therefore is plural.

Today many people try to avoid sex bias by writing sentences like the following:

> If anyone wants a ride, he or she can go in my car.
> If anybody calls, tell him or her that I've left.
> Somebody has left his or her textbook here.

But those sentences are wordy and awkward. Therefore some people, especially in conversation, turn them into sentences that are not grammatically correct.

> If anyone wants a ride, they can go in my car.
> If anybody calls, tell them that I've left.
> Somebody has left their textbook here.

Such ungrammatical sentences, however, are not necessary. It just takes a little thought to revise each sentence so that it avoids sex bias and is also grammatically correct:

> Anyone who wants a ride can go in my car.
> Tell anybody who calls that I've left.
> Somebody has left a textbook here.

Another good way to avoid the awkward *he or she* and *him or her* is to make the words plural. Instead of writing, "Each of the students was in his or her place," write, "All the students were in their places," thus avoiding sex bias and still having a grammatically correct sentence.

EXERCISES
Underline the correct word. Check your answers ten at a time.

☐EXERCISE 1

1. Every one of the students in this class (get gets) to class on time.
2. If they (are is) late, they (miss misses) the one-sentence quiz given at the beginning of the hour.
3. The instructor dictates a sentence, and each of the students (write writes) it on a piece of paper and (hand hands) it in.

4. The sentence (include, includes) some of the points that (are is) in the day's assignment.
5. The instructor then (sort sorts) the papers into two groups—correct and incorrect.
6. One of the women always (get gets) (her their) quiz correct.
7. Two of the men usually (get gets) (his theirs) correct too.
8. Most of the students (like likes) those quizzes because they're short.
9. Even though the quiz (doesn't don't) take long, it's effective.
10. It (give gives) a good idea of a student's progress.

☐EXERCISE 2

1. One of my new interests (are is) geology.
2. Last month I found a couple of fossils that (was were) in the sediment of an old creek bed.
3. They show the outline of some plants that (was were) in this area millions of years ago.
4. I have a book about fossils that (give gives) a lot of information.
5. The exhibits in our college museum also (include includes) some fossils.
6. Some of the exhibits (show shows) both plant and animal fossils.
7. A knowledge of both geology and biology (are is) necessary for a study of fossils.
8. The study of fossils (reveal reveals) the geologic history of an area.
9. The rock formations in many of our national parks (show shows) fossils.
10. One of my goals (are is) to see some of those formations.

☐EXERCISE 3

1. One of the best courses I'm taking this year (are is) typing.
2. Some of my friends (take takes) the same course.
3. All of us (wish wishes) we had learned to type earlier.
4. Typed papers usually (get gets) better grades.
5. Most of my friends now (type types) their papers.
6. One of my friends (has have) even typed her brother's papers.
7. It (doesn't don't) take as much time to type as to write longhand.
8. Two of the men in our class (take takes) computer programming.
9. Each of them (find finds) (his their) typing skills essential.
10. All the students who can't type (wish wishes) they could.

☐EXERCISE 4

1. Each of my sisters (has have) a weekend job to pay for (her their) tuition.

2. One of them (are is) a bagger at Safeway.
3. The other (drive drives) a delivery truck for Macy's.
4. Both of them (has have) had these jobs for about a year.
5. Some of my friends (has have) had trouble finding jobs.
6. Several of them (has have) been out of work all summer.
7. It (doesn't don't) look as if they'll get anything.
8. One thing that (help helps) to get a job is experience.
9. And another thing that (help helps) (are is) knowing the right person.
10. And of course one of the big factors (are is) persistence.

□EXERCISE 5

1. No one in our family (has have) ever been to Yellowstone National Park.
2. For a long time all of us (has have) wanted to see it.
3. The stories about it (has have) impressed us, and each of us (are is) eager to visit it.
4. Therefore all of us (are is) planning to drive to Yellowstone in June.
5. Many of my friends (has have) been there, and one of my friends (are is) going in August.
6. The one thing all of us (want wants) to see most is Old Faithful.
7. Although it's not the largest nor even the most powerful geyser in the park, its fame and popularity (come comes) from its relative regularity of eruption.
8. Ever since it was discovered in 1870, it has erupted every hour, although the time (varies vary) from 61 to 67 minutes.
9. Lately, however, because of earthquakes nearby, the timing of the eruptions (are is) not quite so faithful.
10. I was interested to learn that the term geyser (come comes) from an Icelandic word meaning "to gush."

□EXERCISE 6

1. One of my brothers (want wants) especially to see some of the other geysers.
2. In the park there (are is) more than a hundred active geysers.
3. This concentration of geysers (are is) the greatest in the world.
4. Only in New Zealand and Iceland (are is) there other active geyser regions of any consequence.
5. All of us (look looks) forward to seeing the animals of the park too: the bears, bison, deer, moose, elk, and coyotes.
6. My sister, who is interested in plants, (want wants) to learn about the flora of the area.
7. The main trees in Yellowstone (are is) lodgepole pines, and along the stream banks (grow grows) cottonwoods and willows.

8. All of us (plan plans) to take advantage of the interpretive programs and go on guided tours and listen to campfire talks.
9. Each of us (has have) something different we want to see.
10. But all of us (intend intends) to stay together in our sightseeing.

□EXERCISE 7

1. I especially want to see the petrified forests, which (are is) unique among the petrified forests of the world.
2. In most petrified forests, like the Petrified Forest National Park in Arizona, the trees (lie lies) horizontally.
3. The reason for their lying flat on the ground is that most of them (has have) been carried into the area by streams.
4. In Yellowstone the petrified trees (stand stands) upright just where they grew millions of years ago.
5. Yellowstone's petrified forests are also the largest known and (cover covers) more than 40 square miles.
6. Another thing all of us (are is) eager to do is to take some of the self-guiding trails.
7. Along those trails (are is) hot springs, mud pots, and mud geysers.
8. We have all been reading some books about the park and (hope hopes) to have enough background to get the most from our trip.
9. Our plan to camp out and cook our own meals (suit suits) all of us just fine.
10. Since Yellowstone is our oldest and largest national park, all of us (think thinks) it's time we saw it.

□EXERCISE 8

1. Everybody in our family (are is) going to the races today.
2. Not one of us (want wants) to miss them.
3. There (are is) ten horses in the featured race.
4. All of them (has have) been well trained.
5. Each of them (seem seems) to like to race.
6. Everyone in our family (has have) picked a favorite horse.
7. Luckily it (doesn't don't) look like rain today.
8. Therefore each of us (are is) planning to walk to the stadium.
9. It (doesn't don't) take more than five minutes to walk there.
10. Then everyone (are is) going to be free from parking worries.

JOURNAL WRITING

Write about something that interests you using at least four words from your Personal Spelling List.

CHOOSING THE RIGHT PRONOUN

Of the many kinds of pronouns, the following cause the most difficulty:

SUBJECT GROUP	NONSUBJECT GROUP
I	me
he	him
she	her
we	us
they	them

A pronoun in the Subject Group may be used in two ways:

1. as the subject of a verb:

He is my counselor. (*He* is the subject of the verb *is*.)

Meg is older than *I*. (The sentence isn't written out in full. It means "Meg is older than *I* am." *I* is the subject of the verb *am*.) Whenever you see *than* in a sentence, ask yourself whether a verb has been left off. Add the verb, and then you'll automatically use the correct pronoun. In both writing and speaking, always add the verb. Instead of saying, "She's smarter than (I me)," say, "She's smarter than I am." Then you can't fail to use the correct pronoun.

2. as a word that means the same as the subject:

That was he in the blue car. (*He* means the same as the subject *That*. Therefore the pronoun from the Subject Group is used.)

It was she who phoned. (*She* means the same as the subject *It*. Therefore the pronoun from the Subject Group is used.)

Modern usage allows some exceptions to this rule however. *It is me* and *it is us* (instead of the grammatically correct *it is I* and *it is we*) are now established usage; and *it is him*, *it is her*, and *it is them* are widely used, particularly in informal speech.

Pronouns in the Nonsubject Group are used for all other purposes.
In the following sentence, *me* is not the subject, nor does it mean the same as the subject. Therefore it comes from the Nonsubject Group.

He came with Amanda and *me*.

A good way to tell which pronoun to use is to leave out the extra name. By leaving out *Amanda*, you will say, *He came with me.* You would never say, *He came with I.*

> We saw *him* and Kimberly last night. (We saw *him* last night.)
> The firm gave my wife and *me* a trip to the Virgin Islands. (The firm gave *me* a trip.)

EXERCISES

Underline the correct pronoun. Remember the trick of leaving out the extra name to help you decide which pronoun to use. Use the correct grammatical form even though an alternate form may be acceptable in conversation.

□EXERCISE 1

1. Our instructor asked Jessica and (I me) to organize a panel discussion.
2. Since Lew is such a good speaker, we asked (he him) and Robert to be the leaders.
3. (He Him) and Robert got some pointers from the instructor.
4. Between you and (I me), I think it was a good program.
5. Everyone told Jessica and (I me) that it was interesting.
6. Several students wanted to know when Jessica and (I me) would plan another panel.
7. Most of (we us) students think we should have panel discussions often.
8. (We Us) two began thinking of a subject for another panel.
9. Then our instructor asked whether Jessica and (I me) could get one ready in two weeks.
10. Naturally both Jessica and (I me) were pleased.

□EXERCISE 2

1. My uncle sent my fiancé and (I me) a stereo.
2. Now my fiancé and (I me) are collecting records.
3. We're going to invite (he him) and Aunt Linda to our wedding.
4. We really liked the gift from (he him) and Aunt Linda.
5. It was an expensive gift that (he him) and Aunt Linda sent.
6. My fiancé and (I me) are planning a trip to the Maritimes.
7. It will be the first trip (we us) two have had this year.
8. It will be good for Bart and (I me) to get away for a week.
9. Most of the time it's just work, work, work for Bart and (I me).
10. Now for a change Bart and (I me) will do some sightseeing.

☐EXERCISE 3

1. Carol and (I me) went to a play at the university last night.
2. Carol thought Vicki would be there, and at intermission we saw (she her) and Bob.
3. Bob and (I me) have always been good friends.
4. They came over and spoke to Carol and (I me) and asked us to go out for pizza afterward.
5. When we went out for pizza, Bob and (I me) fought over the check.
6. Then they rode home with Carol and (I me) in my car.
7. They asked Carol and (I me) to go skiing with them next weekend.
8. It didn't take long for Carol and (I me) to accept.
9. (Carol and I, Me and Carol) both like to ski.
10. (We Us) four are sure to have a great weekend.

☐EXERCISE 4

1. (Jason and I, Me and Jason) have parts in the play being put on by the Drama Department.
2. It's something new for both (he him) and (I me).
3. It's been a struggle for Jason and (I me) to learn all our lines.
4. But now both (he and I) (him and me) are sure of them.
5. Neither Jason nor (I me) have ever missed a rehearsal.
6. The director complimented Jason and (I me) on our faithfulness.
7. During the scenes when we're not on stage Jason and (I me) play pinochle.
8. The last game we played was a tie between (he him) and (I me).
9. The entire production has been fun for Jason and (I me).
10. Now both (he him) and (I me) are looking forward to the next play.

☐EXERCISE 5

1. (My brother and I, Me and my brother) take turns shoveling our walks.
2. He is younger than (I me).
3. He thinks the family car should be available to both (he and I, him and me).
4. It was a problem that my dad and (I me) had to work out.
5. Dad and (I me) sat down to talk it over.
6. Dad thought the car should be available equally to my brother and (I me).
7. My brother and (I me) now have an agreement about it.
8. There never has been any trouble between (we us) two.
9. Oh, when we were little, (we us) two used to have fights.
10. But now (he and I, him and me) can always come to an agreement.

MAKING THE PRONOUN REFER
TO THE RIGHT WORD

When you write a sentence, *you* know what it means, but your reader may not. What does this sentence mean?

Kelly told her instructor that she had made a mistake.

Who had made a mistake? We don't know whether the pronoun *she* refers to *Kelly* or to *instructor*. The simplest way to correct such a faulty reference is to use a direct quotation:

Kelly said to her instructor, "I've made a mistake."

Here is another sentence with a faulty reference:

I've always enjoyed helping teach preschoolers, and now I'm actually going to be one.

Going to be a preschooler? There's no word for *one* to refer to. We need to write

I've always enjoyed helping teach preschoolers, and now I'm actually going to be a preschool teacher.

Another kind of faulty reference is a *which* clause that doesn't refer to any specific word, thus making it difficult to tell what part of the sentence it refers to.

He finally landed a job which gave him some self-confidence.

Was it the job that gave him self-confidence or the fact that he finally landed a job? The sentence should read

Finally landing a job gave him some self-confidence.

or

The job that he finally landed gave him some self-confidence.

EXERCISES

Most—but not all—of these sentences aren't clear because we don't know what word the pronoun refers to. Revise such sentences to make the meaning clear. Remember that using a direct quotation is often the easiest way to clarify what a pronoun refers to. Since there are more ways than one to rewrite each sentence, yours may be as good as the one on the answer sheet.

☐EXERCISE 1

1. When Curt showed his father the dented fender, he was upset.

2. He said he would have to get it repaired.

3. She showed us a conch shell and explained how they live in them.

4. The parents take turns supervising the park playground, where they have free use of the swings and slides.

5. He told his instructor that he didn't think he understood the novel.

6. His instructor said that maybe he hadn't read it carefully enough.

7. The clerk told his boss he was too old for the job.

8. When the professor talked with Roland, he was really worried.

9. She told her girlfriend that her record collection needed reorganizing.

10. She asked the job applicant to come back after she had given more thought to the question.

☐EXERCISE 2

1. His motorcycle hit a parked car, but it wasn't damaged.

2. As I went up to the baby's carriage, it began to cry.

3. Rebecca told her mother that her wardrobe was completely out-of-date.

4. As soon as the carburetor of my car was adjusted, I drove it home.

5. I couldn't find the catsup bottle, and I don't like a hamburger without it.

6. His father said he would have to get a bank loan.

7. Susanne told Cynthia that she had failed the exam.

8. She was shy, and it kept her from moving ahead in her profession.

9. He finished his paper, turned off the typewriter, and took it to class.

10. When we couldn't find the cake plate, we decided my husband must have eaten it.

□EXERCISE 3

1. When the dentist pulled the child's tooth, it screamed.

2. I finished my exam, put down my pen, and handed it in.

3. I'm interested in politics and would like to become a politician.

4. I decided to take a different job which my parents disapproved of.

5. When I opened the dog's carrying case at the airport, it ran away.

6. The cars streamed by without paying any attention to the stalled motorist.

7. Darryl told Max that his parakeet was loose in his room.

8. I finally made up my mind to major in math which wasn't easy.

9. When Debbie phoned her mother, she was quite ill.

10. He asked the salesman to come back when he wasn't so rushed.

□EXERCISE 4

1. He told his father that his car needed a tune-up.

2. After I read about Tom Dooley's career in medicine, I decided that that was what I wanted to be.

3. After Alfredo talked to the boss, he was enthusiastic about the project.

4. He loves to wrestle and spends most of his time doing it.

5. The park commission established a hockey rink where they can play free.

6. The doctor told the orderly he had made a mistake.

7. She tried to persuade her sister to take her car.

8. My car hit a truck, but it wasn't even scratched.

9. She told her mother she was working too hard.

10. As we approached the robin's nest, it flew away.

☐EXERCISE 5

1. She told her daughter that she had always been too shy.

2. Erica's mother let her wear her fur coat to the party.

3. He told his dad that he had made a terrible mistake.

4. She slammed her cup into the saucer and broke it.

5. I enjoy figure skating and would like to be one if I could.

6. The president told the chief accountant that he had made an error in

   reporting his income.

7. In Hawaii they have June weather the year around.

8. When her sister came home from college, she was excited.

9. He told his father he thought he should go back to college for a year.

10. His father told him he didn't have enough money.

WRITING ASSIGNMENT

As you get back your writing assignments, are you keeping a list of your misspelled words on the inside back cover of this book?

CORRECTING MISPLACED OR DANGLING MODIFIERS

A modifier gives information about some word in a sentence, and it should be as close to that word as possible. In the following sentence the modifier is too far away from the word it modifies to make sense:

> Playing delightedly with a ball of string, we sat and watched our kitten.

Was it *we* who were playing? That's what the sentence says because the modifier *Playing delightedly with a ball of string* is next to *we*. Of course it should be next to *kitten*.

> We sat and watched our kitten playing delightedly with a ball of string.

Here's another misplaced modifier:

> We saw a deer and a fawn on the way to the shopping center.

Were the deer and fawn going to the shopping center? Who was?

> On the way to the shopping center we saw a deer and a fawn.

The next example has no word at all for the modifier to modify:

> At the age of nine, my dad was transferred to Alabama.

The modifier *At the age of nine* is dangling there with no word to attach itself to, no word for it to modify. We can get rid of the dangling modifier by turning it into a dependent clause.

> When I was nine, my dad was transferred to Alabama.

Here the clause has its own subject—*I*—so that there's no chance of misunderstanding the sentence.

EXERCISES

Most—but not all—of these sentences contain misplaced or dangling modifiers. Some you may correct simply by shifting the modifier so it will be next to the word it modifies. Others you'll need to rewrite. Since there is more than one way to correct each sentence, your way may be as good as the one at the back of the book.

☐EXERCISE 1

1. Garbed in a brief bikini, he watched her strolling along.

2. My brother-in-law took me to the hospital after breaking my leg.

3. Glowing in the dark garden, we watched hundreds of fireflies.

4. After finishing the English assignment, that pizza tasted great.

5. After cleaning the cage and putting in fresh water and seed, my canary began to sing.

6. Sound asleep in the hammock, I discovered my boyfriend.

7. Jerking the leash, I made my dog heel.

8. At the age of six, my mother had another baby.

9. I gave away that blue suit to a charity that I didn't care about any more.

10. While answering the doorbell, my cookies burned to a crisp.

☐EXERCISE 2

1. Hundreds of colorful tropical fish could be seen cruising in the glass-bottom boat.

2. While playing on the floor, I noticed that the baby seemed feverish.

3. After being wheeled out of the operating room, a nurse asked me how I felt.

4. While watching the football game, Mark's bike was stolen.

5. The bank will make loans to responsible individuals of any size.

6. Rounding a bend in the road, a huge glacier confronted me.

7. I could see more than 20 lakes flying at an altitude of 5,000 feet.

8. Having finished mowing the lawn, the lawn chair looked comfortable.

9. Before planting my garden, I consulted a seed catalog.

10. Having broken my right arm, the instructor let me take the test orally.

☐EXERCISE 3

1. After doing all the outside reading, the term paper almost wrote itself.

2. Flitting among the apple blossoms, I spotted a monarch butterfly.

3. After drinking a lot of coffee, the lecture was less boring.

4. Standing there being milked, we thought the cows looked contented.

5. The Museum of Science and Industry is the most interesting museum in the city that I have visited.

6. She was going out with a man who owned a Corvette named Harold.

7. We gave all the meat to the cat that we didn't want.

8. Speeding down the slope, our toboggan hit a rock.

9. Determined to learn to write, the textbook was slowly mastered.

10. After eating a quick lunch, our bus left for Waterbury.

☐EXERCISE 4

1. The little town is in the middle of a prairie where I was born.

2. You may visit the National Cemetery where noted people are buried every day except Friday from nine until five.

3. At the age of three I saw my first circus.

4. She put the clothes back in the traveling bag that she had not worn.

5. Although almost ten years old, he still hangs onto his old car.

6. Completely smashed, I saw that my little car was beyond repair.

7. Barking furiously, I went to see what was the matter with my puppy.

8. Sitting there looking out over the water, her decision was finally made.

9. Crying pitifully, I tried to find the child's mother.

10. Being a boring conversationalist, I always try to avoid him.

☐EXERCISE 5

1. I bought a secondhand car from a man with generator trouble.

2. I read that the hit-and-run driver had been caught in the evening paper.

3. We gave all the newspapers to the Boy Scouts that have been lying around for months.

4. She left the meat on the table that was too tough to eat.

5. A report was made about the holdup by the police.

6. Twittering delightfully, I watched the wren building its nest.

7. Being a conceited fool, I didn't much care for his company.

8. After smelling up the whole house, I finally gave my dog a bath.

9. While watering the geraniums, a bee stung me.

10. Being unsure of the way to correct dangling modifiers, my instructor gave me a low grade.

JOURNAL WRITING

Make up a sentence with a dangling or misplaced modifier, and then write the correction.

USING PARALLEL CONSTRUCTION

Your writing will be clearer if you use parallel construction. That is, when you make any kind of list, put the items in similar form. If you write

She likes cooking, weaving, and to make pottery.

the sentence lacks parallel construction. The items don't all have the same form. But if you write

She likes cooking, weaving, and making pottery.

then the items are parallel. They all have the same form. They are all *ing* words. Or you could write

She likes to cook, to weave, and to make pottery.

Again the sentence has parallel construction because the items all have the same form. They all use *to* and a verb. Here are some more examples. Note how much easier it is to read the column with parallel construction.

LACKING PARALLEL CONSTRUCTION	HAVING PARALLEL CONSTRUCTION
They were looking for a house with six rooms, a full basement, and it should have an all-electric kitchen.	They were looking for a house with six rooms, a full basement, and an all-electric kitchen. (All three items can be read smoothly after the preposition *with*.)
She is intelligent, outgoing, and she likes to help people.	She is intelligent, outgoing, and helpful. (All three words describe her.)
Because I worked hard, had a good attendance record, and I often suggested new ideas, I was promoted.	Because I worked hard, had a good attendance record, and often suggested new ideas, I was promoted. (All three items can be read smoothly after *Because I*.)
I did all my math, studied my Spanish, and then there was that composition to write.	I did all my math, studied my Spanish, and then started my composition. (All items begin with a verb in past time.)

The supporting points for a thesis statement (see p. 209) should always be parallel. For the following thesis statements, the supporting points in the left-hand column are not all constructed alike. Those in the right-hand column are; they are parallel.

NOT PARALLEL	PARALLEL
Playing in the college orchestra has been a valuable experience.	Playing in the college orchestra has been a valuable experience.
1. I've improved my playing.	1. I've improved my playing.
2. Made friends.	2. I've made good friends.
3. Trips.	3. I've had out-of-town trips.
My decision to study at the library was wise.	My decision to study at the library was wise.
1. I have no distractions.	1. I have no distractions.
2. Spend more time.	2. I spend my allotted time.
3. No fridge.	3. I have no fridge to tempt me.

Using parallel construction will make your writing more effective. Note the effective parallelism in these well-known quotations:

> With malice toward none, with charity for all, with firmness in the right as God gives us to see the right. . . .
>
> —Abraham Lincoln

> It was the best of times, it was the worst of times, it was the age of wisdom, it was the age of foolishness, it was the epoch of belief, it was the epoch of incredulity, it was the season of Light, it was the season of Darkness, it was the spring of hope, it was the winter of despair . . .
>
> —Charles Dickens

> Many of us allow our children to eat junk, watch junk, listen to junk, talk junk, play with junk, and then we're surprised when they turn out to be social junkies.
>
> —Jesse Jackson

EXERCISES

Most—but not all—of these sentences lack parallel construction. Cross out the part that is not parallel and write the correction above.

☐EXERCISE 1

1. I like living in Bellevue because I can go fishing, sailing, or take a ski trip without driving very far.

2. Sacramento has a great climate, excellent parks, and you can go to good plays and concerts.

3. He can ski, swim, and he has even learned to sail a boat.

4. The goals of this course are critical reading, careful writing, and being able to think clearly.

5. I haven't decided whether to go into medicine or be a lawyer.

6. I like hiking, mountain climbing, and I especially like camping out.

7. It's not only what you do but the way in which you do it.

8. Expecting a phone call, dreading it, and yet wanting it, I sat there all evening.

9. The orchestra leader asked us to come to practice at 7:00, that we should get our instruments tuned immediately, and to be ready to start practicing at 7:15.

10. I admire her. I love her. I find that I need her.

☐EXERCISE 2

1. This course teaches you how to limit your subject, how to form a thesis statement, how to back it up with several points in well-developed paragraphs, how to write an introduction and conclusion, and then you should think up a good title.

2. When you have finished your paper, proofread it for spelling, fragments, run-together sentences, and see whether it has any lack of parallelism.

3. He liked being the boss and that people came to him for advice.

4. I am learning how to study, the way to organize my time, and how to concentrate.

5. A good salary, that I have pleasant working conditions, and good fringe benefits are among the assets of my job.

6. Since I live 200 miles from campus, since I'm eager to make the most of my time here, and since I really have nothing to go home for, I've decided not to make any weekend trips.

7. She hopes to graduate in June, get a job, and to move to a bigger apartment.

8. They painted the living room beige, the hall green, and the kitchen was a soft blue.

9. My days are filled with working at my job, playing at my hobby, and I have to get some exercise.

10. Whatever the weather, whatever your mood, even though you have obligations, save a few minutes to vote on Election Day.

☐EXERCISE 3

1. His dream was to get his degree, get a good job, and then he would help his younger brother and sister.

2. When I was a child, I was expected to keep my room clean, had to help with the dishes, and to carry out the garbage.

3. I like to go to bed early and getting up early the next morning to study.

4. The speed-reading course has taught me not only to read faster but comprehending more of what I read.

5. The do-it-yourself psychology book sets out to help people handle everyday problems as well as understanding themselves better.

6. He looked at his daughter over his newspaper, put the paper down, got up, walked to the hall closet, and he indulgently handed her the car keys.

7. The weather was perfect with the sun shining, no clouds in the sky, and a cool breeze was coming down from the mountain.

8. The traffic in Los Angeles is heavier than Long Beach.

9. Our system for controlling crime is ineffective, unjust, and it costs too much.

10. Going to summer camp is important for children because it will give them self-confidence, teach them about nature, and they will learn to live with a group of their peers.

□EXERCISE 4

1. They want to move to the country because they want to be near nature, live simply, and to spend less money.

2. They are looking for a house with a good location, with land around it, and a view.

3. They were thinking of buying a lot that was a hundred feet wide and two hundred feet in length.

4. They decided it was too big, too wooded, and that it was more expensive than they needed.

5. They found a house on a smaller lot and decided to buy it and that they would move at the end of the month.

6. Before they move in, they will paint the walls, wash the cupboards, clean the rugs, and the windows have to be washed inside and out.

7. Moving to a new community, making new friends, and to find work for everyone in the family may prove difficult.

8. The senator works in Washington, lives in Maryland, and he often goes home to North Carolina for weekends.

9. I like a movie that has strong characters, a good plot, and that has a message.

10. He is succeeding through hard work, persistence, and maybe he's also having a bit of luck.

□EXERCISE 5

1. She was the kind of employee any boss would like—efficient, knowledgeable, friendly, and she always got to work on time.

2. You can depend on her to work hard, introduce new ideas, and she will promote the firm.

3. Your credentials file should include a transcript of your credits, letters of recommendation, and you ought to include a summary of your experience.

4. Travel lets one learn about other cultures, see distant places, meet other nationalities, and one also gets a better understanding of one's own country.

5. The visitors to the island were impressed with the quiet friendliness of the people, the lack of hard-sell tactics in the stores, the absence of billboards and neon lights, and of course they liked the balmy weather.

6. The speaker said that applause before a speech is faith, during a speech is hope, and after a speech is charity.

7. In Mount Ranier National Park in Washington are flower-covered meadows, luxuriant alpine forests, and there are also a host of birds and animals.

8. The park is famed for its 40 square miles of glaciers that are still active but that are only a remnant of the vast rivers of ice of the past.

9. Glaciers move from a fraction of an inch to as much as 100 feet a day depending on the thickness of the ice, the atmospheric temperature, and it also depends on the degree of slope down which the glacier is moving.

10. Besides the 32 national parks, the National Park Service administers more than 260 other areas including national monuments, national historical parks, national seashores, and also included are national cemeteries and national memorials.

Make the supporting points of these thesis statements parallel.

□EXERCISE 6

1. Recycling cans and bottles has been worthwhile.

    1. It has reused valuable resources.

    2. Prevents littering.

    3. It has made Americans conscious of ecological problems.

2. Air bags should be standard equipment on new cars.

    1. Tests have proved them more effective than seat belts.

    2. They would reduce injuries.

    3. Worth the cost.

3. My summer job on the playground for the handicapped was valuable.

    1. It provided funds for my first year of college.

    2. It provided experience for my career.

    3. Opportunity to do something for society.

4. A camping trip in Estes Park gave me some new insights.

    1. I now know I'm capable of coping with hardship.

    2. New interest in nature.

    3. Ecology.

5. Improving one's vocabulary is important.

    1. It will lead to improvement in academic grades.

    2. Lead to a more successful career.

    3. Give one personal satisfaction.

JOURNAL WRITING

Write two sentences with parallel construction, one telling why you think you'd enjoy a certain career and the other telling why you'd like to live in a certain place.

CORRECTING SHIFT IN TIME

If you begin writing a paper in past time, don't shift now and then to the present; and if you begin in the present, don't shift to the past. In the following paragraph the writer starts in the present and then shifts to the past and then back to the present again.

> In Eudora Welty's short story "A Worn Path," old Phoenix Jackson encounters all sorts of hazards on her long walk to Natchez to get some medicine for her grandson. But she overcame them all and at the doctor's office was given not only the medicine but also a nickel, which she plans to spend on a paper windmill for her grandson.

It should be all in the present:

> In Eudora Welty's short story "A Worn Path," old Phoenix Jackson encounters all sorts of hazards on her long walk to Natchez to get some medicine for her grandson. But she overcomes them all and at the doctor's office is given not only the medicine but also a nickel, which she plans to spend on a paper windmill for her grandson.

Or it could be all in the past:

> In Eudora Welty's short story "A Worn Path," old Phoenix Jackson encountered all sorts of hazards on her long walk to Natchez to get some medicine for her grandson. But she overcame them all and at the doctor's office was given not only the medicine but also a nickel, which she planned to spend on a paper windmill for her grandson.

EXERCISES

These sentences have shifts in time, either from past to present or from present to past. Make all the verbs in each sentence agree with the first verb used. Cross out the incorrect verb and write the correct one above it.

☐EXERCISE 1

1. Only a few feet in front of me I saw a quail, and I walk quietly forward, hoping not to frighten it away.

2. After I finished studying, I decide to jog a few miles.

3. We were enjoying the game tremendously, and then it begins to rain.

4. I tried to keep a study schedule, but sometimes I give up.

5. I closed my book, had a snack, and then decide to call it a day.

6. I wanted to register for that course, but it was full, so I register for this one.

7. He thought he wanted a job, but then he finally come back to college.

8. I added something to my knowledge of nature today; I learn the difference between cumulus and nimbostratus clouds.

9. In *The Grapes of Wrath* John Steinbeck wrote about the dust bowl days. He describes how one family left their home in Oklahoma and migrated to California.

10. When I was seven, I ran away and stayed away until dark; then I come home.

These selections shift back and forth between present and past time. Change the verbs to agree with the first verb used.

□EXERCISE 2

1. Eric Berne's *Games People Play* shows how people play games instead of acting frankly. It explained that people play the game of Blemish by pointing out other people's faults in order to enhance their own image.

2. We visited the old one-room schoolhouse that had been built in 1877. Old schoolbooks were lying on the desks, and the coal oil lamps on the wall have oil in them.

3. Mark Twain gives us a saga of the Mississippi River in his novel *The Adventures of Huckleberry Finn.* The story was told by Huck and recounts the adventures of the two most famous boys in American literature.

4. Hans Selye, a world authority on stress, says that life without stress would be boring and meaningless, but he also said that it must be the right kind of stress.

☐EXERCISE 3

Having heard about the unusual Boston Children's Museum, I decided to visit it. Children were everywhere, running, screaming, laughing. With no "Do Not Touch" signs to stop them, they were climbing, feeling, pushing, pulling, and operating the exhibits. Some children were taking off their shoes to go into an authentic Japanese house; some were filling a gas tank; some were examining a house sliced in two from cellar to attic to show its plumbing, gas lines, and electric lines.

Still other children were experimenting in the "What If You Couldn't?" room. One little girl is finding her way blindfolded with a white cane. One boy is tapping out his name on a Braille typewriter. One is trying to propel a wheelchair along a gravel path and up a slight incline. Another is walking with metal crutches. Thus they are gaining an understanding of and a compassion for the handicapped.

In this museum the children were all educating themselves by doing.

The following student papers shift back and forth between past time and present. Change the verbs to agree with the first verb used, thus making the whole paper read smoothly. (The verbs in direct quotations, of course, must not be changed. They must be left exactly as the speaker said them.)

☐EXERCISE 4

MY BEARSKIN BLANKET

One cold March evening I came home late and got ready for bed. I think I must have switched myself onto automatic as I went through the familiar routine of taking off my clothes, brushing my teeth, and setting my clock radio. At least I know I must not have been very aware of anything.

I turned out the lights, crawled into bed, and reach for my bearskin blanket, which keeps me toasty warm on the coldest of nights. I reach but can't find it. I check the floor to see if it has fallen off the bed. Nothing. My mind wakes out of its half-asleep-already state. I pause and try to think where in my room it was. I shook my head and peered into the darkness, but I can't see a thing.

"Something strange here," I thought.

I get up, grope for the light switch, and see that my desk drawers are all open and ransacked. And there is no bearskin blanket anywhere.

"What's been going on? Someone's been in my room," I thought.

Now my mind races as I scan the room. My stereo was still there, and my TV is OK, and I didn't have anything else valuable, but someone has been in my room. I found a few other things missing: my camera, some change from a jar, and a half bottle of wine from the cupboard. I was furious. I had left my door unlocked, so I really was angry at myself too. But the worst part was the idea that someone has been looking through my things. I felt as if my privacy had been invaded.

Well, after a few days of rage, I finally calmed down and give up ever recovering my bearskin blanket. Now I lock my door when I go out.

□**EXERCISE 5**

THE DAY I FLEW

I had always wanted to fly a plane, so I grab at my chance. I had saved the money for lessons, and I had enough enthusiasm to fly a jumbo jet.

That first time I flew I remember the sensation of leaving the ground and feeling the air pull us off the runway and float us upward and cushion us from the effects of gravity. It was an amazing sensation, a feeling of escaping the ground and of leaving gravity behind. It was a wonderful feeling to hear the engine drone as we moved higher and see the earth get smaller below.

My instructor let me do most of the flying even on my first lesson. It seems so easy and yet so impossible that a little plane could get off the ground. I kept trying to remember just what kept us up, and I nervously try to reassure myself that airplanes do work and we aren't going to suddenly fall out of the sky.

I learn to turn left and right and go up or down. In only half an hour I learn the thrill of flying. Then I am reminded how much more there is to flying when my instructor asks me if I know where we are. It has been only a few minutes since we were over the airport, but now I have no idea how to get back.

"There's a lot more to learn," he said as he took over and flew us back.

And he was right. I learned a lot more in future lessons, but that first time I flew will always be special to me.

JOURNAL WRITING

Write a brief paragraph telling about something that happened to you recently. Then describe the same incident as if it is happening to you at this moment.

CORRECTING SHIFT IN PERSON

You may write a paper in

First person—*I, we*
Second person—*you*
Third person—*he, she, they, one, anyone, a person, people*

but do not shift from one group to another.

Wrong: In writing a paper, *one* should first write a thesis statement; otherwise *you* may have difficulty organizing your paper.

Right: In writing a paper, *one* should first write a thesis statement; otherwise *one* may have difficulty organizing the paper.

Right: In writing a paper, *you* should first write a thesis statement; otherwise *you* may have difficulty organizing your paper.

Wrong: Few *people* get as much enjoyment out of music as *they* could. *One* need not be an accomplished musician to get some fun out of playing an instrument. Nor do *you* need to be very far advanced before joining an amateur group of players.

Right (but stilted): Few *people* get as much enjoyment out of music as *they* could. *One* need not be an accomplished musician to get some fun out of playing an instrument. Nor does *one* need to be very far advanced before joining an amateur group of players.

(Too many *one*'s in a paragraph make it sound stilted and formal. Sentences can be revised to avoid using either *you* or *one*.)

Better: Few *people* get as much enjoyment out of music as *they* could. It's not necessary to be an accomplished musician to get some fun out of playing an instrument. Nor is it necessary to be very far advanced before joining an amateur group of players.

Also, too frequent use of the expressions *he or she* and *him or her* can make a paper sound awkward. Turn back to page 115 to see how a sentence can be revised to avoid sex bias without using those expressions.

> Wrong: A student should not cut classes; otherwise *you* may miss something important.
>
> Right (but awkward): A student should not cut classes; otherwise *he or she* may miss something important.
>
> Better: Students should not cut classes; otherwise *they* may miss something important.

Often students write *you* in a paper when they don't really mean *you, the reader.*

You could tell that the speaker wasn't well prepared.

Such sentences are always improved by getting rid of the *you.*

It was obvious that the speaker wasn't well prepared.

Sometimes, however, a shift to *you* is permissible. The first paragraph of Exercise 3 on page 191 begins with *I* and continues quite satisfactorily with *you,* and the paper beginning on page 193 shifts in the next-to-the-last sentence to *your* and *yourself.* The shift seems more natural than using the correct *my,* and *myself.*

As a rule, though, a shift in person should be avoided.

EXERCISES

Change the pronouns (and verbs when necessary) so that there will be no shift in person. Cross out the incorrect words and write the correct ones above. Sometimes you may want to change a sentence from singular to plural to avoid using too many *one*'s or the awkward *he or she* (see p. 115). Sentences 7 and 8, which follow, are examples.

☐**EXERCISE 1**

1. I enjoy jogging because you feel so good when you quit.

2. In high school our English teacher wouldn't give you more than a C.

3. I like going out with her because she really makes you feel important.

4. I used to think my parents were fussy, but as you grow older, you become more tolerant.

5. I'm finding you have to do a lot of memorizing if you want to be a good speller.

6. I like living in Florida because you have good weather all year long.

7. Often a person can find work if you are willing to take what you can get.

8. It's wise for a beginning driver to stay out of heavy traffic until you have more experience.

9. If you want to play the guitar well, one really needs lessons.

10. All those who intend to graduate should order your gowns immediately.

☐EXERCISE 2

1. When our instructor gives an assignment, she expects you to finish it by the next day.

2. If one has done all the exercises in this book, you should be able to get a perfect score on the final grammar test.

3. At the Oriental Institute one can see the great Winged Bull from Iraq, and you can also see many other Middle East antiquities.

4. When we looked down, you could see the little farms growing smaller and smaller.

5. We were on the plane six hours, and you get tired of sitting that long.

6. We tried to move around, but there was not much you could do.

7. Our car was in the middle of a traffic jam, and you could see that we weren't going to make our appointment.

8. When we opened the door that morning, one could see rabbit tracks in the snow.

9. One should always look up the spelling of a word you aren't sure of.

10. I like being with a person you can talk perfectly frankly with.

When students write *you* in a paper, they usually don't mean *you, the reader*. Rewrite these sentences, eliminating the *you* and stating the sentences as simply as possible. Getting rid of the *you* will usually get rid of wordiness also.

☐EXERCISE 3

1. You should have seen the mess my room was in.

2. You can imagine how terrified I was.

3. Swimming is the best exercise you can take.

4. You don't need to be a member of the Kiwanis Club to attend their breakfast.

5. Your paper will always be more interesting if you put in specific details.

6. Her paper was excellent; you could tell she had spent time on it.

7. If you want to succeed in college, you need a good vocabulary.

8. Your vocabulary will improve if you read widely.

9. You feel absolutely foolish after you have said such a thing.

10. You can imagine how I looked forward to that weekend.

☐EXERCISE 4

1. When you watch television for a whole evening, you realize how much violence is on the programs.

2. After you finish that course in psychology, you're a different person.

3. I spent two days in Williamsburg, but you really need more time if you want to see everything.

4. You need to exercise every day if you want to keep fit.

5. Anyone interested can call this number if you want more information.

6. If you want to prevent air pollution, you should take your car in for a tune-up twice a year.

7. From the above facts you can see that many companies still discriminate in their hiring.

8. You can't imagine how frustrating it was to be unable to get there on time.

9. You should have seen the elegant costume she wore to the masquerade.

10. After an escape like that, you feel pretty lucky to be alive.

Get rid of the shift in person toward the end of this paragraph.

☐EXERCISE 5

As I drove on a deserted blacktop road, I saw horned larks feeding on the surface of the road and along the shoulders. This road, used by farmers for transporting grain from fields to elevators, furnished a bountiful table for these little cold-weather birds. As I came along, the larks rose up from the road and with a low, slightly undulating flight disappeared into a plowed field. I drove to the side of the road and waited. In a few moments the larks came circling back and dropped down to the road again, running all over the road and in the ditches searching for food. You could see the black mark or "whisker" on each side of the head and the black collar below the light throat. On a few of them you could even see the tiny feather "horns" and, as they flew off, the black feathers in the tail, which distinguish them from other birds of the open fields.

JOURNAL WRITING

1. Write a brief paragraph telling someone how to learn to spell. It will, of course, be a "you should" paragraph.
2. Then write the same paragraph to yourself—an "I should" paragraph.
3. Finally write the same paragraph using "students should" and using the pronoun *they.*

CORRECTING WORDINESS

Good writing is concise writing. Don't say something in ten words if you can say it as well, or better, in five. "In this day and age" is not as effective as simply "today." "At the present time" should be "at present" or "now."

Another kind of wordiness comes from saying something twice. There is no need to say "in the month of July" or "7 A.M. in the morning" or "my personal opinion." July *is* a month, 7 A.M. *is* the morning, and my opinion obviously *is* personal. All you need to say is "in July," "7 A.M.," and "my opinion."

Still another kind of wordiness comes from using expressions that add nothing to the meaning of the sentence. "The fact of the matter is that I'm tired" says no more than "I'm tired."

Here are more examples of wordiness.

WORDY WRITING	CONCISE WRITING
at that point in time	then
there is no doubt but that	no doubt
he is a person who	he
a person who is honest	an honest person
there are many boys who	many boys
he was there in person	he was there
personally I think	I think
surrounded on all sides	surrounded
ten pounds in weight	ten pounds
brown in color	brown
refer back	refer
repeat again	repeat
two different kinds	two kinds
free complimentary copy	complimentary copy
free gift	gift
very unique	unique
past history	history
end result	result
and etc.	etc.
usual custom	custom
new innovation	innovation
the field of electronics	electronics
an unexpected surprise	a surprise
each and every	each
due to the fact that	because

EXERCISES

Cross out words or rewrite parts of each sentence to get rid of the wordiness. Doing these exercises can almost turn into a game to see how few words you can use without changing the meaning of the sentence.

☐EXERCISE 1

1. A player who had experience would have had an idea about what to do.

2. The girl who had roomed with me during my college years now was going to make a trip to see me.

3. Personally I think that the field of electronics is a good field to go into.

4. In the month of May two of the members of our family have birthdays.

5. The story I am going to tell you is a story that I heard from my grandfather.

6. It seems to me that the government should be able to work out some way to speed up the judicial process in the courts of our land.

7. What I'm trying to say is that I think justice should be swift and sure.

8. I grew up as a child in an ordinary small town.

9. Owing to the fact that I had a lot of work to do, it wasn't possible for me to accept their invitation.

10. I was unaware of the fact that she was leaving.

☐EXERCISE 2

1. History is a subject that interests me a great deal.

2. The professor is a man who makes his subject interesting to everyone.

3. I have no doubt but that he spends a great deal of time preparing each lecture and getting ready to present it to the class.

4. This polish will double the life of your shoes and make them last twice as long.

5. A personal friend of mine has a very unique invention.

6. There was a lot of objection on the part of the taxpayers.

7. It was 5 A.M. in the morning when we started, and we got there at 6 P.M. that evening.

8. In the month of August most of the employees of this institution of ours take a vacation.

9. The fact of the matter is that I have not had time to prepare an agenda for the program for our meeting this afternoon.

10. I want to repeat my final conclusion again.

☐EXERCISE 3

1. The purple martin circled around and around the martin house for half an hour and then disappeared from view.

2. He was arrested for driving his car in an intoxicated condition.

3. At the present time modern present-day medicine has practically wiped out polio from our country.

4. There were a number of spectators who couldn't get seats.

5. It is my opinion that the grandstand is not as large as it should be.

6. As you may be aware, a fly has a little suction cup on each of its six feet, and this enables it to walk on the ceiling without falling off.

7. The hardest exam that I had last semester was a psychology exam.

8. That exam included a number of questions about things that I had forgotten about completely.

9. The magpie is a bird that is quite large and has a black head, a long greenish tail, and white wing patches on its wings.

10. She is a person who will always do whatever she promises that she'll do.

☐EXERCISE 4

1. In spite of the fact that I hadn't eaten since morning, I wasn't hungry.

2. I'm hoping that I'll be able to find a job in the not-too-distant future.

3. Due to the fact that there was no announcement of the meeting, not many came.

4. There were ten people who were planning to come.

5. Within a period of three months, six of the people in the department have handed in their resignations.

6. I learned to identify three different kinds of ivy on the field trip that I went on this morning.

7. I've gained ten pounds in weight since I first began this diet.

8. Each and every person who attended the opening of the new store received a free gift.

9. I'm convinced of the fact that I use entirely too many words in many of the sentences that I write.

10. There is no doubt but that many people do the exact same thing.

These paragraphs are from a university publication about a new library. On a separate sheet, revise them to get rid of the wordiness, and then see how much more effective they are. The material as it stands has 241 words; the revision at the back of the book has 126—just about half as many. Can you make a revision that concise and still keep the essential information? Finish your revision and count the words before you check with the one at the back of the book.

☐EXERCISE 5

1. Whatever has been accomplished has been made possible because of the cooperation of the university administration, faculty, students, and the library staff working together.

2. Periodicals do not circulate because of the heavy use by all students, and this provision guarantees that they will always be available. Many divisions provide photoduplication facilities so that articles from the periodicals can be easily reproduced.

3. The Information Center is a general reference area which assists faculty and students in the use of the card catalogue, basic reference books, bibliographies, and indexes. There is an orientation program for the purpose of instructing students on library procedures as well as the Inter-Library Loan service.

4. The Reserve Reading Room houses and circulates those books and

materials which the faculty has chosen as required reading for current courses.

5. In the Music Division there are at present ten listening stations, and six of these are equipped with cassette recorders which can be used to record a particular piece of music so that the listener can play it back several times in order to study it.

6. Much of the material essential to a new library is no longer available in printed form. Technology has overcome this problem with the development of microfilms, microcards, and microfiche. The library contains over one million items of microfilms, and the students soon discover the very attractive rooms which house the latest equipment for accommodating these items, as well as microprint machines if copies are required.

AVOIDING CLICHÉS

A cliché is an expression that has been used so often it has lost its originality and effectiveness. Whoever first said "light as a feather" had thought of an original way to express lightness, but today that expression is outworn and boring. Most of us use an occasional cliché in speaking, but clichés have no place in writing. The good writer thinks up fresh new ways to express ideas.

Here are a few clichés. Add some more to the list.

better late than never
busy as a bee
crazy as a loon
down in the dumps
few and far between
fit as a fiddle
fresh as a daisy
green with envy
heavy as lead
in seventh heaven
not my cup of tea
one fell swoop
put his foot down
quick as a wink
raised the roof
safe and sound
sick as a dog

sink or swim
slick as a whistle
sold like hotcakes
thank my lucky stars
the last straw
under the weather

Clichés are boring because the reader always knows what's coming next. What comes next in these expressions?

all her eggs in one . . .
all work and no . . .
born with a silver . . .
bring home the . . .
burning the midnight . . .
easier said than . . .
fighting a losing . . .
fit to be . . .
hot as . . .
jump from the frying pan . . .
more fun than a barrel of . . .
no sooner said than . . .
pretty as a . . .

On a separate sheet rewrite these sentences to get rid of the clichés.

☐EXERCISE 1

1. We had planned to go to the lake, and I was up bright and early, raring to go.
2. But my wife was sleeping like a log, and our son was dead to the world.
3. I started the breakfast, but I was all thumbs and couldn't get the orange juice can open to save my life.
4. Finally I did get the breakfast on the table and called the others. I was determined to get rolling, come hell or high water.
5. When they finally came downstairs, they were hungry as bears, but they complained that the toast was cold.
6. I told them they were making a mountain out of a molehill and that they should be grateful for small favors.
7. Eventually we got in the car and took off, but as luck would have it, we had gone only a mile when it began raining cats and dogs.
8. Finally though, the skies cleared, and we got to the lake safe and sound.
9. Our son immediately jumped into the lake because he swims like a fish.
10. My wife soon followed him, but I just sat on the beach and took a well-earned rest.

JOURNAL WRITING

One way to become aware of clichés so that you won't use them in your writing is to see how many you can purposely put into a paragraph. Write a paragraph describing your difficulties trying to make an eight o'clock class every morning. Use all the clichés possible while still keeping your account smooth and clear. What title will you give your paragraph? Why, a cliché of course. Writing such a paragraph should make you so aware of clichés that they'll never creep into your writing again.

Review of Sentence Structure

Only one sentence in each pair is correct. Read both sentences carefully before you decide. Then write the letter of the *correct* sentence in the blank. You may find any one of these errors:

run-together sentence
fragment
wrong verb form
lack of agreement between subject and verb and pronoun
wrong pronoun
faulty reference of pronoun
dangling modifier
lack of parallel construction
shift in time or person

_____ 1. A. They invited Juan and me to go along.
      B. They invited Juan and I to go along.

_____ 2. A. He ask his parents for more money, and they gave it to him.
      B. They gave an award to him and his brother.

_____ 3. A. One cannot make people learn; you can only show them the way.
      B. I've worked really hard and think I'll pass the course.

_____ 4. A. The director asked Ed and me to help with the publicity.
      B. I can't decide whether to be a secretary, a nurse, or go into teaching.

_____ 5. A. Having finished washing the car, I found the swimming pool inviting.
      B. Kirk told the professor that his watch was wrong.

_____ 6. A. Have you finish your assignment yet?
      B. He invited my brother and me to go for a ride in his boat.

_____ 7. A. Most of the class were prepared for the exam.
      B. I finished my math then I spent the rest of the evening watching TV.

_____ 8. A. Racing down the hill, I fell and sprained my ankle.
      B. You're suppose to turn in a paper every Friday.

_____ 9. A. He has walk to campus ever since his car broke down.
      B. We got an invitation from him and his wife.

_____ 10. A. A list of required readings was posted in the library.
      B. They asked whether you was planning to go.

_____ 11. A. Making the most of every opportunity that came his way.
        B. When I turned in for the night, I fell asleep immediately.

_____ 12. A. There's no use complaining it's too late now.
        B. I certainly didn't choose an easy course.

_____ 13. A. The instructor gave A's to both Melissa and me.
        B. It don't make any difference to me what you do.

_____ 14. A. Most of my friends are going to work this summer.
        B. I was driving along at the speed limit when I see a cop following me.

_____ 15. A. He likes classical music he doesn't like rock.
        B. Of course they blamed my friend and me.

_____ 16. A. There was nothing more to do the outcome was settled.
        B. Our team had worked hard but couldn't compete with them.

_____ 17. A. Getting an A made me happy and caused me to have more self-confidence.
        B. Each of my sisters have their own phone now.

_____ 18. A. When one writes a thesis statement, you should make the points parallel.
        B. I worked until midnight and even then didn't finish.

_____ 19. A. She's beautiful, talented, and has lots of money.
        B. The car belongs to my fiancé and me.

_____ 20. A. Graduating from college, and then being unable to find a job.
        B. Each of my three friends has a scholarship.

_____ 21. A. I had been studying since morning I had to have a break.
        B. I wish they'd invite my husband and me sometime.

_____ 22. A. The rain dampen the heads but not the spirits of the cheering crowd.
        B. I enjoy math and psychology, but I find history and English difficult.

_____ 23. A. Each of his children is interested in music.
        B. She order an expensive suit, and then she couldn't pay for it.

_____ 24. A. The instructor asked Ross and me to lead a group discussion.
        B. I came around a turn in the road, and there I see a pheasant in front of me.

_____ 25. A. You was here before I was, so you should go in first.
        B. They offered my wife and me their cottage for a week.

Punctuation
and
Capital Letters

3　Punctuation and Capital Letters

PERIOD, QUESTION MARK, EXCLAMATION MARK, SEMICOLON, COLON, DASH

Every mark of punctuation should help your reader. Just like Stop and Go signals at an intersection, marks of punctuation will keep the reader, like the traffic, from getting snarled up.

Here are the rules for six marks of punctuation. The first three you have known for a long time and have no trouble with. The one about semicolons you learned when you studied independent clauses (p. 72). The one about the colon may be less familiar.

Put a period at the end of a sentence and after most abbreviations.

Mr.	A.D.	Dr.	Wed.	sq. ft.
Mrs.	etc.	Jan.	P.M.	lbs.

Put a question mark after a direct question (but not after an indirect one).

What time is it? (the exact words of the speaker)
He asked what time it was. (not the exact words)

Put an exclamation mark after an expression that shows strong emotion.

Help! I'm lost!

Put a semicolon between two closely related independent clauses unless they are joined by one of the connecting words *and, but, for, or, nor, yet, so.* (Refer to pp. 72–73 for more information about the semicolon.)

The day was bitter cold; we didn't venture outdoors.
I need to study; therefore I'm going to the library.

Actually you can write quite acceptably without ever using semicolons because a period and capital letter can always be used instead of a semicolon.

The day was bitter cold. We didn't venture outdoors.
I need to study. Therefore I'm going to the library.

Put a colon after a complete statement when a list or quotation follows.

In the trunk of our car were the following items: two sleeping bags, a camp stove, a bag of provisions, and a cooler. (*In the trunk of our car were the following items* is a complete statement. You can hear your voice fall at the end of it. Therefore we put a colon after it before adding the list.)

In the trunk of our car were two sleeping bags, a camp stove, a bag of provisions, and a cooler. (*In the trunk of our car were* is not a complete statement. It needs the list to make it complete. Therefore, since we don't want to separate the list from the first part of the sentence, no colon is used.)

The professor closed his lecture on writing with a quotation from Donald M. Murray: "Maple syrup is the product of boiling 30 or 40 gallons of sap to get one of syrup, and in writing there's a great deal of sap that needs to be boiled down." (*The professor closed his lecture on writing with a quotation from Donald M. Murray* is a complete statement. Therefore we put a colon after it before adding the quotation.)

Donald M. Murray said, "Maple syrup is the product of boiling 30 or 40 gallons of sap to get one of syrup, and in writing there's a great deal of sap that needs to be boiled down." (*Donald M. Murray said* is not a complete statement. Therefore we don't put a colon after it.)

Use a dash to indicate an abrupt change of thought or to throw emphasis upon what follows. Use it sparingly.

And then came the last act—what a letdown.

A Portuguese proverb says that visits always give pleasure—if not in the coming, then in the going.

EXERCISES

Add the necessary punctuation to these sentences (period, question mark, exclamation mark, semicolon, colon, dash). Not all sentences require additional punctuation. Also your answer may not always agree with the one at the back of the book because independent clauses can be separated either with a semicolon or with a period and capital letter. In general use a period and capital letter. Use a semicolon only if the clauses are closely related in meaning.

☐EXERCISE 1

1. My favorite outdoor hobbies are gardening, hiking, and canoeing.
2. My indoor interests are these chess, bridge, and checkers.
3. Checkers isn't a difficult game it demands concentration however.
4. We've bought a place in the country it's only three miles from town.
5. It's a run-down farmhouse it's really only a shell.
6. We enjoy remodeling we'll make something of it.
7. Sure, it will take work it will take money too.
8. But eventually it should pay off at least that's what we're counting on.
9. We'll work at it slowly there's no hurry.
10. Meantime we'll enjoy our surroundings we like the country.

☐EXERCISE 2

1. Did you know there are more than half a million snowflakes in each cubic foot of snow.
2. And did you know that glaciers are formed by snowflakes being compressed for thousands of years into hard ice.
3. Snow delights children it often annoys or inconveniences adults.
4. People think of snow as sterile actually it teems with microorganisms.
5. There are various kinds of snow the Eskimos have more than two dozen words for snow.
6. The U.S. record for snowfall in a period of 24 hours was 75.8 inches in Silver Lake, Colorado, in 1921.
7. Snow begins with ice crystals they are formed in the clouds.
8. They may have various shapes their basic shape is determined by the temperature of the air in which they grow.
9. Several ice crystals may join to form a snowflake the size of the snowflake may be even as large as an inch in diameter.
10. No two snowflakes are alike most are six-pointed however.

☐EXERCISE 3

1. Don't you collect aluminum cans the recycling center pays good money for them.

2. Last week I made four dollars on them some weeks I make more.
3. I took a sack out to the park and filled it with empties in 25 minutes.
4. One man told me that he found 300 cans in a forest preserve another found almost that many in vacant lots.
5. Some people hunt mushrooms others hunt aluminum cans.
6. Who's your favorite jazz trombonist.
7. My favorite George Benson albums are these *Breezin'*, *Weekend in L.A.*, and *Benson Burner.*
8. The needle on my stereo has been damaging my records I really need a new needle.
9. I spend a lot of time at our local record store I spend a lot of money there too.
10. I don't think I'll have much money this summer I'll probably just vacation at home.

☐EXERCISE 4

1. I always thought that spiders were pests now I've learned that they're useful.
2. Among the harmful insects that spiders destroy are the following mosquitoes, flies, grasshoppers, and garden insects.
3. Spiders are found in almost all parts of the world they're the spinners and engineers of nature.
4. Their webs are marvels of geometric design their suspension bridges over streams are amazing.
5. Spider thread is stronger than silkworm thread it can't be obtained, however, in large enough quantities to make cloth.
6. Spiders use their thread in the following ways to spin webs, to catch insects, to line their nests, and to make cocoons for their eggs.
7. About 40,000 kinds of spiders live throughout the world some are the size of a pinhead some are eight inches long.
8. A spider that loses a leg is in no great difficulty it simply grows a new one.
9. The female is larger than the male sometimes she eats her mate.
10. Spiders are important in the balance of nature they shouldn't be thoughtlessly killed.

☐EXERCISE 5

1. Are you tired of the long winters some geologists say the winters are getting shorter.
2. In North America 20,000 years ago, ice and snow covered the land the year round there were summers though.

3. The summers were simply too cool to melt the winter snow therefore the snow piled up year after year.
4. In the cold summers only mosses and lichens could grow a few fast-blooming plants also appeared.
5. Today we have remnants of that ice age the Antarctic and Greenland.
6. Most of Greenland is covered by an ice cap the Antarctic also is covered by a sheet of ice.
7. And we have icebergs they are the broken-off ends of glaciers.
8. Some are tiny others are mountains a mile across.
9. The part below the water is as much as seven times larger than the part above the water also the part below may extend farther than the visible part.
10. The *Titanic* struck a part of an iceberg not visible above the water the ship went down near Newfoundland in 1912 with 1,513 people aboard.

□EXERCISE 6

1. Do you enjoy driving slowly along a country road.
2. Most states are busy building efficient highways one state, however, is also preserving some old country roads.
3. The idea was first presented to the people of Wisconsin in 1973 they gave the proposal their enthusiastic support.
4. The legislature liked the idea too the governor then signed the Rustic Roads Act into law.
5. Now the state has 27 rustic roads moreover requests for more are growing.
6. Along these roads are remnants of the past old stone barns, old mills, log buildings, rusting farm plows and hay rakes, as well as fields of wild flowers.
7. The rustic character of the road is never changed plank bridges are kept, and if one wears out, it is simply replaced with another plank bridge.
8. Life goes on as it always has visitors can drive along and enjoy the countryside, sharing it with squirrels, deer, beavers, and turtles.
9. Travelers will never see any signs of commercialism billboards, signs, motels, souvenir shops.
10. Wisconsin now has two kinds of roads those for leisurely travel and those for people in a hurry.

□EXERCISE 7

1. I've been learning some word roots it's a good way to increase one's vocabulary.

2. Words didn't just happen they grew from roots.
3. Yesterday I learned four roots CRED, LOGY, PATH, and TELE.
4. CRED means "to believe" about 15 common words contain that root.
5. Something that is *credible* is believable anything that is *incredible* is not believable.
6. A *creed* is a statement of one's beliefs *credentials* are documents that cause others to believe in one.
7. LOGY means "study of" it is found at the end of hundreds of words.
8. GEO means "earth" therefore *geology* is a study of the earth.
9. ARCH means "ancient" therefore *archeology* is a study of ancient cultures.
10. And ASTR means "star" *astrology* is a pseudoscience claiming to tell the future by the stars.

☐EXERCISE 8

1. Another root I've learned is PATH it means "feeling."
2. SYM means "together" therefore *sympathy* is literally a feeling together with someone.
3. ANTI means "against" thus *antipathy* is a feeling against someone or something.
4. The root TELE meaning "far" is found in many common words *telephone, telegraph, television, telescope,* and *telepathy.*
5. A *telephone* (PHON sound) lets one hear far sounds a *telegraph* (GRAPH to write) is literally an instrument for far writing.
6. *Television* (VIS to see) lets one see pictures from afar a *telescope* (SCOP to look) lets one look at far objects.
7. *Telepathy* (PATH feeling) is the supposed communication between two people far apart that is, they sense each other's feelings from afar.
8. Other words containing the root TELE are *teletypewriter, telemetry,* and *telephoto.*
9. I now intend to learn more roots they help me remember difficult words.
10. They also surprise me I find more meaning in words I already know.

☐EXERCISE 9

1. Her table was set with sterling, china, and crystal.
2. Mine was set with the following plastic dishes from Woolworth's, stainless steel flatware, and giveaway glasses.
3. My dad says there are two kinds of people single and worried.
4. My brother received his B A then he began work on his M A.

5. But besides his academic field, he has other interests he plays a good game of tennis and a fair game of golf.
6. Also he loves to cook he says that he's at home on the range.
7. The Scots-born veterinarian James Herriot has named his best-sellers after the lines in an old hymn *All Things Bright and Beautiful, All Creatures Great and Small, All Things Wise and Wonderful, The Lord God Made Them All.*
8. There are only two lasting things we can give our children roots and wings.
9. There are two kinds of pain the pain that leaves as soon as the wound heals and the pain that lasts a lifetime.
10. Money giving, says Karl Menninger, is a good criterion of a person's mental health generous people are rarely mentally ill people.

JOURNAL WRITING

Write two sentences, the first requiring a colon and the second not requiring a colon, in which you list the things you have to do this coming weekend. Make sure, of course, that the items are parallel.

WRITING ASSIGNMENT

Continue your writing assignments from the latter part of the book.

COMMAS

Students often sprinkle commas through their papers as if they were shaking pepper out of a pepper shaker. Don't use a comma unless you know a rule for it. But commas are important. They help the reader. Without them, a reader would often have to go back and reread a sentence to find out what the writer meant.

Actually you need only six comma rules. MASTER THESE SIX RULES, and your writing will be easier to read. The first rule you have already learned (p. 73).

1. Put a comma before *and, but, for, or, nor, yet, so* when they connect two independent clauses.

They started to play Trivial Pursuit, and that ended their studying.
I may try out for the next play, or I may wait until the following one.

But be sure such words do connect two independent clauses. The following sentence is merely one independent clause with one subject and two verbs. Therefore no comma should be used.

He wanted to try out for the play but didn't have the time.

2. Put a comma between items in a series.

She ordered ice cream, cake, and an éclair.
He opened the letter, read it hastily, and gave a shout.

Some words "go together" and don't need a comma between them even though they do make up a series.

The tattered old plush album had belonged to her grandmother.
Large bright blue violets bordered the path in the woods.

The way to tell whether a comma is needed between two words in a series is to see whether *and* could be used naturally between them. It would sound all right to say *ice cream and cake and an éclair*. Therefore commas are used between the items. But it would not sound right to say *tattered and old and plush* album or *Large and bright and blue violets*. Therefore no commas are used. Simply put a comma where an *and* would sound right.

It's permissible to omit the comma before the *and* connecting the last two members of a series, but more often it's used.

If an address or date is used in a sentence, treat it as a series, putting a comma after every item, including the last.

> He was born on May 17, 1966, in Madison, Wisconsin, and grew up there.
> She lived in Gresham, Oregon, for two years.

When only the month and year are used in a date, the commas are omitted.

> In May 1984 he moved to Casper, Wyoming.

3. **Put a comma after an introductory expression that doesn't flow smoothly into the sentence, or before an afterthought that is tacked on.** It may be a word, a group of words, or a dependent clause.

> No, I'm not interested.
> Well, that's finished.
> Racing to the finish line, she won the 100-meter dash.
> When I entered, the house was in darkness.
> It's important, isn't it?

When you studied dependent clauses, you learned that a dependent clause at the beginning of a sentence needs a comma after it. In the fourth example you can see that a comma is necessary. Otherwise the reader would read *When I entered the house* . . . before realizing that that was not what the writer meant. A comma prevents misreading.

EXERCISES
Punctuate these sentences according to the first three comma rules. Correct your answers ten at a time.

☐**EXERCISE 1**

1. You always have two choices.
2. You always have had and you always will have.
3. You could have gone to college or you could have taken a job.
4. You chose college and you still have two choices.
5. You can choose to work or you can choose to slide.
6. If you choose to work you still have two choices.
7. You can work for a grade or you can work to learn.
8. If you choose to learn you still have two choices.
9. You can do something with your learning or you can forget it.
10. As far as you can see into the future you will always have two choices.

☐EXERCISE 2

1. I used to think great writers just sat down and wrote without errors but now I understand that they have to write and write and rewrite.
2. In preparation for each class hour we write one of the following: a complete thesis statement a rough draft or a final draft.
3. A few rough drafts are read aloud and we all learn from our discussion of them.
4. We turn our final drafts in on Friday and we usually get them back on Monday.
5. I like getting my paper back promptly for then I still remember my struggles with it.
6. A few papers are read aloud to the class but the instructor never reads the writer's name.
7. Sometimes my paper sounds better than I thought it was and sometimes it sounds worse.
8. One thing is sure and that is that each paper I write is an improvement over the last one.
9. I now no longer fear writing a paper for I know how to go about it.
10. If I work out a good thesis statement the rest is easy.

☐EXERCISE 3

1. No matter what the devastation nature always makes a comeback.
2. After the eruption of Mount Saint Helens 150 square miles of countryside lay dead.
3. Everything was covered with gray ash and no green was seen anywhere.
4. But only two months after the eruption small ferns pushed through the ash.
5. And a year later tiny fir trees pink fireweed and lupine appeared.
6. Animals began reestablishing themselves too: pocket gophers elk and deer.
7. And ladybugs black ants and honeybees were found at work.
8. People too began to come back for there was cleaning up to do.
9. Some salvaged the fallen timber and others prepared for the tourists.
10. It may take years but the area around Mount Saint Helens will someday be green again.

☐EXERCISE 4

1. I've been reading about the history of some common things and I've had some surprises.
2. I thought ice cream was a modern invention but I discover that it's had a long history.

3. Alexander the Great enjoyed a chilled mixture of milk honey and fruit juice in 335 B.C.
4. The first ad for ice cream appeared in 1777 and in 1848 a hand-cranked ice-cream freezer was patented.
5. The freezer was a large wooden bucket filled with chipped ice and in the center was the container with the cream sugar eggs and vanilla.
6. The ingredients had to be stirred constantly by a dasher turned by a crank and this stirring made the ice cream freeze smoothly.
7. In the early part of this century every household had an ice-cream freezer and before a meal someone always got the job of cranking the freezer.
8. After perhaps half an hour the ice cream was frozen and one of the children was then given the treat of licking the dasher.
9. The homemade ice cream melted rapidly but that never caused a problem.
10. Before it had a chance to melt it was gone.

☐EXERCISE 5

1. When we think of birds we usually think of frail little creatures.
2. Actually birds are stronger than humans in many ways and they have set records beyond human capability.
3. For example the tiny New England blackpoll flies nonstop 2,300 miles to its winter home in South America.
4. To have the strength for such a flight it nearly doubles its body weight before taking off.
5. Without stopping for food or drink it covers the distance in 105 to 115 hours.
6. To match that feat a human would have to run four-minute miles for 80 consecutive hours without food or drink.
7. Although most birds fly at low altitudes even small birds can fly as high as 21,000 feet.
8. In comparison humans begin to experience shortness of breath and exhaustion at 14,000 feet.
9. Smaller birds fly at 25 to 30 miles an hour but larger birds can fly at speeds of more than a mile a minute.
10. Setting the distance record the Arctic tern flies 11,000 miles each way between its breeding ground in the Arctic and its winter home in the Antarctic.

☐EXERCISE 6

1. I always thought totem poles were just freestanding poles but now I know they had many uses.

2. When I visited the Museum of Anthropology in Vancouver I saw many totem poles and learned that the Northwest Coast Indians used them in various ways.
3. A totem pole might be a corner post of a house or it might support one of the roof beams.
4. A pole with an opening at the base was an entrance to a plank house and other poles simply stood against exterior or interior walls.
5. Some poles were large freestanding memorial poles in honor of deceased high-ranking people and inside such poles might be coffins with human remains.
6. A family totem pole might display figures from family legends or it might have representations of a raven bear beaver frog or a supernatural bird with a huge beak.
7. Humans were also represented and the size of the head was always exaggerated.
8. The southern and central groups of the Northwest Coast Indians made humans with heads one-third the body height but the northern group enlarged the head to one-half the body height.
9. Besides having such personal uses some totem poles stood on seashores or riverbanks to welcome visitors.
10. Carved from the trunks of red cedar trees the totem poles tell us something of the history and customs of the Northwest Coast Indians.

□EXERCISE 7

1. Carl Sandburg was born in Galesburg Illinois on January 6 1878.
2. Between the ages of 13 and 17 he was successively a driver of a milk wagon porter in a barbershop sceneshifter in a theater and truck operator at a brick kiln.
3. Then he went west, where he harvested wheat in the Kansas wheat fields washed dishes at hotels in Kansas City Omaha and Denver and worked as a carpenter's helper in Kansas.
4. Eventually he went to college became a newspaper reporter and began writing poetry.
5. After the publication of his poem "Chicago" he became recognized.
6. He chose to write about ordinary things and the public liked his themes.
7. Of all his poems "Fog" is the one most people memorize.
8. Although he is best known for his poetry he also wrote a biography of Lincoln.
9. People who died in 1929—just over 50 years ago—had never heard of jet airplanes Polaroid cameras food freezers frozen vegetables radar V-8 engines electric razors electric typewriters drive-in movie theaters color television the United Nations the atomic bomb or bubble gum.

10. The United States is a bit presumptuous in calling itself America. A big chunk of America is Canada and a big chunk is Mexico and if you look at a map of the North American continent you'll see that the United States is really just a swath across the middle.

☐EXERCISE 8

1. For every ton of newspaper that is recycled 17 trees are not cut down.
2. The Nature Conservancy the Wilderness Society the Sierra Club and other conservation groups are making some headway in saving the redwoods.
3. The lowest naturally occurring temperature ever recorded was −126.9°F. in Vostok Antarctica on August 24 1960.
4. Yes and we're complaining that it's cold here.
5. The highest temperature ever recorded in the shade was 136.4°F. in Azizia Libya on September 13 1922.
6. The wettest place on earth is Mt. Waialeale Hawaii. It rains there 350 days a year and the average yearly rainfall is 451 inches.
7. We heard a carillon recital from the Bok Singing Tower at Lake Wales Florida.
8. The carillon was designed built and installed in 1928 by a company in England.
9. Its 53 tuned bronze bells range in size from 22,000 pounds to 17 pounds and they play a chromatic scale.
10. While the history of carillons in Europe dates back more than 300 years it is only in this century that carillons have become popular on this continent.

Punctuate this paragraph according to the first three comma rules.

☐EXERCISE 9

In the issue of *Saturday Review* that appeared on the newsstands the week before Robert Kennedy was killed Richard L. Tobin gave the following report of an eight-hour monitoring of three TV networks and half a dozen local outlets: "We marked down ninety-three specific incidents involving sadistic brutality murder cold-blooded killing sexual cruelty and related sadism. . . . We encountered seven different kinds of pistols and revolvers three varieties of rifle three distinct brands of shotgun half a dozen assorted daggers and stilettos two types of machete one butcher's clever a broadax rapiers galore a posse of sabers an electric prodder and a guillotine. Men (and women and even children) were shot by gunpowder burned at the stake tortured over live coals trussed and beaten in relays dropped into molten sugar cut to ribbons (in color) repeatedly kneed in the groin beaten while being held defenseless by other hoodlums forcibly drowned whipped with a leather belt. . . . By the end of the stint we were quite insensitive, almost immune to the shock of seeing a human being in pain."

JOURNAL WRITING

Write a brief paragraph about some valuable information you've gained from a course. In your account make use of the first three comma rules.

WRITING ASSIGNMENT

As you get back your writing assignments, are you keeping a list of your misspelled words on the inside back cover of this book?

COMMAS (continued)

4. Put commas around the name of a person spoken to.

> I hope, Michelle, that you're going with me.
> David, you're an hour late.
> I'm ready for a game of Scrabble, John.

5. Put commas around an expression that interrupts the flow of the sentence (such as *however, moreover, finally, therefore, of course, by the way, on the other hand, I am sure, I think*).

> I hope, of course, that the rumor isn't true.
> We decided, therefore, to leave without him.
> The entire trip, I think, will take only an hour.

Read the preceding sentences aloud, and you will hear how those expressions interrupt the flow of the sentence. Sometimes, however, such expressions flow smoothly into the sentence and don't need commas around them. Whether an expression is an interrupter or not often depends on where it is in the sentence. If it's in the middle of a sentence, it's more likely to be an interrupter than if it's at the beginning or the end. The expressions that were interrupters in the preceding sentences are not interrupters in the following sentences and therefore don't require commas.

> Of course I hope that the rumor isn't true.
> Therefore we decided to leave without him.
> I think the entire trip will take only an hour.

Remember that when one of the above words like *however* comes between two independent clauses, that word always has a semicolon before it. It may also have a comma after it, especially if there seems to be a pause between the word and the rest of the clause. (See p. 72.)

> I wanted to go; however, I didn't have the money.
> Everyone liked the speaker; furthermore, they asked her to return.
> I'm going out for track; therefore I'm spending hours running.
> I worked for days on my term paper; finally I finished it.

Thus a word like *however* or *therefore* may be used in three ways:

1. as an interrupter (commas around it)
2. as a word that flows into the sentence (no commas needed)
3. as a connecting word between two independent clauses (semicolon before it and often a comma after it).

6. Put commas around nonessential material.

Such material may be interesting, but the main idea of the sentence would be clear without it. In the following sentence

Kay Carter, who edits the college paper, chaired the meeting.

the clause *who edits the college paper* is not essential to the main idea of the sentence. Without it, we still know exactly who the sentence is about and what she did: Kay Carter chaired the meeting. Therefore the nonessential material is set off from the rest of the sentence by commas to show that it could be left out. But in the following sentence

The girl who edits the college paper chaired the meeting.

the clause *who edits the college paper* is essential to the main idea of the sentence. Without it the sentence would read: The girl chaired the meeting. We would have no idea which girl. The clause *who edits the college paper* is essential because it tells us which girl. It couldn't be left out. Therefore commas are not used around it. In this sentence

The suit I'm wearing, which I bought two years ago, is still my favorite.

the clause *which I bought two years ago* could be left out, and we'd still know the main meaning of the sentence: The suit I'm wearing is still my favorite. Therefore the nonessential material is set off by commas to show that it could be left out. But in this sentence

The suit that I bought two years ago is still my favorite.

the clause *that I bought two years ago* is essential. Without it, the sentence would read: The suit is still my favorite. We'd have no idea which suit. Therefore the clause couldn't be left out, and commas are not used around it.

The trick in deciding whether material is essential is to say, "Interesting, but is it necessary?"

EXERCISES

Look back now at Rules 4 and 5. Punctuate the next two exercises according to those two rules.

☐EXERCISE 1

1. Yes Gregg I know the car needs washing.
2. I'm too busy this evening however to wash it.
3. It will have to wait therefore until tomorrow.
4. Therefore it will have to wait until tomorrow.
5. However much I'd like to wash it I'm simply too busy now.
6. I wish Felipe that I could be out surfing now.
7. Surfing however won't get you a college degree Gregg.
8. Neither will watching television Felipe.
9. Well there's nothing to do I guess but turn it off.
10. Yes we can't go on this way.

☐EXERCISE 2

1. I heard a lecture on maturity yesterday by a psychologist who I understand has written a book on the subject.
2. Maturity the lecturer explained is the ability to establish helping relationships.
3. The immature person is as a rule egocentric and gives no thought to the other person.
4. The mature person on the other hand is concerned about the development, the well-being, and the happiness of the other person.
5. The great difference in people therefore is in their maturity and their ability to care.
6. He said furthermore that maturity is essential for settling any quarrel.
7. In any disagreement he said there is just one question to ask, and that question is "What's important here?"
8. But only one of the two people disagreeing needs to be mature he said in order to solve the problem.
9. The one mature person can distinguish the important from the unimportant the lecturer continued and can then use that knowledge to settle the quarrel.
10. The basis of all good relationships it seems is maturity.

The rest of the exercises include not only Comma Rules 4 and 5 but also Comma Rule 6. Make sure you understand the explanation of Rule 6 before you begin the exercises.

□EXERCISE 3

1. This is the car that I bought three years ago.
2. This car which I bought three years ago has gone 50,000 miles.
3. We're going to our cottage which we all love.
4. The cottage that we bought last summer is near Muskegon.
5. Frederick Stock the great conductor of the Chicago Symphony always tried to fix the mistake and not the blame.
6. *The Door into Summer* a novel by Robert A. Heinlein is a good introduction to science fiction.
7. The origin of games which have always been a part of civilization is unknown.
8. The games of hopscotch, blindman's buff, and tug-of-war which we think of as modern were actually played by the children of ancient Rome.
9. None of the early games however were as difficult as Rubik's Cube.
10. And none of the ancients moreover ever thought of such a game as Trivial Pursuit.

□EXERCISE 4

1. Avalanches I thought were accidents of nature that could not be prevented.
2. Now however I have learned that their hazards can at least be lessened.
3. Snow safety workers have developed techniques that control avalanches to some extent.
4. They study the factors that can start an avalanche: the kind of snow, the amount of snowfall, and the force of the wind.
5. Then they shoot explosives into a likely spot and start small avalanches which are not so destructive as large ones.
6. And ski patrollers who carry hand charges of explosives in their jackets scour any area where there has been heavy snow.
7. A resort area 25 miles southeast of Salt Lake City is the spot that has more avalanches than any other populated area on this continent.
8. The thousands who ski there are safer today undoubtedly because of the new methods of avalanche control.
9. But this continent doesn't have the hazardous avalanches that occur in the Alps.

10. In Switzerland for example in the winter of 1950–51 which was the worst avalanche year in modern times 279 people were killed by avalanches.

□EXERCISE 5

1. The idea that touching a toad may cause warts is a superstition.
2. A toad's skin however is dry and covered with warts.
3. A frog's skin on the other hand is moist and smooth.
4. The toad which spends most of its life on land has feet that are not fully webbed for swimming.
5. The toad flicks out its tongue which is long and sticky to catch insects.
6. When a toad sings, its vocal sac enlarges into a balloon that is larger than its head.
7. The toad's song which is used to attract females is heard in May and June.
8. The female lays thousands of eggs which look like strings of beads.
9. In a few days the eggs hatch into tiny tadpoles which are often eaten by other creatures.
10. Those that survive turn into little toads which are at first no bigger than a shirt button.

□EXERCISE 6

1. The reason students can't write some people say is that they haven't been taught enough grammar.
2. They should some think learn to diagram sentences the way their grandparents did.
3. Authorities tell us however that extensive drill on grammar has virtually no effect on writing skills.
4. Too much drill on grammar can in fact be harmful because it will take time that should be spent on writing.
5. Of course students need to know the fundamentals of grammar.
6. But more important than a lot of grammar drill we are told is giving students more opportunity to write.
7. The standardized test which can be graded by a computer has almost replaced the essay exam.
8. What is necessary it seems clear is for students to write more in all their classes and not only in English classes.
9. When students write about a subject, they learn more undoubtedly than if they merely read about it and answer some true-false questions.
10. Hayakawa says that one doesn't know anything clearly unless one can state it in writing.

□EXERCISE 7

1. Cherry cobbler which is really easy to make is always a popular dessert.
2. Cherry pie on the other hand takes longer to make and isn't any better.
3. Foods that take a long time to prepare I have found are often no tastier than simpler recipes.
4. Spending a lot of time in the kitchen as you can see isn't my idea of the good life.
5. Most American homes it seems to me are cluttered with too many things.
6. We could take a lesson I think from the Japanese whose homes are decorated simply.
7. The traditional Japanese room is decorated with only one picture which is changed frequently so that it won't become monotonous.
8. One picture and one vase of flowers are as a rule the sole ornaments in a room.
9. Western ways however are rapidly gaining popularity in Japan.
10. Before long I fear much of the traditional beauty of Japanese life will be gone.

□EXERCISE 8

1. Anthropologist Mary Leakey wife of famed Louis Leakey has made some new discoveries in Africa about the origin of humans.
2. Forty years ago she and Louis excavated for a time in Laetoli a remote area of Tanzania but found little of interest.
3. They moved on to Olduvai Gorge 25 miles to the north where they made most of their discoveries.
4. Now however Mrs. Leakey has returned to Laetoli and has uncovered jawbones, teeth, and other fossils.
5. Her greatest find is the footprint of a creature that was a direct ancestor of humans.
6. The footprint according to radioactive dating was made more than three million years ago.
7. It's wider than the footprints of Neanderthal man which were left 80,000 years ago and which had always been accepted as the earliest human footprints.
8. And now a still more recent discovery is a skeleton that was found in Ethiopia in 1974 by Donald Johanson.
9. This skeleton which was named "Lucy" after a Beatles' song is 3.5 million years old and is the most nearly complete prehistoric skeleton ever found.

10. The bones of all these finds belonged to erect walkers who were not human but who were the ancestors of humans.

☐EXERCISE 9

1. The world was shocked quite naturally at the disaster in the pesticide plant in India in 1984.
2. But fully as frightening according to the environmentalists is the ever-growing buildup of poisonous wastes upon our land.
3. Some 90 billion pounds of toxic waste according to the Environmental Protection Agency are produced annually in the United States.
4. This waste is produced by giant companies of course but also by small companies such as local dry cleaners.
5. Only 10 percent of the chemical wastes regardless of their potency are disposed of properly.
6. The rest which are dumped into rivers, abandoned mine shafts, swamps, or fields are endangering everyone.
7. There are according to the Natural Resources Defense Council as many as 50,000 toxic-waste dumps around the United States.
8. At least 14,000 of these it is estimated are or soon could be dangerous.
9. Their contents are slowly dripping into the soil or water supplies.
10. The full effects of these gradual seepages may not be felt for 10 or 15 years which is the time it takes for some cancers to develop.

Source: *Time*, December 17, 1984.

JOURNAL WRITING

A question of punctuation arose in writing the Republican Party platform in 1984. The first draft said that Republicans "oppose any attempts to increase taxes which would harm the recovery." A revised draft said that Republicans "oppose any attempts to increase taxes, which would harm the recovery." Can you explain the difference in meaning between the two drafts? Write a paragraph giving your explanation.

Review of the Comma

THE SIX COMMA RULES

1. Put a comma before *and, but, for, or, nor, yet, so* when they connect two independent clauses.
2. Put a comma between items in a series.
3. Put a comma after an introductory expression or before an afterthought.
4. Put commas around the name of a person spoken to.
5. Put commas around an interrupter, like *however, moreover*, etc.
6. Put commas around nonessential material.

Add the necessary commas to these sentences.

1. When it comes to eating people differ in their tastes.
2. The United States needs to add order to liberty and Russia needs to add liberty to order.
3. She cried when she lost her contact lens for her insurance policy on it had run out.
4. Professor Gonzalez whom I've known for four years is retiring.
5. The earliest parking meters ever installed were those put in the business district of Oklahoma City Oklahoma on July 19 1935.
6. While I was watching a pretty face at the curb the light turned green and cars behind me began to honk.
7. Yes I'd like to go with you Melanie if you can wait a few minutes.
8. After mending Julie's mitten finding lunch money for Tim and locating a lost workbook I finally sent the children on their way.
9. The book that I had requested at the library came in.
10. The tallest inhabited building in the world is the Sears Tower on Wacker Drive in Chicago with 110 stories.
11. Some experiments have been conducted with chimpanzees and the results are surprising.
12. A chimpanzee can aim a ball at a target almost as well as a person can but the chimpanzee can't concentrate as long.
13. If the first few shots are unsuccessful the person tries harder.
14. The chimpanzee however rapidly loses patience.
15. If the aiming tests are made too difficult the chimpanzee may even wreck the apparatus.

QUOTATION MARKS

Put quotation marks around the exact words of a speaker (but not around an indirect quotation).

> She said, "I'm ready." (her exact words)
> She said that she was ready. (not her exact words)

Whenever *that* precedes the words of a speaker (as in the last example), it indicates that the words are not a direct quotation and should not have quotation marks around them.

If the speaker says more than one sentence, quotation marks are used only before and after the entire speech.

> She said, "I'm ready. I'll be there in a minute. Don't go without me."

The words telling who is speaking are set off with a comma unless, of course, a question mark or exclamation mark is needed.

> "I'm ready," she said.
> She said, "I'm ready."
> "Do you want me to go?" she asked.
> "Come here!" she shouted.

Every quotation begins with a capital letter. But when a quotation is broken, the second part doesn't begin with a capital letter unless it's a new sentence.

> "The best way out," wrote Robert Frost, "is always through."
> "People always get what they ask for," wrote Aldous Huxley. "The only trouble is that they never know, until they get it, what it actually is that they have asked for."

Begin a new paragraph with each change of speaker.

> "Let's try some Carl Rogers psychology," he said.
> "Do you mean his idea about stating the other person's opinion?" she asked.
> "That's right," he said.

Put quotation marks around the name of a story, poem, article, or other short work. For longer works such as books, newspapers, magazines, plays, or movies, use underlining, which means they would be italicized in print.

> I like Amy Lowell's poem "Patterns."
> Have you seen the movie *A Passage to India?*
> In our short story class we read James Joyce's "Eveline," which is found in his book *Dubliners.*
> Do you read *National Geographic* magazine?

EXERCISES

Punctuate the quotations, and underline or put quotation marks around each title. Correct each group of ten sentences before going on.

☐EXERCISE 1

1. A college education is one of the few things a person is willing to pay for and not get said William Lowe Bryan, former president of Indiana University.

2. Americans have more timesaving devices and less time than any other group of people in the world wrote Duncan Caldwell.

3. If all misfortunes were laid in a common heap said Socrates whence everyone must take an equal portion, most people would be content to take their own and depart.

4. Our guide said that the Cathedral of St. John the Divine in New York City is one of the two largest cathedrals in the world.

5. I have been brought up to believe that how I see myself is more important than how others see me said Anwar Sadat.

6. Speaking of his life of unceasing effort, the great pianist Paderewski said before I was a master, I was a slave.

7. An excellent plumber is infinitely more admirable than an incompetent philosopher says John Gardner.

8. Alfred North Whitehead said that education is a movement of the mind from freedom through discipline to freedom again.

9. The secret of happiness is not in doing what one likes said James M. Barrie but in liking what one has to do.

10. The toastmaster said that marriage is oceans of emotions surrounded by expanses of expenses.

☐EXERCISE 2

1. In an art gallery a man said to his wife I know what that artist is trying to say. He's trying to say he can't paint worth a damn!

2. The important thing in life is not the person one loves. It is the fact that one loves said Marcel Proust in his novel Remembrance of Things Past.

3. A diplomat is someone who remembers a lady's birthday but forgets her age said the speaker.

4. By working faithfully eight hours a day said Robert Frost you may eventually get to be a boss and work twelve hours a day.

5. My dad says that our forefathers didn't need as much machinery to run a farm as we need to mow a lawn.

6. Alexander Woollcott said all the things I really like to do are either immoral, illegal, or fattening.

7. More and more I come to value charity and love of one's fellow beings above everything else said Albert Einstein.

8. A man who uses a great many words to express his meaning is like a bad marksman who, instead of aiming a single stone at an object, takes up a handful and throws at it in hopes he may hit said Samuel Johnson.

9. A Sioux Indian prayer says Great Spirit, help me never to judge another until I have walked in his moccasins for two weeks.

10. In describing the Taj Mahal, Rufus Jones said only a few times in one's earthly life is one given to see absolute perfection.

□EXERCISE 3

1. What's the most important thing you've learned in this class Brenda asked.

2. Learning to write a complete thesis statement Alex said because it's going to help me in my writing for other courses.

3. I know that's important Brenda replied but it's not most important for me.

4. What's most important for you Alex asked.

5. My biggest improvement has been learning to write concisely. My papers used to be so wordy.

6. That never was my problem he said my biggest achievement besides learning about thesis statements is that I finally decided to learn to spell.

7. And have you improved?

8. Tremendously he said now I just spell every other word wrong. I used to spell every word wrong.

9. Come on! You're not that bad. I read one of your papers, and there wasn't a single misspelled word.

10. I'm getting there Alex said.

☐EXERCISE 4

1. Do commas and periods go inside the quotation marks Alex asked.

2. Of course Brenda replied they'd look lost on the outside.

3. I guess they would he said.

4. Is there anything more you want to know about punctuation she asked.

5. What do you do if you want to quote a whole paragraph from a book he asked.

6. If the quotation is more than five lines long, then you punctuate it differently from ordinary quotations she said.

7. How he asked.

8. You indent the whole quotation five spaces, single-space it, and forget about the quotation marks she said.

9. I suppose that makes it stand out clearly as quoted material.

10. Exactly she said.

☐EXERCISE 5

1. And what have you been doing with yourself Kevin wanted to know.

2. Oh, I've been doing a lot of reading for one thing Natalie said.

3. Still learning new words Kevin asked.

4. Sure, I'm always learning new words Natalie said yesterday I learned what *energize* means.

5. And what does it mean?

6. Well, the root *erg* means a unit of energy or work, and *energize* means to give energy to. For example, some people find cold showers energizing Natalie said.

7. I prefer to get my energy some other way Kevin said I suppose that same root *erg* is in *energy* and *energetic.*

8. Right. And it's also in *metallurgy*, which means working with metals. Another interesting word is *George. Geo* means earth, and *erg* means work. Therefore *George* is an earth worker or farmer.

9. I never knew that before Kevin said it really helps to know word roots.

10. It helps me Natalie replied.

☐EXERCISE 6

1. When I go baby-sitting, I always take along some books.

2. The moment I get in the door, the children shout are you going to read to us?

3. Don't I always I say.

4. I often begin with one of their favorite poems like Jabberwocky.

5. And then I may read a book like Mr. Popper's Penguins.

6. Curious George is another of their favorite books.

7. When I try to stop, they shout, More. Read some more.

8. You have to get to sleep I say.

9. Read just one more poem they beg.

10. I read them The Swing from Robert Louis Stevenson's book A Child's Garden of Verses, and then I say That's absolutely all for tonight.

☐EXERCISE 7

1. I had three chairs in my house: one for solitude, two for friendship, and three for society wrote Henry David Thoreau in his book Walden.

2. Sometimes wrote Thoreau as I drift idly on Walden Pond, I cease to live and begin to be.

3. If a man does not keep pace with his companions Thoreau said perhaps it is because he hears a different drummer.

4. Victor Hugo wrote the greatest happiness of life is the conviction that we are loved, loved for ourselves, or rather loved in spite of ourselves.

5. No matter what happens said Marcus Aurelius you can control the situation by your attitude.

6. It's very hard to take yourself too seriously when you look at the world from outer space said Astronaut Thomas K. Mattingly II.

7. If I could choose one degree for the people I hire, it would be English says a senior vice president of the First Atlanta Corporation. I want people who can read and speak in the language we're dealing with.

8. It's hard said Bill Vaughan for the modern generation to understand Thoreau, who lived beside a pond but didn't own water skis or a snorkel.

9. Subsidies for growing and promoting tobacco are maintained, but school health programs are slashed. Social benefits are denounced as handouts, but it is proposed to open up vast areas of public lands to developers in what may be the greatest giveaway in our history said Norman Cousins.

10. Birds sing after a storm said Rose Kennedy why shouldn't we?

JOURNAL WRITING

To practice using quotation marks, record a conversation you had with a friend recently. Start a new paragraph with each change of speaker.

CAPITAL LETTERS

Capitalize

1. The first word of every sentence.

2. The first word of every direct quotation.

> He said, "The tour starts at six."
> "The tour starts at six," he said, "and latecomers will be left behind."
> (The *and* is not capitalized because it doesn't begin a new sentence.)
> "The tour starts at six," he said. "Latecomers will be left behind."
> (*Latecomers* is capitalized because it begins a new sentence.)

3. The first, last, and every important word in a title. Don't capitalize prepositions, short connecting words, the *to* in front of a verb, or *a, an, the.*

> *The New Grove Dictionary of Music and Musicians*
> *To Have and Have Not*

4. Names of people, places, languages, races, and nationalities.

Aunt Christine	English	Indian
Central America	Chicano	Chinese

5. Names of months, days of the week, and special days, but not the seasons.

September	Memorial Day	fall
Tuesday	Labor Day	winter

6. A title of relationship if it takes the place of the person's name, but not otherwise. If *my* (or a similar word) is in front of the word, a capital is not used.

I know Dad will go.	*but*	I know my dad will go.
She talked to Uncle Fred.	*but*	She talked to her uncle.
I phoned Mom this evening.	*but*	I phoned my mother.

7. Names of particular people or things, but not general ones.

I spoke to Professor Randall.	*but*	I spoke to the professor.
We sailed on the Hudson River.	*but*	We sailed on the river.
Are you from the South?	*but*	We turned south.
I take Art 300 and History 101.	*but*	I take art and history.
I go to San Mateo High School.	*but*	I'm in high school now.
He goes to Westland College.	*but*	He's going to college now.

EXERCISES

Add the necessary capital letters.

☐EXERCISE 1

1. I subscribe to both *time* and *newsweek.*
2. Last year I attended Pasadena city college.
3. Next year I'm going to Moorpark college.
4. Many people now attend community colleges and later transfer to universities.
5. This summer I'm taking european history, english, and mythology.
6. My most difficult subjects are english 101 and chemistry 101, both of which meet in Simpkins hall.
7. The professor who teaches chemistry makes the course interesting.
8. She's a graduate of Hawaii pacific college in Honolulu.
9. For english I have professor Heyeck, who has really helped me with my writing.
10. In my mythology class our text is *age of fable* by Bulfinch.

☐EXERCISE 2

1. Our neighbors are sending their daughter to college in the east.
2. She makes quite a splash when she comes home and walks down the avenue.
3. She looks as if her clothes came from fifth avenue.
4. My cousin went to high school in Petersburg, Virginia.
5. Now he's a freshman at Tidewater community college.
6. He plans to go to the university of Montana eventually.
7. We heard a senator give a speech in the elks hall last night.
8. I think senator Cranston is going to speak on TV tomorrow.
9. Don't you want me to do that mowing, dad?
10. Do you mind, uncle Dave, if I borrow your car for a few minutes?

☐EXERCISE 3

1. "What happens," my counselor said, "is not so important as how you react to what happens."
2. I have been reading Kenneth Clark's *civilisation* for my art history class.
3. Art history 201 requires a lot of reading.
4. My english and history courses require a great deal of reading too.
5. I'm glad I have professor Jellinck for english.
6. My instructor last year was Dr. Reynolds, who gave me a good start.
7. My sister graduated from high school in Monticello, Utah.

8. Then she attended Brigham Young university.
9. My best friend is a sophomore at Nassau community college.
10. He takes college very seriously.

□EXERCISE 4

1. Northern Virginia community college offers courses in adult education.
2. Many adults are going to night school at community colleges.
3. My mother is going to a community college to prepare herself for a new career.
4. Do you know Edna St. Vincent Millay's poem "my candle burns at both ends"?
5. We tell mom she's burning her candle at both ends.
6. But we're all proud of what mom's doing.
7. On labor day we decided to go fishing in the Huron river.
8. I had never fished in a river before; I had always fished in lakes.
9. One lake where I have fished is Duck lake in Michigan.
10. I went fishing there one fourth of July, and by the fifth of July I had my quota of fish.

□EXERCISE 5

1. On memorial day weekend we went to visit my wife's parents, who live 600 miles north of here.
2. They used to live in the south, but they moved to the northwest two years ago.
3. You can find where they live by consulting an atlas. Here's the *Rand McNally world atlas.*
4. Our address is 2100 second avenue.
5. All the houses on our avenue are duplexes.
6. At the end of our street is a high school.
7. And only a few miles away is Belleville area college.
8. We're glad there's a college not too far away.
9. Tonight a famous arctic explorer is speaking at the Presbyterian church.
10. He wrote a book entitled *saga of the north.*

□EXERCISE 6

1. Yesterday dean Lewis gave a talk at the Kiwanis club luncheon.
2. He speaks three languages: english, german, and spanish.
3. He got his degree from western Michigan university in Kalamazoo.
4. He said that more social rights legislation was passed under president Johnson than under any other president.

5. He closed his speech by saying, "don't let anyone make your decisions for you."
6. For years aunt Jayne has been my favorite aunt.
7. She grew up in the midwest but went to the west coast after her marriage.
8. My father spends his leisure time at the country club.
9. I think dad is almost a pro at golf.
10. "I learned a long while ago," said Eleanor Roosevelt, "not to make judgments on what other people do."

☐EXERCISE 7

1. After graduating from high school, I decided to go to DeVry institute of technology in Columbus, Ohio.
2. But I went south for my Christmas holidays.
3. And in the summer I went to rocky mountain national park.
4. That old brick building at the corner of main and third avenue is being torn down.
5. You must mean the old Garwood building.
6. William Lyon Phelps said, "this is the final test of a gentleman: his respect for those who can be of no possible service to him."
7. Canada is a bilingual country with both english and french as official languages.
8. She plans to go to Victor valley college next fall.
9. I've been reading a book on astronomy called *cosmos*.
10. Will you need the car tonight, dad?

☐EXERCISE 8

1. I've attended three colleges since I graduated from high school.
2. First I went to a college in Vermont; then I transferred to Dean junior college and finally to Berkshire community college in Massachusetts.
3. I gained from my experience at each of these colleges.
4. At first I was going to major in business administration, but then I changed to biology.
5. I've just read a book entitled *extinction* by Paul and Anne Ehrlich.
6. Its subject is ecology, and one chapter is entitled "should we mourn the dinosaurs?"
7. The last section of the book is entitled "what are we doing and what can we do?"
8. Since I'm interested in ecology, I'm concerned about conservation.
9. My dad and my uncle are planning a fishing trip to Vermont.
10. I know dad will enjoy it, but I'm not sure about uncle Doug.

Review of Punctuation and Capital Letters

Punctuate these sentences and paragraphs. They include all the rules for punctuation and capitalization you have learned. Correct your answers carefully by those at the back of the book. Most sentences have several errors. Some have none.

☐EXERCISE 1

1. A comma is required when a dependent clause comes first in a sentence.

2. When a dependent clause comes first in a sentence put a comma after it.

3. The proper use of commas I've found prevents misreading.

4. Stop I'll go with you can you wait until 5 P M.

5. In speaking of his childhood as one of seven children of a poor oil field worker in Texas Franklin Pollard says We had three rooms and a path.

6. He's attending Massasoit community college this summer.

7. He memorized William Butler Yeats' poem The Lake Isle of Innisfree.

8. When Eric Heiden was a sophomore at the university of Wisconsin in Madison he became the first skater to win three world championships in one year.

9. Heiden an 18-year-old skated his way to three world championships in one stunning season against the best speed skaters of Europe.

10. I think dad that I've finally decided on my major.

11. Birds are not only fast fliers but also fast walkers an adult roadrunner which is only nine inches tall can keep pace with a human sprinter.

12. Life lived at its best is full of daily forgivin' and forgettin' said Edward Hill.

13. Canada is the second largest country in the world only the Soviet Union is larger.

14. Not more than one-third of Canada is developed much of the land is mountainous or rocky or located in an Arctic climate.

15. Commas are like pounds you either have too many or too few or you have them in the wrong places.

□EXERCISE 2

1. A study has shown that children whose TV viewing was cut back to no more than one hour a day improved their grades in school and seemed happier they played more with other children and increased their concentration in school one child changed from a passive loner into a friendly playmate then when the study was concluded she went back to her former TV habits and became a loner again.

2. A hundred years ago when Edison was working on his first tin horn phonograph he wasn't even thinking about music he just wanted to make a dictating machine in fact it took almost a whole generation for musicians to get interested in recordings fortunately Edison lived long enough (until 1931) to get the first inkling of the big change his invention was making in the world of music.

3. An Assyrian stone tablet of about 2800 B C makes the following statements our earth is degenerate in these latter days bribery and corruption are common children no longer obey their parents the end of the world is evidently approaching.

□EXERCISE 3

1. Yesterday I had my first solo flight at the Flying Club it's an amazing feeling when your instructor tells you to go flying alone then after you take off you look around and find you really are alone at that point it's too late to change your mind you've got to land by yourself sooner or later it's a great sensation it's like the time you first rode a bicycle— quite a thrill.

2. The federal budget speaks in terms of billions but how much is a billion dollars if a man stood over a big hole in the ground and dropped in a $20 bill every minute day and night it would take him 95 years to throw a billion dollars into the hole.

3. There have been six basic changes in the tools people write with since the cavemen used sharp stones to scratch pictures on their stone walls first came the quill pen then came the lead pencil next came the fountain pen in about 1870 came the first typewriter by 1960 the electric typewriter was taking over and now it's the word processor.

Proofreading Exercise 1

Proofread this student paper. You will find only a few errors—13 in fact—but correcting those few errors will improve the paper (the shift to *your* and *yourself* in the last paragraph is not counted an error). This is the kind of careful proofreading you should do before you call your own papers finished. See if you can find all 13 errors before checking with the answers.

THE BIG GRIN ON MY FACE

One afternoon I was driving my car when I notice a pinging noise in my engine. In a few days the pinging grew to a thumping and then to a loud clunking that couldn't be ignored.

My knowledgeable friends broke the news to me that it was undoubtedly my main engine bearings and in the same breath they mentioned sums like four or five hundred dollars. Being a poor student, I had only two alternatives—walk or fix it myself.

Necessity force me to chose the latter alternative and I found myself up to my elbows in grease and grime for the next few days. With the help of a lot of free advice from friends, who claimed to be undiscovered mechanical geniuses, and the guidance of a library book on engines, I removed and disassembled the whole thing.

An engine is something I take for granted as long as it goes, and only when it fails, do I really appreciate how intricate and complicated it is. Their are all kinds of odd-shaped, highly polished parts, each one for some function. My taking the engine apart was like a little boy fixing an alarm clock each new piece was so interesting and so completely unfathomable.

Then when it was all in pieces the reassembly with new parts began, along with the job of trying to remember where each nut and bolt belonged. This work was a lot slower and required more help but it was encouraging to watch the motor grow with each new piece.

Finally it was all connected in the car and ready to be tested. It had taken weeks of late evenings of work but now it was ready at last. My friends stood around offering final advice and checking to make sure I had remembered everything. I held my breath and turned the key—the engine started and turned, a little rough at first, but soon it ran smoothly.

"Eureka! I've done it!" I shouted.

I was overwhelm with a great feeling of accomplishment and I couldn't hide the big grin on my face.

There's an indescribable feeling of pride in having rebuilt your own engine yourself. It was worth it, not just for saving money but for the experience.

Proofreading Exercise 2

Here is another student paper to proofread. This one has eight errors. You're on your own now. No answers are provided at the back of the book for this exercise.

MUDDY McBRIDE

Sometimes I take a shortcut across McBride Park even though its muddy now in the rainy weather. I walk through the old softball diamond. It seems bleak with the benches empty, their green paint peeling after a summer's softball season. Three muddy puddles in the field mark where the three bases used to be and a bumpy little hill is all that's left of the pitchers mound. The park is like a tree that has lost its leaves in the fall.

I can remember the excitement and the fun of those games. I can imagine my teammates sitting on the bench yelling at the other team and I can almost see, behind the backstop, a few people who have come to watch. I can feel my turn to bat coming up and I remember how I always felt. I'd stand beside the plate right where that puddle has been made by a whole season of batters and would wait for each pitch. I remember the cheers and yells that came with every hit I made in that hot summer sun.

But the windy weather is brisk now and those sunny Sunday afternoons seem a long time ago. Now theres litter piled up against the backstop fencing, and the light drizzle of rain is all the cheering I hear. There aren't any fielders standing in the grass waiting for each hit there are only some birds looking for worms that the rain has brought up.

I miss those softball games when I walk through muddy McBride.

Proofreading Exercise 3

This student paper has been rewritten three times but still has 13 errors. You may have to read the paper several times to find all the errors. Challenge your instructor to find all 13 on the first try! No answers are provided at the back of the book.

THE ROLLING STONES

Although I've been a fan of the Rolling Stones for years, I never thought I'd see them perform in a live concert. Even when I learn that their tour of the United States would include two concerts at the local football stadium, I knew I wouldn't bother to wait in line all night for tickets that would sell out in a few hours. But a last-minute decision by the promoters to sell 3,000 extra tickets on the day before the second concert allowed me to get a ticket after all—and without waiting in line.

I arrive at the stadium three hours ahead of time, but two-thirds of the seats were all ready filled. Security at the gates was tight each person was frisked and police were everywhere. But the fans were all well-behaved and just out for a rollicking afternoon of music in the sun.

Across one entire end of the stadium, a huge stage with pastel-painted 40-foot screens had been erected. A high fence separated the crowd from the stage, and burly guards in yellow T-shirts were kept busy pushing overeager fans off the fence.

Somehow the hours past, and the Stones finally appeared at about 4:30 P.M. The crowd of 90,000 was more than ready, and each song was greeted with a roar of recognition. Some people danced in the aisles others just tapped there feet. The music was great. Mick Jagger's singing matched his strutting and striding around the huge stage and Keith Richard's lead guitar was stunning. The rest of the band seem content to create the music and leave the visual effects to Jagger.

The stones clearly intended to give the fans their moneys worth, and they were still playing as the sun went down and as the huge banks of lights around the stage went into action. At one point, after darkness fell, the fans spontaneously lit matches or lighters so that the whole stadium seemed blanketed by fireflies.

As the end of the concert approached, the sky was lit up with a dazzling display of fireworks. For his final song, Jagger scrambled up the scaffolding of the stage to hop into the basket of a huge crane, which later deposited him, still singing, back on the stage. After a thundering encore, the Stones were lifted away in helicopters and the tired but satisfied crowd let out a final cheer and headed home.

Comprehensive Test on Entire Text

In these sentences you will find all the errors that have been discussed in the entire text. Correct them by adding apostrophes, punctuation, and capital letters and by crossing out incorrect expressions and writing the corrections above. Most sentences have several errors. A perfect—or almost perfect—score will mean you have mastered the text.

1. We girls made the deserts for the party everyone like them.

2. The altos carried the melody the sopranos sung the accompaniment.

3. Joe Namath was a talented quarterback in high school his team won lots of championships.

4. When we got to the end of the detour we turn south and then West.

5. Which turned out to be the wrong thing to do.

6. Each of her trophies are displayed in it's proper place on the shelf.

7. Working hard that semester my grades improved.

8. I enjoy math social studies and gym but I find chemistry and english difficult.

9. Making the most of every opportunity that came her way.

10. He spends most of his time however reading comic books and you cant do that and get satisfactory grades.

11. I cant decide whether to get a job take a trip or whether I should just loaf this summer.

12. Yes personally I think Amys costume is more striking than Beverlys.

13. She took to many cloths along on her trip party dresses beachwear and half a dozen other outfits.

14. Her mother and father send her to a exclusive school but she dont appreciate it.

15. Leroy told his father he was embarrassed by his old car.

16. Their quiet pleased with there new car although it was to expensive.

17. Kurt you was driving to fast when we past that cop.

18. We didnt like the amendment furthermore we refuse to vote for it.

19. James invitation to my girlfriend and me came as a surprise.

20. Each of the leaves are quite unique in their vein patterns.

21. Ive been wondering about you and hoping for a letter.

22. She memorized Masefield's poem Sea Fever from his book Salt Water Ballads.

23. John Masefield who became poet laureate of England was born on June 1 1878 in Ledbury Herefordshire England.

24. Life's always a struggle if anything's easy it's not likely to be worthwhile said Hubert Humphrey.

25. When you get to the end of your rope said Franklin D. Roosevelt tie a knot and hang on.

26. If I had known you was coming I would of prepared a special meal.

27. Last week they develop a plan and then they proceed to carry it out.

28. He decided to join Fritz and me on the golf course.

29. There house is in a better location than our's.

30. When you wind up a watch you start it when you wind up a speech you end it.

4

Writing

4 Writing

You learn to write by writing—not by reading long discussions *about* writing. Therefore the instructions in this section are brief. In fact, they are boiled down to just eight steps that you need to take to write good papers. Take these eight steps, one at a time, and you'll write more effectively and also more easily. Here are the steps:

EIGHT STEPS TO BETTER WRITING

    I. Do some free writing.
    II. Limit your topic.
    III. Write a thesis statement.
    IV. Support your thesis with reasons or points.
    V. Organize your paper from your thesis.
    VI. Organize each paragraph.
    VII. Write and rewrite.
    VIII. Proofread ALOUD.

I. DO SOME FREE WRITING

"Writing is good for us," Oliver Wendell Holmes said, "because it brings our thoughts out into the open, as a boy turns his pockets inside out to see what is in them." Try "turning your pockets inside out" by writing as fast as you can for five minutes. Write anything that comes into your mind. Put your thoughts down as fast as they come. What you write may not make sense, but that doesn't matter. Write fast. Don't stop a moment. Don't even take your pen off the page. If you can't think of anything to write, just write, "I can't think of anything to write," over and over until something occurs to you. Look at your watch and begin.

This free writing should limber up your mind and your pen so that you'll write more freely.

Now try another kind of free writing—focused free writing. Write for five minutes as fast as you can, but this time stick to one subject—music.
Look at your watch and begin.

Did you focus on music that long? Did you think not only of music you like but of music you don't like, of music your mother tried to teach you, of music you've heard on special occasions, of your struggles to play some instrument, of conflicts you've had with someone concerning music?

You didn't have time to include all those things of course. Now write for ten minutes and add more to your discussion of music.

Focused free writing is a good way to begin writing a paper. When you are assigned a paper, write for ten minutes putting down all your thoughts on the subject. It will let you see what material you have and will help you figure out what aspect of the subject (what topic) to write about.

II. LIMIT YOUR TOPIC

Finding the right topic is sometimes the hardest part of writing. For one thing, you need to limit your topic so that you can handle it in a paper of 300 to 500 words. The subject music, which you used for free writing, was obviously too big. You could limit it by saying

My stereo collection
Music I hate
The important place music had in our high school

but even those topics are too big. Keep making your topic smaller

Our high school marching band

and smaller

My first week with our high school marching band

and smaller

The day I made the marching band.

Now you have a topic limited enough to write about in a short paper.

Usually the more you limit your topic, the better your paper will be, for then you'll have room to add plenty of specific details. And it's specific details that will interest your reader.

EXERCISE 1   Make each of these topics more and more limited until it would be a possible topic for a short paper. Then compare your topics with those suggested at the back of the book.

1. Painting a room

Preparation for painting a room

New tools to help you paint a room

2. Baking is my hobby

_____

3. Buying a car

_____

4. Camping out

_____

5. My trip to Washington, D.C.

_____

6. Growing your own vegetables

_____

7. My German heritage

_____

8. Dancing for fun

_____

9. Saving our forests

_____

The following two assignments emphasize the first two Steps to Better Writing—doing some free writing and limiting your topic.

Assignment 1   A Moment I'd Like to Relive

What moment in your life, if you could live one moment over again, would you most enjoy reliving? It might be a moment when you won a sports event, a moment when you made a big decision, a moment when you achieved something you didn't think you could, a moment when you did something courageous. . . . It need not be a dramatic moment; it might be a very simple one, but it should be a moment that had great meaning for you.

First do some free writing telling about the experience. Put down all the details you can think of. For example, if you are going to tell about the time you won a trophy, you'll want to say more than that it was a great moment. You'll want to tell what you saw at that moment, what you heard, how you felt. If you are groping for details, think of your five senses—sight, hearing, smell, taste, and touch. Each of them may call forth some details you hadn't thought of before. Remember that it's specific details that will help your reader experience your moment with you.

When you've done all the free writing you can, then make sure your topic is limited. If you're writing about winning a trophy, you won't tell about the entire season but only about actually receiving the award.

Before you start to write, you might like to read a student paper on this assignment. At first this writer was having so much trouble with sentence structure and wordiness that the paper was difficult to read, but after four rewritings, it is now clear. The writer had something interesting to say, and it was worth her while to get rid of errors so that her paper can be read easily.

I TOLD HER OFF

When we moved from one side of Elk Grove to the other, all the children in our new neighborhood seemed to have their own friends, and I wasn't one to go out of my way to meet people. From the first day of fourth grade until the beginning of junior high, I kept my mouth shut. Then I met Suzette. Suzette tried to gain popularity by making fun of people, this time someone who wouldn't talk back, someone who was shy. She ridiculed me in front of her friends, who in turn ridiculed me in front of the whole school. She pointed out how I dragged my feet on the ground, how I had a soft voice, and how unattractive I was.

At the end of eighth grade came the most embarrassing moment of my life. At our junior high graduation, where my father was one of the speakers, Suzette had planned for everyone to clap for me. Although clapping is usually good, this time everyone, including my father, realized it wasn't meant for praise.

As I walked home that evening, I knew I couldn't take being ridiculed any more. Despite my shyness I had to tell Suzette what I thought. The next day as I stood at her doorstep trying to get courage to ring the bell, I knew I wasn't shaking because of the cold. Suddenly, with the next shiver, my finger jerked far enough forward for the bell to ring. As the door opened, I must have looked confident because Suzette didn't. None of her friends were there to back her up, and the impossible happened. I told her how she had ruined three years of my life. I explained how, because I was shy, I had no close friends, no one to talk over my problems with.

I got my point across because Suzette ridiculed me no more. But what makes me feel even better is that if I hadn't spoken to Suzette, I would still be that shy little girl who wouldn't speak up for herself.

Now write your paper for this assignment. Imagine that you are telling someone about the moment you'd like to relive, and write what you would say.

Finally, spend some time thinking of a good title. Just as you are more likely to read a magazine article with a catchy title, so your reader will be more eager to read your paper if you give it a good title. (And remember that every important word in a title is capitalized.) Which of these titles from student papers would make you want to read further?

It's Not Just Pumping Gas   A Place I Love
Ready! Wrestle!   Is There College after Marriage?
An Interesting Experience

Assignment 2   A Place I Like to Remember

What place means more to you than any other place in the world? It might be a place you know now or one you knew in childhood—a play-room, your workshop, a backyard, a playing field . . . .

Do some free writing to bring to your mind specific details that will help your reader see your place. Telling some things that happened there will also help your reader participate in your memory of it.

After you have done all the free writing about it that you can, ask yourself whether your topic is limited enough. Take it through several steps of limiting to see whether you can turn it into a more manageable topic.

Here is a student paper, a third draft. With each draft the writer added specific details about what she saw, what she did, and how she felt. Now you can visualize the place and understand how the writer feels about it.

THE HENHOUSE

When I was six, I was sent to live with my grandparents at the edge of a small town on the North Dakota prairie. Besides the trauma of being pulled away from my family, I faced the terror of a new environment among elderly people, with no children nearby to play with. I spent some desperately lonely days.

And then I discovered the henhouse.

In years gone by, someone had kept chickens, and the old henhouse in the backyard had never been torn down. Although the latch was too high for me to reach, I found that I could get into the henhouse by crawling through the small opening for the chickens. It was little more than a foot square, but I could squeeze through.

Inside I found a dream house—a dirt floor that from years of use had become as hard and slick as linoleum, a small window with four dirty square panes, an old packing box just high enough to be a table, a couple of smaller boxes that became chairs, and, best of all, eight square cubby-holes with remnants of straw nests, where the hens had laid their eggs.

I immediately cleaned out the straw, and the cubbyholes became my cupboard. In a vacant lot nearby I found a treasure of dishes and glasses, some of them not even broken, which filled the "shelves" of my cupboard. Soon I began growing things. I would fill each dish with dirt, carefully dig up a tiny weed, transplant it into the dish, put it on the top shelf where the sun would shine on it, water it daily, and wait for it to grow. Occasionally one did.

And then one day, calamity! The big door to the henhouse was suddenly yanked open, and there stood Grandma.

"What are you doing in here?" she shouted.

My eyes welled with tears. I couldn't speak. My delightful domain had been invaded.

Grandma looked around. Then . . . slowly . . . quietly . . . she closed the door—and never bothered me again.

And day after day I smiled as I planted my weeds and crawled in and out of my henhouse.

Now write a description of your place that will help your reader picture it and feel its importance to you. Remember that fully as important as making your paper mechanically correct is making it so interesting that your readers will enjoy it.

III. WRITE A THESIS STATEMENT

For any kind of writing, and particularly for writing that explains something or defends an idea, you need to know what point you want to get across to your reader.

The limited topic on page 201, "The day I made the marching band," doesn't make any point. What about that day? What did it do for you? What point about that day would you like to present to your reader? You might write

Making the marching band gave me new confidence.

or

Making the marching band gave me something to work for.

or

The day I made the marching band I decided to major in music.

Now you have said something. **When you write in one sentence the point you want to present to your reader, you have written a thesis statement.**

All good writers have a thesis in mind when they begin to write. Whether they are writing articles, novels, short stories, poems, or plays, they have in mind an idea they want to present to the reader. They may develop it in various ways, but back of whatever they write is their ruling thought, their reason for writing, their thesis.

For any writing assignment, after you have done some free writing and limited your topic, your next step is to write a thesis statement. As you write it, keep two things in mind.

1. A thesis statement must be a sentence (not merely a topic).

TOPIC	THESIS
The day I made the marching band	The day I made the marching band I decided to major in music.
Saving gas	I've learned three ways to save gas.
Exercising for health	I jogged my way back to health.

2. A thesis statement must be a statement that you can explain or defend (not simply a fact that no one would deny).

FACT	THESIS
The price of food is going up.	I've found two ways to save on groceries.
Our college is hosting the state music festival.	I'll be competing against three great performers in the state music festival.
Downtown traffic is increasing.	The city should take steps to decrease downtown traffic.

EXERCISE 2 Which of the following are merely topics or facts, and which are thesis statements that you could explain or defend? In front of each, write TOPIC, FACT, or THESIS. Check your answers with those at the back of the book.

_____ 1. Figure skating

_____ 2. Getting my own apartment gave me a sense of responsibility

_____ 3. The Alaska pipeline is now in operation

_____ 4. The Rock and Mineral Show

_____ 5. My summer vacation in Montana

_____ 6. Teaching a six-year-old to ride a bike

_____ 7. Americans should conserve paper to save our forests

_____ 8. I am going to quit my job for three reasons

_____ 9. This winter has been the coldest in ten years

_____ 10. Making a pizza

_____ 11. Transactional analysis has helped me solve some problems

_____ 12. For making a perfect high dive, three steps are necessary

_____ 13. It takes practice to master an orchestral instrument

_____ 14. My trip to Oregon taught me something about volcanoes

EXERCISE 3 Now make thesis statements from all the preceding that are only topics or facts. Compare your thesis statements with those suggested at the back of the book.

IV. SUPPORT YOUR THESIS WITH REASONS OR POINTS

Now you are ready to support your thesis with reasons or points. That is, you will think of ways to convince your reader that your thesis is true. How could you convince your reader that making the marching band gave you confidence? You might write

Making the marching band gave me new confidence. (because)*
1. It was the first competition I ever won.
2. I won over peers I had always felt inferior to.
3. It was an achievement to get into one of the best bands in the state.

The points supporting a thesis are not always reasons. They may be examples (to make your thesis clear), steps (in a how-to paper), descriptions (in a descriptive paper), or anecdotes (in a narrative paper). Whatever they are, they should convince your reader that your thesis is true for you.

EXERCISE 4 Add supporting points (sentences) to these thesis statements.

I've decided to change my major to computer science.

　　　　　　1.

(reasons)　　2.

　　　　　　3.

Acid rain is harming the country in many ways.

　　　　　　1.

　　　　　　2.

(examples)　3.

　　　　　　4.

　　　　　　5.

I'm doing three things to improve my study habits.

　　　　　　1.

(steps)　　 2.

　　　　　　3.

---

* (Sometimes if you imagine a "because" at the end of your thesis statement, it will help you write your reasons clearly and in parallel form.)

Learning to write a good thesis statement with supporting points is perhaps the most important thing you can learn in this course. Most writing problems are not really writing problems but thinking problems. Whether you are writing a term paper or merely an answer to a test question, working out a thesis statement is always the best way to organize your thoughts. If you take enough time to think, you will be able to write a clear thesis statement with supporting points. And if you have a clear thesis statement with supporting points, organizing your paper won't be difficult.

Of course not all writing follows this "thesis and support" form. Experienced writers vary their writing. Using this form, however, is an excellent way to begin learning to write because it will help you think logically, and logical thinking is important for all writing.

Assignment 3   Two Thesis Statements with Supporting Points

Think of some decision you are trying to make. Are you wondering what major to choose, whether to drop out of college for a time, whether to give up smoking, whether to try out for the next dramatic production? Think of a decision that really matters to you. Only then will you be able to write something others will care to read. When you have decided on a topic, write a thesis statement for *each side*. For example, if you are wondering whether to drop out of college for a semester, you might write

I've decided to drop out of college for a semester and take a job.

I've decided to stick with college.

These statements now need to be supported with reasons. You might write

I've decided to drop out of college for a semester and take a job (because)
1. I need to make some money.
2. I want some experience in my field.
3. I might come back to college with a clearer purpose.

I've decided to stick with college (because)
1. I don't want to waste time merely making money.
2. I'm now getting used to studying.
3. If I left, I might never come back.

Three reasons usually work well, but you could have two or four. Be sure your reasons are all sentences.

V. ORGANIZE YOUR PAPER FROM YOUR THESIS

Once you have worked out a good thesis with supporting points, organizing your paper will be easy.

First, you need an introductory paragraph. It should catch your reader's interest and should either include or suggest your thesis statement. It may also list the supporting points, but usually it's more effective to let them unfold paragraph by paragraph rather than to give them all away in your introduction. (Your instructor may ask you to write your complete thesis statement with supporting points at the top of your paper so that it may be referred to easily.) Even if your supporting points don't appear in your introduction, your reader will easily spot them later in the paper if your paper is clearly organized.

Your second paragraph will present your first supporting point—everything about it and nothing more.

Your next paragraph will be about your second supporting point—all about it and nothing more.

Each additional paragraph will develop another supporting point.

Finally you'll need a brief concluding paragraph. In a short paper it isn't necessary to restate all your points. Even a single clincher sentence to round out the paper may be sufficient.

Paragraph 1. Introduction arousing your reader's interest and indicating your thesis

Paragraph 2. First supporting point

Paragraph 3. Second supporting point

Additional paragraphs for additional supporting points

Final concluding paragraph

Learning to write this kind of paper will teach you to write logically. Then when you are ready to write a longer paper, you'll be able to organize it easily. A longer paper may divide each of the supporting points into several paragraphs, and it may not present the thesis statement until later in the paper. But no matter how the material is presented, it will still have some kind of logical pattern.

Here are the introductory and concluding paragraphs from a student paper. Note that the introductory paragraph arouses the reader's interest and suggests the thesis statement. And the concluding paragraph simply wraps the paper up in one good sentence.

Introductory paragraph	My superman doesn't soar through the sky or leap tall buildings in a single bound. My superman is my dad. I think my dad is super because he shows that he cares with the little things he does.
	(The paper tells in three paragraphs the kinds of little things the father does.)
Concluding paragraph	My dad may not change clothes in a telephone booth or rescue the earth from alien attack, but he's still superman to me.

You should now have written (for Assignment 3 on page 210) two thesis statements about a decision you are trying to make, and each thesis statement should have good supporting points. You will later write a paper on one of these thesis statements, but first we must consider the organization of paragraphs.

VI. ORGANIZE EACH PARAGRAPH

Organizing a paragraph is easy because it's organized just the way an entire paper is. Here's the way you learned to organize a paper:

Thesis statement in introductory paragraph
First supporting point
Second supporting point
Additional supporting points
Concluding paragraph

And here's the way to organize a paragraph:

Topic sentence
First supporting detail or example
Second supporting detail or example
Further supporting details or examples
Concluding sentence if needed

You should have at least two or three points to support your topic sentence. If you find that you have little to say after writing your topic sentence, ask yourself what details or examples will make your reader see that your topic sentence is true for you.

The topic sentence doesn't have to be the first sentence in the paragraph. It may come at the end or even in the middle, but having it first is the most common way.

Each paragraph should contain only one main idea, and no detail or example should be allowed to creep into the paragraph if it doesn't support the topic sentence. Note how the following paragraph is organized.

Amazing as it seems, one of the largest archeological treasures in the United States lies under the city of Phoenix. As new highways and shopping centers are being built, remains of the ancient Hohokam Indian culture are being found. The Hohokam, who lived in the area from about 300 B.C. to the fifteenth century A.D., had one of the most advanced Indian cultures in North America, but it is a culture we know little about. They lived in two dozen large towns in or near what is now Phoenix. Because modern houses in Phoenix are built without basements, only the top foot of soil has been disturbed, thus leaving archeological remains that may go as deep as nine feet. If Phoenix had been a city with deep basements, the remains would have been completely destroyed. But now, if developers will give archeologists a chance to do some probing, something may be learned about that ancient culture.

Source: Daniel B. Adams, "Last Ditch Archeology," *Science 83*, December 1983.

The topic sentence states that the largest archeological treasure in the United States lies under the city of Phoenix. Sentences explaining that statement follow, and the final sentence gives added emphasis to it.

EXERCISE 5   Here is the topic sentence for a paragraph:

Galileo lived the last nine years of his life under house arrest because of his beliefs.

Which of the following statements support that topic sentence and therefore should be included in the paragraph? Mark them S (support). Check your answers with those at the back of the book.

_____ 1. In 1633 the Inquisition condemned Galileo, a famous Italian scientist, for his beliefs.

_____ 2. Galileo believed that the earth revolves around the sun.

_____ 3. Everyone at that time believed that the sun revolves around the earth.

_____ 4. Today even small children know that the earth revolves around the sun.

_____ 5. The belief that the earth, and not the sun, is the center of our universe was called the geocentric theory.

_____ 6. The Inquisition condemned Galileo as a heretic because he dared to oppose the geocentric theory.

_____ 7. Today we allow freedom of belief even if the belief seems absurd.

_____ 8. When Galileo was condemned for his belief, he was 69 years old.

_____ 9. Since the Inquisition often had heretics burned at the stake, Galileo was lucky to escape with only house arrest.

_____ 10. Today we are learning more about the universe through space travel.

Transition Expressions

Transition expressions within a paragraph help the reader move from one detail or example to the next.

EXERCISE 6 Here are some transition expressions that would make the following paragraph read more smoothly. In each blank in the paragraph write the transition expression you think appropriate. Check your answers with those at the back of the book.

Also	Furthermore
As for me	In the first place
Finally	Then too

Last summer we decided to take a family vacation and to drive to California. _____, we hadn't had a family vacation for four years, and we all thought it would be a great idea. _____, no one in our family had ever been west of the Rockies. _____, my brother wanted to see the campus at San Diego State University because he was hoping to go there in another year. _____, my mother had a friend living in Long Beach and had always wanted to visit her. _____, I was eager to see a new part of the country and thought I might even look for a job while we were out there. _____, my dad clinched the idea by saying that he'd pay all the expenses.

Transition expressions are also important in a paper. They help the reader move from one supporting point to the next. It's a good idea to start each supporting paragraph in a paper with a transition expression such as

My first reason	Another example
Second	Furthermore
Also	Finally
Even more important	

Assignment 4　Writing a Paragraph

For practice in writing paragraphs, choose one of these topic sentences and add support sentences. You may alter each topic sentence slightly if you wish.

1. The main reason I prefer to travel by car is that I see more.
2. For me, a job must be challenging, or I don't want it.
3. The first step in preparing a meal is to have a plan.
4. My psych course has taught me not to waste time on regrets.
5. I've learned not to make a big thing of small things.
6. A near-accident made me a careful driver.
7. The most important thing I've learned in college is to concentrate.
8. Learning to use a thesis statement has improved my writing.

The easiest and most natural way to practice writing paragraphs is to write them as part of a paper. You'll have an opportunity to practice writing paragraphs in the assignments that follow.

Assignment 5　A Decision I Have Made

Return to the two thesis statements with supporting points about a decision you are trying to make (Assignment 3, p. 210). Choose one of those thesis statements to write about. Even if your mind is not really made up, you must choose one side for this assignment. You may mention in your introduction the arguments on the other side, but you must focus on one side if your paper is to be effective.

Write a rough draft of your paper, giving enough specific details in each of your supporting paragraphs to convince your reader that you have made the right decision.

Then take Step VII, which follows.

VII. WRITE AND REWRITE

If possible, write your paper several days before it's due. Let it sit for a day. When you reread it, you'll see ways to improve it. After rewriting it, put it away for another day, and again try to improve it.

Great writers don't just sit down and write their books in a first draft. They write and rewrite. Hemingway said, "I wrote the ending to *Farewell to Arms*, the last page of it, 39 times before I was satisfied." And Leo Tolstoy wrote, "I can't understand how anyone can write without rewriting everything over and over again."

Here's a checklist of questions to ask yourself as you begin to rewrite:

1. Will my introductory paragraph make my reader want to read further?
2. Does each paragraph support my thesis statement?
3. Does each paragraph contain only one main idea?
4. Do I have enough specific details in each paragraph to support the topic sentence, and are all the details relevant?
5. Have I used transition expressions to tie my paragraphs together?
6. Does my concluding paragraph sum up my paper in a persuasive way?
7. Are my sentences properly constructed and clear?
8. Have I checked all questionable spellings?
9. Is my punctuation correct?
10. Is my title interesting?

Don't call any paper finished until you have worked through it two or three times. **REWRITING IS THE BEST WAY TO LEARN TO WRITE.**

Your final rewriting should be typed, double-spaced or written legibly in ink on 8½-by-11-inch paper on one side only. A 1½ inch margin should be left on each side of the page for your instructor's comments. Paragraphs should be indented about five spaces.

Part of the success of a paper depends on how it looks. The same paper written sloppily or neatly might well receive different grades. If, however, when you do your final proofreading, you find a word repeated or a word left out, don't hesitate to make neat corrections in pen. So long as your paper gives a neat appearance, no one will mind a few minor corrections.

VIII. PROOFREAD ALOUD

Finally, read your finished paper ALOUD. If you read it silently, you're sure to miss some errors. Read it aloud slowly, word by word, to catch omitted words, errors in spelling and punctuation, and so on. Make it a rule to read each of your papers aloud before handing it in.

As you do the following assignments, be sure to take each of the EIGHT STEPS TO BETTER WRITING.

Assignment 6   A Letter to Someone Who Has Influenced Me

What person, other than a parent, has been of great influence in your life? Has someone—perhaps a teacher or a counselor or a coach—encouraged you in athletics or music, influenced you in the choice of a career, given you confidence in yourself? Write a thesis statement saying that a certain person has influenced you, and organize under two or three main points the ways in which you were influenced. Then write a letter of appreciation to that person. Even though you are writing a letter, it will still be in essay form, with an introduction, a paragraph for each supporting point, and a conclusion. And remember to include specific examples.

Assignment 7   In Praise of Something

Write a paper praising something. It might be a job you enjoyed, an activity such as dramatics or music from which you have benefited, a sport that has done something for you, a kind of motorcycle or car you think is superior. . . . Be sure to limit your subject. Basketball, for example, would not be a possible subject because it's too broad. You might limit it to what playing on a particular basketball team did for you. After limiting your subject, work out a good thesis statement with two or three supporting points. Then write your paper using plenty of specific details.

Before you hand your paper in, read it aloud *slowly* word by word to catch errors.

Assignment 8   A Letter to Myself

One reason for wriitng is to gain knowledge about ourselves. For this assignment, instead of looking outward, look inward. Have a talk with yourself. What are some things you've been telling yourself you should or should not do? Ten minutes of free writing will be a good way to find out what material you have. Then work out a thesis statement and write a letter to yourself. One student began his letter, "Dear Ben, Why don't you wise up?" Then he went on to tell three things he knew he should be doing. It's always harder to analyze oneself than someone else, but it can be fun and perhaps productive.

Assignment 9   Something I Can Do

What is something you can do well? Bake brownies? Make jewelry? Play chess? Do high dives? Play the trombone? Throw a Frisbee? Give your reader the benefit of your expertise and explain in several steps just how to master your skill.

Assignment 10   On My Mind

What's on your mind? What do you talk about to your friends or to your family? If it's a problem, or even if it isn't a problem, talk about it on paper. Write a thesis statement and then support it with several points. Sometimes putting something down on paper is the best way to get it off your mind.

Assignment 11   An Aspect of My Major

Talk to the general reader about some problem or aspect of your major, something you can explain that the reader will find of interest. It might be some aspect of computer science, a phase of environmental control, a new concept in advertising art, a practice in business administration, a method of playing the drums. . . .

Assignment 12   A Prejudice

Most of us have prejudices of some kind. Show how one of your prejudices is based on emotion rather than reason. Are there any steps you could take to overcome your prejudice if you wanted to?

Assignment 13   Advice That Hits Home

Look through the quotations on pages 180–85 and find one that you could profit from following. Or find one that you have followed. Then write a thesis statement explaining either how you have benefited from the quotation or how you might benefit from it. Back up your thesis statement with supporting points, and write your paper.

Assignment 14   My Opinion on a Current Problem

Choose one of the following problems and present your arguments for one side. Write a carefully thought-out thesis statement, supported by reasons, before you begin to write your paper. In your introduction or conclusion you may want to mention briefly the reasons you can see for the opposite side.

A. A couple, both alcoholics and totally unable to care for their infant son, were forced by the court to place him in a foster home. Ten years later the couple, by then completely rehabilitated, asked to have their child returned to them. The boy had come to think of his foster parents as his real parents, and they in turn thought of him as their son. But the courts gave the boy, against his wishes, back to his natural parents. If you had been the judge, what would you have done?

B. The most important football game of the season is coming up, with the outcome depending largely on one top player. Unfortunately that player, although he has put forth considerable effort, has been flunking chemistry all term and now has failed the final exam. He is eager to play because he hopes to have a career in professional football and knows that scouts from professional teams will be watching. If he receives an F or even an Incomplete, he will be ineligible. If you were the chemistry professor, what grade would you give him?

C. A bill is before Congress to create a national park in an area where a commercial lumbering company is ready to move in. The congressman from that district, a conservationist, strongly favors the park and would like to vote for the bill. His constituents, however, are writing him asking that he oppose the bill because they want the commercial lumbering company to come in and create jobs. If you were the congressman, what would you do?

WRITING A SUMMARY

A good way to learn to write concisely is to write 100-word summaries. Writing 100 words sounds easy, but actually it isn't. Writing 200- or 300- or 500-word summaries isn't too difficult, but condensing all the main ideas of an essay or article into 100 words is a time-consuming task—not to be undertaken the last hour before class. If you work at writing summaries conscientiously, you'll improve both your reading and your writing. You'll improve your reading by learning to spot main ideas and your writing by learning to construct a concise, clear, smooth paragraph. Furthermore, your skills will carry over into your reading and writing for other courses.

Assignment 15   A 100-Word Summary

Your aim in writing your summary should be to give someone who has not read the article a clear idea of it. First read the article, and then follow the instructions given after it. Note that difficult words are defined in the margin.

The Jeaning of America— and the World

Carlin C. Quinn

This is the story of a sturdy American symbol which has now spread throughout most of the world. The symbol is not the dollar. It is not even Coca-Cola. It is a simple pair of pants called blue jeans, and what the pants symbolize is what Alexis de Tocqueville called "a manly and legitimate passion for equality. . . ." Blue jeans are favored equally by bureaucrats and cowboys; bankers and deadbeats; fashion designers and beer drinkers. They draw no distinctions and recognize no classes; they are merely American. Yet they are sought after almost everywhere in the world—including Russia, where authorities recently broke up a teen-aged gang that was selling them on the black market for two hundred dollars a pair. They have been around for a long time, and it seems likely that they will outlive even the necktie.

de Tocqueville (1805–1859)—a French historian who wrote about America

This ubiquitous American symbol was the invention of a Bavarian-born Jew . . . Levi Strauss. He was born in Bad Ocheim, Germany, in 1829, and during the European political turmoil of 1848 decided to take his chances in New York, to which his two brothers already had emigrated. Upon arrival, Levi soon found that his two brothers had exaggerated their tales of an easy life in the land of the main chance. They were landowners, they had told him; instead, he found them pushing needles, thread, pots, pans, ribbons, yarn, scissors, and buttons to housewives. For two years he was a lowly peddler, hauling some 180 pounds of sundries door-to-door to eke out a marginal living. When a married sister in San Francisco offered to pay his way West in 1850, he jumped at the opportunity, taking with him bolts of canvas he hoped to sell for tenting.

It was the wrong kind of canvas for that purpose, but while talking with a miner down from the mother lode, he learned that pants—sturdy pants that would stand up to the rigors of the diggings— were almost impossible to find. Opportunity beckoned. On the spot, Strauss measured the man's girth and inseam with a piece of string and, for six dollars in gold dust, had them tailored into a pair of stiff but rugged pants. The miner was delighted with the result, word got around about "those pants of Levi's," and Strauss was in business. The company has been in business ever since.

When Strauss ran out of canvas, he wrote his two brothers to send more. He received instead a tough, brown cotton cloth made in Nìmes, France—called *serge de Nìmes* and swiftly shortened to "denim" (the word "jeans" derives from *Gênes*, the French word for Genoa, where a similar cloth was produced). Almost from the first, Strauss had his cloth dyed the distinctive indigo that gave blue jeans their name, but it was not until the 1870's that he added the copper rivets which have long since become a company trademark. The rivets were the idea of a Virginia City, Nevada, tailor, Jacob W. Davis, who added them to pacify a mean-tempered miner called Alkali Ike. Alkali, the story goes, complained that the pockets of his jeans always tore when he stuffed them with ore samples and demanded that Davis do something about it. As a kind of joke, Davis took the pants to a blacksmith

ubiquitous—present everywhere

eke out—to make with great effort
marginal—low quality

mother lode—main vein of ore in a district

and had the pockets riveted; once again, the idea worked so well that word got around; in 1873 Strauss appropriated and patented the gimmick— and hired Davis as a regional manager.

appropriate—to take possession of

By this time, Strauss had taken both his brothers and two brothers-in-law into the company and was ready for his third San Francisco store. Over the ensuing years the company prospered locally, and by the time of his death in 1902, Strauss had become a man of prominence in California. For three decades thereafter the business remained profitable though small, with sales largely confined to the working people of the West—cowboys, lumberjacks, railroad workers, and the like. Levi's jeans were first introduced to the East, apparently, during the dude-ranch craze of the 1930's, when vacationing Easterners returned and spread the word about the wonderful pants with rivets. Another boost came in World War II, when blue jeans were declared an essential commodity and were sold only to people engaged in defense work. From a company with fifteen salespeople, two plants, and almost no business east of the Mississippi in 1946, the organization grew in thirty years to include a sales force of more than twenty-two thousand, with fifty plants and offices in thirty-five countries. Each year, more than 250,000,000 items of Levi's clothing are sold—including more than 83,000,000 pairs of riveted blue jeans. They have become, through marketing, word of mouth, and demonstrable reliability, the common pants of America. They can be purchased pre-washed, pre-faded, and pre-shrunk for the suitably proletarian look. . . .

ensuing—following

demonstrable— capable of being proved

proletarian—working class

The pants have become a tradition, and along the way have acquired a history of their own—so much so that the company has opened a museum in San Francisco. There was, for example, the turn-of-the-century trainman who replaced a faulty coupling with a pair of jeans; the Wyoming man who used his jeans as a towrope to haul his car out of a ditch; the Californian who found several pairs in an abandoned mine, wore them, then discovered they were sixty-three years old and still as good as new and turned them over to the Smithsonian as a tribute to their toughness. And then there is the particularly terrifying story of the careless construction worker who dangled fifty-two stories above the street until

Smithsonian—a museum in Washington, D.C.

rescued, his sole support the Levi's belt loop through which his rope was hooked.

Today "those pants of Levi's" have gone across the seas—although the company has learned that marketing abroad is an arcane art. The conserva-tive-dress jeans favored in northern France do not move on the Côte d'Azur; Sta-Prest sells well in Switzerland but dies in Scandinavia; button fronts are popular in France, zippers in Britain.

arcane—secret

Though Levi Strauss & Co. has since become Levi Strauss International, with all that the corporate name implies, it still retains a suitably fond regard for its beginnings. Through what it calls its "Western Image Program," employing Western magazine advertisements, local radio and television, and the promotion of rodeos, the company still pursues the working people of the West who first inspired Levi Strauss to make pants to fit the world.

A good way to begin a summary is to figure out the author's thesis, the major idea the author wants to present to the reader. Usually it is suggested in the first paragraph. Reread the first paragraph of the article, and decide what the author's main idea is. Write that idea down **BEFORE YOU READ FURTHER.**

You probably wrote something like this: *An American symbol of equality now spreading throughout the world is a simple pair of pants called blue jeans.*

Using that thesis statement as your first sentence, summarize as briefly as you can the rest of the article, which is simply the history and present status of blue jeans. Your first draft may be 150 words or more. Now cut it down by including only essential points and by getting rid of wordiness. Keep within the 100-word limit. You may have a few words less but not one word more. By forcing yourself to keep within the 100 words, you will get to the kernel of the author's thought and understand the article better.

When you have written the best summary you can, then, *and only then*, compare it with the summary on page 304. If you look at the model sooner, you'll cheat yourself of the opportunity to learn to write summaries because once you read the model, it will be almost impossible not to make yours similar. So do your own thinking and writing, and *then* compare.

Even though your summary is different from the model, it may be just as good. If you are not sure how yours compares, ask yourself these questions:

Did I include as many important ideas?
Did I omit all unnecessary words and phrases?
Does my summary read as smoothly?
Would someone who had not read the article get a clear idea of it from
    my summary?

Assignment 16 A 100-Word Summary

A well-organized article, like the following, is not difficult to summarize. You're on your own now. No model summary is given at the back of the book. After you finish writing, simply ask yourself whether someone who hadn't read the article would get a clear idea of it from your summary.

As you read the article, note the effective sentences. For example, in the first paragraph note the sentences with parallelism.

Move Over, Ol' MacDonald
Jean Ayres Hartley

In a few years there is going to be a new look down on the farm. The hands that run the tractors, harvest the hay, and milk the cows will likely be women's hands. Agriculture is one of the fastest growing, most vital industries in the United States, and more and more women are owning farms, managing them, operating them, teaching about them, breeding cattle, harvesting crops, and doing everything else agricultural. Farmyards and fields no longer are "males only" territory.

Judging from university and college enrollments, an enormous female work force is being readied for the farm. The mounting interest of women in agricultural careers is evidenced by the fact that in 1969 only about two percent of U.S. undergraduates majoring in agricultural programs were women. In 1979 that figure had jumped to 33 percent.

According to a recent study by O. E. Thompson and Zoe McCandless-Grossman of the University of California at Davis, enrollment of women in agriculture courses at high school and college levels in California has increased at least three times faster than the enrollment of men. The number of female students in agricultural economics has risen at an annual rate of 72 percent since 1975.

What has brought about this trend of ascending female interest in agriculture? It can be attributed to a number of things:

Labor experts say it is part of a larger movement that has seen an ever-expanding percentage of all women seeking independence and working outside the home.

Agriculture is expanding faster than most sectors in the U.S. economy, bringing greater opportunities. More than 260 different types of occupations are available in agriculture-related work. It's a brisk job market.

Passage of equal-opportunity laws in the past decade has given more women the courage to enter any field they wish. Single women seeking to buy farms find that credit is more readily available to them than in the past. The American Banking Association reports that more than 40 female loan officers are specializing in agricultural endeavors in the U.S.

In 1969, the Future Farmers of America (an organization of students enrolled in vocational agriculture in high schools) decided to allow girls in its membership; that has had a big influence in turning girls toward agricultural careers. Now FFA's membership is more than 38 percent female. Some FFA national officers and many state presidents are female. The FFA state adviser for California, Don Wilson, says, "Membership in the FFA is responsible for great numbers of girls choosing agricultural majors, then following careers in agriculture."

The pull to the farm is strong in this age. It represents an opportunity to breathe clean air, to grow one's own food, and to escape city pressures and crime. Rural parents find they have more time to spend with their children and the less sophisticated atmosphere of the farm seems to make for stronger family ties. Those values are important to many of today's young women.

Before the 1970s agriculturally related businesses and government agencies did not hire women to do professional jobs, but employers now are beginning to recognize that women are as qualified as men to fill many of their positions. The assistant dean of agriculture at Ohio State University reports, "Many college women graduates are being recruited by agribusiness and the USDA. More and more women are being placed in responsible jobs that used to be held only by men."

Generally, the employment picture of the future looks bright for the great numbers of women studying agricultural subjects. According to the U.S. Department of Labor, 40,000 to 50,000 new farm and ranch operators will be needed each year through the 1980s. There is a great job diversity, and salaries are higher than at any time in history.

With colleges turning out women in great numbers who are fully prepared to run the machinery, research the crops, identify the parasites, analyze the soil, and apply their other technical skills to the rigors and problems of farm life, it looks as though today's bumper crop of women farmers is here to stay.

Assignment 17   A 100-Word Summary

Write a 100-word summary of this essay, which was written more than 100 years ago by a student of the Harvard zoologist Louis Agassiz. You will probably decide that the point the writer makes is as important today as it was then.

No summary is provided at the back of the book for this article nor for the one that follows.

Look Again, Look Again!
Samuel Scudder

It was more than fifteen years ago that I entered the laboratory of Professor Agassiz, and told him I had enrolled my name in the Scientific School as a student of natural history. He asked me a few questions about my object in coming, the mode in which I afterwards proposed to use the knowledge I might acquire, and, finally, whether I wished to study any special branch. To the latter I replied that, while I wished to be well grounded in all departments of zoology, I purposed to devote myself specially to insects.

"When do you wish to begin?" he asked.

"Now," I replied.

This seemed to please him, and with an energetic "Very well!" he reached from a shelf a huge jar of specimens in yellow alcohol. "Take this fish," he said, "and look at it; we call it a haemulon; by and by I will ask what you have seen."

With that he left me, but in a moment returned with explicit instructions as to the care of the object entrusted to me.

"No man is fit to be a naturalist," said he, "who does not know how to take care of specimens."

I was to keep the fish before me in a tin tray, and occasionally moisten the surface with alcohol from the jar, always taking care to replace the stopper tightly. Those were not the days of ground-glass stoppers and elegantly shaped exhibition jars; all the old students will recall the huge neckless glass bottles with their leaky, wax-besmeared corks, half eaten by insects, and begrimed with cellar

dust. Entomology was a cleaner science than ich- *entomology*—the
thyology, but the example of the Professor, who branch of zoology that
had unhesitatingly plunged to the bottom of the deals with insects
jar to produce the fish, was infectious; and though *ichthyology*—the
this alcohol had a "very ancient and fishlike smell," deals with fish
I really dared not show any aversion within these *infectious*—catching
sacred precincts, and treated the alcohol as though *aversion*—intense
it were pure water. Still I was conscious of a pass- dislike
ing feeling of disappointment, for gazing at a fish
did not commend itself to an ardent entomologist.
My friends at home, too, were annoyed when they
discovered that no amount of eau-de-Cologne
would drown the perfume which haunted me like
a shadow.

In ten minutes I had seen all that could be seen in
that fish, and started in search of the Professor—
who had, however, left the Museum; and when I
returned, after lingering over some of the odd animals stored in the upper apartment, my specimen
was dry all over. I dashed the fluid over the fish
as if to resuscitate the beast from a fainting fit, and *resuscitate*—to revive
looked with anxiety for a return of the normal
sloppy appearance. This little excitement over,
nothing was to be done but to return to a steadfast
gaze at my mute companion. Half an hour passed
—an hour—another hour; the fish began to look
loathsome. I turned it over and around; looked it
in the face—ghastly; from behind, beneath, above,
sideways, at a three-quarters' view—just as ghastly.
I was in despair; at an early hour I concluded that
lunch was necessary; so, with infinite relief, the fish
was carefully replaced in the jar, and for an hour I
was free.

On my return, I learned that Professor Agassiz
had been at the Museum, but had gone, and would
not return for several hours. My fellow-students
were too busy to be disturbed by continued conversation. Slowly I drew forth that hideous fish,
and with a feeling of desperation again looked at
it. I might not use a magnifying-glass; instruments
of all kinds were interdicted. My two hands, my two *interdicted*—
eyes, and the fish: it seemed a most limited field. forbidden
I pushed my finger down its throat to feel how
sharp the teeth were. I began to count the scales in
the different rows, until I was convinced that that
was nonsense. At last a happy thought struck me—

I would draw the fish; and now with surprise I began to discover new features in the creature. Just then the Professor returned.

"That is right," said he; "a pencil is one of the best of eyes. I am glad to notice, too, that you keep your specimen wet, and your bottle corked."

With these encouraging words, he added:

"Well, what is it like?"

He listened attentively to my brief rehearsal of the structure of parts whose names were still unknown to me: the fringed gill-arches and movable operculum; the pores of the head, fleshy lips and lidless eyes; the lateral line, the spinous fins and forked tail; the compressed and arched body. When I finished, he waited as if expecting more, and then, with an air of disappointment:

operculum—the gill cover in fishes

"You have not looked very carefully; why," he continued more earnestly, "you haven't even seen one of the most conspicuous features of the animal, which is as plainly before your eyes as the fish itself; look again, look again!" and he left me to my misery.

I was piqued; I was mortified. Still more of that wretched fish! But now I set myself to my task with a will, and discovered one new thing after another, until I saw how just the Professor's criticism had been. The afternoon passed quickly; and when, towards its close, the Professor inquired:

piqued—offended

"Do you see it yet?"

"No," I replied, "I am certain I do not, but I see how little I saw before."

"That is next best," said he, earnestly, "but I won't hear you now; put away your fish and go home; perhaps you will be ready with a better answer in the morning. I will examine you before you look at the fish.

This was disconcerting. Not only must I think of my fish all night, studying, without the object before me, what this unknown but most visible feature might be; but also, without reviewing my discoveries, I must give an exact account of them the next day. I had a bad memory; so I walked home by Charles River in a distracted state. . . .

disconcerting—upsetting

The cordial greeting from the Professor the next morning was reassuring; here was a man who seemed to be quite as anxious as I that I should see for myself what he saw.

"Do you perhaps mean," I asked, "that the fish has symmetrical sides with paired organs?"

His thoroughly pleased "Of course! of course!" repaid the wakeful hours of the previous night. After he had discoursed most happily and enthusiastically —as he always did—upon the importance of this point, I ventured to ask what I should do next.

"Oh, look at your fish!" he said, and left me again to my own devices. In a little more than an hour he returned, and heard my new catalogue.

"That is good, that is good!" he repeated; "but that is not all; go on"; and so for three long days he placed that fish before my eyes, forbidding me to look at anything else, or to use any artificial aid. "Look, look, look," was his repeated injunction.

injunction—command

This was the best entomological lesson I ever had—a lesson whose influence has extended to the details of every subsequent study; a legacy the Professor had left to me, as he has left it to many others, of inestimable value, which we could not buy, with which we cannot part. . . .

subsequent—following

inestimable— incapable of being measured

Assignment 18   A 100-Word Summary

The following essay is the Preface to the book *Extinction* by Paul and Anne Ehrlich. Dr. Ehrlich is a professor of biological sciences at Stanford University and a noted authority on ecology. Write a 100-word summary.

The Rivet Poppers
Paul and Anne Ehrlich

As you walk from the terminal toward your airliner, you notice a man on a ladder busily prying rivets out of its wing. Somewhat concerned, you saunter over to the rivet popper and ask him just what the hell he's doing.

saunter—to stroll

"I work for the airline—Growthmania Intercontinental," the man informs you, "and the airline has discovered that it can sell these rivets for two dollars apiece."

"But how do you know you won't fatally weaken the wing doing that?" you inquire.

"Don't worry," he assures you. "I'm certain the manufacturer made this plane much stronger than it needs to be, so no harm's done. Besides, I've taken lots of rivets from this wing and it hasn't fallen off yet. Growthmania Airlines needs the money; if we didn't pop the rivets, Growthmania wouldn't be able to continue expanding. And I need the commission they pay me—fifty cents a rivet!"

"You must be out of your mind!"

"I told you not to worry; I know what I'm doing. As a matter of fact, I'm going to fly on this flight also, so you can see there's absolutely nothing to be concerned about."

Any sane person would, of course, go back into the terminal, report the gibbering idiot and Growthmania Airlines to the FAA, and make reservations on another carrier. You never *have* to fly on an airliner. But unfortunately all of us are passengers on a very large spacecraft—one on which we have no option but to fly. And, frighteningly, it is swarming with rivet poppers behaving in ways analogous to that just described.

gibbering—chattering
FAA—Federal Aviation Administration

analogous—similar

From *Extinction: The Causes and Consequences of the Disappearance of Species*, by Paul R. Ehrlich and Anne H. Ehrlich. Copyright © 1981 by Paul R. and Anne H. Ehrlich. Reprinted by permission of Random House, Inc.

. . . . .

Rivet-popping on Spaceship Earth consists of aiding and abetting the extermination of species and populations of nonhuman organisms. The European Lion, the Passenger Pigeon, the Carolina Parakeet, and the Sthenele Brown Butterfly are some of the numerous rivets that are now irretrievably gone; the Chimpanzee, Mountain Gorilla, Siberian Tiger, Right Whale, and California Condor are prominent among the many rivets that are already loosened. The rest of the perhaps ten million species and billions of distinct populations still more or less hold firm. Some of these species supply or could supply important direct benefits to humanity, and all of them are involved in providing free public services without which society could not persist.

abetting—assisting

irretrievably— unchangeably

The natural ecological systems of Earth, which supply these vital services, are analogous to the parts of an airplane that make it a suitable vehicle for human beings. . . . A dozen rivets, or a dozen species, might never be missed. On the other hand, a thirteenth rivet popped from a wing flap, or the extinction of a key species involved in the cycling of nitrogen, could lead to a serious accident.

ecological—pertaining to the relation of organisms to their environment

In most cases an ecologist can no more predict the consequences of the extinction of a given species than an airline passenger can assess the loss of a single rivet. But both can easily foresee the long-term results of continually forcing species to extinction or of removing rivet after rivet. No sensible airline passenger today would accept a continuous loss of rivets from jet transports. Before much more time has passed, attitudes must be changed so that no sane passenger on Spaceship Earth will accept a continuous loss of populations or species of nonhuman organisms.

ecologist—one who studies the relation of organisms to their environment

Over most of the several billion years during which life has flourished on this planet, its ecological systems have been under what would be described by the airline industry as "progressive maintenance." Rivets have dropped out or gradually worn out, but they were continuously being replaced; in fact, over much of the time our spacecraft was being strengthened by the insertion of more rivets than were being lost. Only since about ten thousand years ago has there been any sign that that process might be more or less permanently reversed. That was when a single species, *Homo sapiens*, began its meteoric rise to planetary dominance. And only in about the last half-century has it become clear that humanity has been forcing species and populations to extinction at a rate greatly exceeding that of natural attrition and far beyond the rate at which natural processes can replace them. In the last twenty-five years or so, the disparity between the rate of loss and the rate of replacement has become alarming; in the next twenty-five years, unless something is done, it promises to become catastrophic for humanity.

Homo sapiens—human being
meteoric—swift like a meteor

attrition—gradual reduction in numbers

disparity—difference

. . . As nature is progressively impoverished, its ability to provide a moderate climate, cleanse air and water, recycle wastes, protect crops from pests, replenish soils, and so on will be increasingly degraded. The human population will be growing as the capacity of Earth to support people is shrinking. Rising death rates and a falling quality of life will lead to a crumbling of postindustrial civilization. The end may come so gradually that the hour of its arrival may not be recognizable, but the familiar world of today will disappear within the life span of many people now alive.

Of course, the "bang" is always possible. For example, it is likely that destruction of the rich complex of species in the Amazon basin would trigger rapid changes in global climatic patterns. Agriculture remains heavily dependent on stable climate, and human beings remain heavily dependent on food. By the end of the century the extinction of perhaps a million species in the Amazon basin could have entrained famines in which a billion human beings perished. And if our species is very unlucky, the famines could lead to a thermonuclear war, which could extinguish civilization.

entrain—to pull along after itself

Fortunately, the accelerating rate of extinctions can be arrested. It will not be easy; it will require both the education of, and concerted action by, hundreds of millions of people. But no tasks are more important, because extinctions of other organisms must be stopped before the living structure of our spacecraft is so weakened that at a moment of stress it fails and civilization is destroyed.

concerted—planned together

WRITING AN APPLICATION

Assignment 19   A Letter of Application

You may not need to do much writing in the career you have chosen, but almost certainly you will at some time need to write a letter of application. Write a letter of application now, either for a job this coming summer or for a job you might want to apply for after you finish college. Then write a separate personal data sheet. Follow the forms given here.

Lincoln Hall
West Adams Street
Macomb, IL 61455
January 25, 1986

Mr. Wayne White, Director
Argyle State Park
Rural Route 1
Colchester, IL 62326

Dear Mr. White:

A friend of mine, Christopher Ransom, was one of the
leaders in your Summer Interpretive Program three
years ago, and he has told me so much about it that
I'd like to apply for a position in the program for
the coming summer.

Chris explained that you try to keep your park
visitors, particularly young people, busy and happy
by showing them how to make things from natural
sources. He said he took a group to a clay bank and
helped them make clay pottery, that he showed them
how to weave simple mats from blue stem grass, that
he helped them make dye from walnut shells, and that
he helped them start a fire from the sun's rays. And
of course he took them on nature hikes and bird walks
and stargazing trips. All these are activities I
enjoy and am capable of leading.

My college courses in botany and biology have given
me a background in nature study, and last summer I
gained some experience in working with young people
as a counselor at Camp Timberidge of the YMCA in Glen
Ellyn, where I helped with crafts and nature study.

Since I'm majoring in biology and am planning to go
into some kind of conservation work eventually, the
experience I would get in your program would be
valuable to me, and I hope that what I can offer
would be valuable to your visitors.

I have listed my training and experience on the
attached sheet and will be glad to come for a
personal interview at your convenience. I'll phone
you soon to see if I can make an appointment.

Sincerely,

Jack Doe

Jack Doe

PERSONAL DATA SHEET

```
Jack Doe
Lincoln Hall
West Adams Street
Macomb, IL  61455
Tel. 000-000-0000
```

PERSONAL
     Age 19, unmarried
     Height 5' 9", weight 145 pounds

EDUCATION
     1985-86   Freshman at Western Illinois
                   University, Macomb, Illinois
               Majoring in biology; minoring in
                   special education
     1981-85   Student at Community High School,
                   District 94, West Chicago, Illinois

WORK EXPERIENCE
     1985 summer   Counselor at Camp Timberidge of the
                       B. R. Ryall YMCA in Glen Ellyn,
                       Illinois
     1984 summer   Bagger at Krogers in Glen Ellyn,
                       Illinois

ACTIVITIES
     1985-86   Participant in all field trips of
                   Department of Biological Sciences
               Member of the Varsity Swim Team

REFERENCES
     Professor John Warnock
     Institute for Environmental Management
     Western Illinois University
     Macomb, IL 61455

     Professor Robert D. Henry
     Department of Biological Sciences
     Western Illinois University
     Macomb, IL 61455

     Ms. Judy Bucci
     Camp Director
     B. R. Ryall YMCA
     Glen Ellyn, IL 60137

WRITING AN EVALUATION

Assignment 20   An Evaluation of My Performance

Do five minutes of free writing in preparation for writing a short paper on your performance in this course. Don't evaluate the course—it may have been bad or good—but simply evaluate how you performed. Although you may need to mention some weakness or strength of the course, the emphasis should be on how you reacted to that weakness or strength.

Don't be afraid to be honest. This isn't an occasion for apple-polishing. If you've gained little, you'll write a better paper by saying so than by trying to concoct phony gains. Someone who has gained little may write a better paper than someone who has gained much. How well the paper is organized and whether there are plenty of specific examples will determine the effectiveness of the paper.

Before starting your paper, write your thesis statement, listing your supporting points. If you've made gains, list the kinds—gain in writing skill, gain in confidence, gain in study habits . . . . Or, if you've gained little, list the reasons why—lack of time, lack of interest, getting off to a bad start . . . .

Since no one will have all gains or all losses in any course, you may want to include in your introduction or conclusion a sentence about the other side.

Answers

Answers

Words Often Confused (p. 10)

EXERCISE 1

1. Our, new, all ready
2. Its, an, it's
3. forth
4. course, feel
5. know, effect
6. hear
7. an, our
8. choose, our
9. conscious
10. do, have

EXERCISE 2

1. fourth, chose, an
2. our, are, Desert
3. course, an
4. hear, it's, an
5. know, already
6. It's, clothes, choose, new
7. chose, complements
8. course, compliment
9. accept, advice, an
10. break

EXERCISE 3

1. have, course
2. It's, an, effect
3. new
4. Our, advice, accept
5. do, course
6. know, it's, accept
7. hear, course, courses
8. chose, or, have
9. conscience, forth
10. already, compliment

EXERCISE 4

1. an, course, already
2. knew, or
3. know, are
4. have, course, does
5. It's
6. know
7. course, conscious
8. do, know
9. accept, advice, an
10. choose, an, effect

EXERCISE 5

1. an
2. conscious
3. choose, are
4. an
5. an, effect
6. course, already, knew, know
7. does, it's, break
8. accept, advice, conscience, do
9. or
10. have

EXERCISE 6
1. an, accept
2. new, fourth
3. course, already
4. break, know
5. does, here
6. clothes, choose
7. advice, desert
8. or, effect
9. have, feel, conscience
10. do, it's

EXERCISE 7
1. An, our
2. its
3. It's, it's
4. effect
5. due
6. course, are, accept
7. feel, do, break
8. effect
9. already, no
10. does

EXERCISE 8
1. choose, choose
2. know, have
3. have, compliment
4. conscience
5. course, forth, course
6. accept
7. complement
8. know, do, course, it's
9. hear, effect, our
10. already, an

EXERCISE 9
1. knew, except
2. an
3. choose
4. feel
5. or
6. except
7. an
8. It's, or
9. course, accept, accept
10. compliment

EXERCISE 10
1. an
2. conscious
3. knew
4. chose, do
5. forth, hear
6. effect
7. new, hear
8. advice
9. an
10. It's, an, have

Words Often Confused (continued) (p. 19)

EXERCISE 1

1. hear, an
2. course, have
3. due, does
4. quite, right
5. whether, new
6. you're, or
7. Who's, woman
8. personnel
9. morale, led
10. there, too, past

EXERCISE 2

1. piece, loose
2. It's, effect
3. threw, where
4. weather, or
5. You're, right
6. passed, quite
7. principal, lose
8. Then, right
9. there, too, our
10. It's, than

EXERCISE 3

1. an, new
2. It's, it's
3. An, its
4. than
5. through
6. you're
7. It's, quite, an, through
8. course, through
9. Then, past, where
10. knew

EXERCISE 4

1. past, know
2. too, choose
3. new, through
4. know, whether, lose
5. principal, course, there, too
6. It's, hear
7. led, quite, course, lead
8. piece, accept, advice
9. write, compliments
10. already, choose

EXERCISE 5

1. knew
2. know, they're, through
3. It's
4. led, an
5. an
6. passed
7. Then
8. There, than, accept
9. their
10. were, new

EXERCISE 6

1. quite, an
2. past
3. their, than
4. forth
5. course, there, no, their
6. there, where
7. Then
8. were
9. right
10. know, whose

EXERCISE 7

1. an, course
2. quite, lose
3. new, they're, too
4. already, than
5. choose, write, where
6. It's, know, our, principal, past
7. quite, than
8. conscious, course
9. It's, personal
10. Who's, or

EXERCISE 8

1. past
2. principal, their
3. where, were
4. Then, quite, an
5. chose

6. led, where
7. There
8. are
9. Already, there, an
10. It's, effect

EXERCISE 9

1. principal
2. quite, past
3. Through, already
4. passed, our
5. They're, where, there, or

6. Then
7. through, to
8. piece, desert
9. led, where
10. Through, their, know, personal

EXERCISE 10

1. It's, too, know
2. Our, lose
3. It's, weather
4. Our, principles
5. know, moral, accept

6. an, past
7. women
8. whether
9. through, chose
10. Where, women

Proofreading Exercise (p. 24)

I LEARNED TO PAINT

Yesterday I learned to paint. Oh, I had painted before, and I thought I ~~new~~ *knew* how. But that was before yesterday.

Yesterday a friend ~~whose~~ *who's* a professional painter helped me paint my apartment. First of all, we spent hours filling all the cracks and removing all the hooks and nails and outlet covers. We washed the kitchen walls to get off any grease, and we lightly sanded one wall that was rough. Of ~~coarse~~ *course* we had ~~all ready~~ *already* moved all the furniture away from the walls. We didn't even open the paint cans until the day was half over. ~~Than~~ *Then* we used paintbrushes to paint all the corners and edges that a roller wouldn't get to. Finally, in the very last hour of ~~are~~ *our* long . . . .

Contractions (p. 26)

EXERCISE 1
1. Where's, What's
2. He's, he's
3. He's, Everybody's
4. Let's
5. There's

6. Who's, who's
7. It's, it's
8. wasn't, it's
9. he's, it's
10. I'm, it's, he'd

EXERCISE 2
1. We're, I'm
2. shouldn't
3. isn't
4. That's
5. I'm

6. that's
7. everybody's
8. It'd, you'd
9. We're, it's
10. That's, It's

EXERCISE 3
1. We've
2. they're
3. It's, that's
4. It's
5. It's, I'm

6. I'm, I'll
7. I'll, I'll
8. It's
9. It's
10. won't, I'll

EXERCISE 4
1. I've
2. Won't, doesn't
3. it's, that's
4. he's
5. it's

6. That's
7. I've, I've
8. That's, haven't
9. Let's
10. I'll, can't, I'm

EXERCISE 5
1. It's, you're
2. you'll, you'll
3. Don't
4. It's, you're
5. you've

6. They're, you'll
7. you'll
8. It's, you've
9. it's
10. It's

EXERCISE 6
1. haven't, I'm
2. I'll, you'll
3. you'd
4. Let's, doesn't
5. Don't, it's, we'll

6. Wouldn't
7. don't, it's
8. That's, it's
9. you'd, I'm
10. I've, here's

EXERCISE 7
1. I'm
2. It's, that's
3. don't
4. I'm, I've, I'm
5. It's, don't

6. don't, there's
7. you've, it's
8. I've
9. That's, I'm
10. that's, it's

EXERCISE 8

1. We've, we've
2. It's, I'm
3, I'm, we've
4. You're, you'd
5. you'll

6. You'll, I've
7. I'm
8. It's, that's
9. It's, they're, they're
10. They're

EXERCISE 9

1. There's, you've
2. that's, wouldn't
3. It's, it'll, won't
4. It's, I'm, wouldn't
5. It's, it's, it'll

6. I've, haven't
7. I've, it's
8. I've, I'm
9. It's (first one)
10. I've

EXERCISE 10

1. don't
2. don't
3. they're
4. It's
5. I've, they're

6. aren't
7. I've, that's
8.
9. That's
10. doesn't

Possessives (p. 33)

EXERCISE 1
1. everybody's
2. Jennifer's
3.
4. Jerome's, Allen's
5. Andy's

6. day's
7. Everybody's
8. Andy's
9. Ashley's
10. people's

EXERCISE 2
1.
2. Ray's
3. Roger's
4. Roger's, Guy's
5. Tchaikovsky's

6.
7. Lisa's
8. father's
9. night's, today's
10. Tonight's

EXERCISE 3
1. everyone's
2. person's, person's
3. students'
4. Derek's, instructor's
5. student's

6. one's
7.
8.
9. Dickens'
10. Sandburg's

EXERCISE 4
1. brother's
2. everybody's
3. mom's
4. sister's
5. dad's

6. brother's, friends'
7. everybody's
8. dad's
9. brother's
10, anybody's

EXERCISE 5
1. Ivan's
2. daughter's
3. children's
4. Ivan's
5. afternoon's

6. monkeys'
7.
8.
9.
10.

EXERCISE 6
1. Caroline's
2. semester's
3. Women's
4. Caroline's
5. parents'

6. Barbara's
7.
8. girls'
9. Barb's, sister's
10.

EXERCISE 7
1. Ohio's
2.
3.
4. Greeks'
5.

6. today's
7. Rockne's
8. Ohio's
9. Namath's
10. Dempsey's

EXERCISE 8

1. brother's
2. family's
3. day's
4. beginner's
5. brother's
6. family's
7. dad's
8. sister's
9. week's
10. brother's

EXERCISE 9

1. Japan's
2. child's
3. Japan's
4. parents'
5. country's
6. People's
7. women's, men's
8. Children's
9. Women's
10. Japan's

EXERCISE 10

1.
2. Jones'
3. department's
4. student's
5. student's
6. Jones'
7. Sunday's
8. week's
9.
10. department's

Review of Contractions and Possessives (p. 37)

EXERCISE 1

1. There'll, I'm
2. Loren's, doesn't, he's
3. He'd, he'll
4. Women's
5. speaker's, chairperson's
6. children's
7. child's
8. Rogers', children's
9. It's
10.
11. Rogers'
12. It's, that's
13. Reeds'
14. It's, Reed's
15. Reed's

EXERCISE 2

There's a little lake with steep rocky sides and crystal clear water that you can see down into forever. Some say it's bottomless, but everyone agrees it's deep.

There's one spot where a big tree grows over the lake, and someone's tied a rope to one of its branches to swing on. It's a great sensation, I discovered, to swing out over the water and then let go. I think everyone gets an urge to yell as loud as possible to enhance an awkward dive. It's a great feeling to cast off from the high rocks holding onto the rope as it swings out over the water. Just before the farthest point of the rope's travel is the best place to let go and drop into the water. Those with initiative try flips and twists as they dive, but however it's done, it's a great sensation. Some say it's for kids, but I hope I never grow too old to have fun at it.

Proofreading Exercise (p. 38)

SUGAR RAY LEONARD

People find it hard to believe that Sugar Ray Leonard, the boxing champion, grew up in poverty. They think that anyone who speaks as well as he does must ~~of~~ *have* come from at least a middle-class home. But ~~Leonards~~ *Leonard's* parents were poor. He was one of seven children and ~~didnt~~ *didn't* go beyond high school. He was eager to succeed, however, and his ambition ~~lead~~ *led* him to work on language skills. . . .

Rule for Doubling a Final Consonant (p. 41)

EXERCISE 1

1. putting
2. controlling
3. admitting
4. mopping
5. planning
6. hopping
7. jumping
8. knitting
9. marking
10. creeping

EXERCISE 2

1. returning
2. swimming
3. singing
4. benefiting
5. loafing
6. nailing
7. omitting
8. occurring
9. shopping
10. interrupting

EXERCISE 3

1. beginning
2. spelling
3. preferring
4. interpreting
5. hunting
6. excelling
7. wrapping
8. stopping
9. wedding
10. screaming

EXERCISE 4

1. feeling
2. murmuring
3. turning
4. weeding
5. subtracting
6. streaming
7. expelling
8. missing
9. getting
10. stabbing

EXERCISE 5

1. forgetting
2. misspelling
3. fitting
4. planting
5. pinning
6. trusting
7. sipping
8. flopping
9. reaping
10. fighting

Progress Test (p. 42)

1. B
2. A
3. B
4. B
5. A
6. A
7. B
8. B
9. A
10. B
11. A
12. B
13. B
14. A
15. B

Finding Subjects and Verbs (p. 57)

EXERCISE 1

1. I visited
2. trip was
3. dunes shift
4. lake was
5. I watched

6. I walked
7. I saw
8. voices broke
9. dunes are
10. stars seem

EXERCISE 2

1. sun is
2. "black holes" were
3. "black hole" is
4. gravity crushed
5. gravity crushed

6. it "disappeared"
7. It became
8. It is
9. galaxies are
10. (You) try

EXERCISE 3

1. names have
2. Monday is
3. Tuesday is
4. Wednesday is
5. Thursday is

6. Friday is
7. Saturn gave
8. day is
9. people say
10. (You) think

EXERCISE 4

1. I went
2. space is
3. buses bring
4. races are
5. It takes

6. outriders toss
7. they jump
8. wagon starts
9. accidents are
10. It is

EXERCISE 5

1. Litter is
2. mountain has
3. camp is
4. Climbers leave
5. They leave

6. They leave
7. Nepal hopes
8. rule requires
9. job is
10. expedition plans

EXERCISE 6

1. Scientists wanted
2. It is
3. Antarctica is
4. Temperatures go
5. scientists brought

6. They succeeded
7. dog became
8. chicks nestle
9. chick nestled
10. scientists have

EXERCISE 7

1. nighthawks swoop
2. They become
3. they fly
4. nighthawk emits
5. It has
6. nighthawk opens
7. It catches
8. nighthawks nest
9. They sit
10. (You) listen

EXERCISE 8

1. sleds are
2. racing is
3. races are
4. racers call
5. dogs have
6. They love
7. dogs run
8. they stay
9. mushers prepare
10. It is

EXERCISE 9

1. libraries are
2. library contains
3. exhibits include
4. Gerald Ford is
5. One is
6. other is
7. latter offers
8. Library overlooks
9. It draws
10. people visited

EXERCISE 10

1. Library has
2. Library contains
3. Center illustrates
4. home is
5. Library is
6. reason is
7. Library celebrated
8. It contains
9. people are
10. (You) visit

Subjects Not in Prepositional Phrases (p. 62)

EXERCISE 1

1. One of the most interesting places on our trip was the Japanese garden in the East-West Center in Honolulu.
2. We followed a bamboo-shaded path through the garden.
3. Clumps of ferns bordered the path.
4. Near the path flowed a little stream.
5. In small pools beside the stream were orange and black and white tropical fish.
6. Here and there were Japanese stone lanterns.
7. At the top of the garden was a small waterfall.
8. Stone slab steps beside the waterfall led to a Japanese teahouse.
9. An atmosphere of peace enveloped the garden.
10. Some of the best things in life are still free.

EXERCISE 2

1. Behind our house is a row of tall poplar trees.
2. In the front are some blue spruces.
3. In the summer dozens of birds nest in our trees.
4. Among the noisiest are the jays.
5. In winter many birds visit our feeder for grain and seeds.
6. Of them all, the magpies are the most colorful.
7. From branch to branch hop small gray squirrels.
8. During the holidays bird lovers flock to woods and marshes and meadows for the National Audubon Society's Christmas bird count.
9. Most of the participants are experienced bird-watchers.
10. The results of the bird count are important for conservation purposes.

EXERCISE 3

1. The largest island in the world is Greenland.
2. New Guinea in the Pacific is the second largest.
3. Both of these islands contain unexplored regions.
4. The interior of Greenland is under an ice cap.
5. In New Guinea a rugged interior discourages travel.
6. Some of the primitive people in New Guinea still use stone tools.
7. Their small thatched houses often stand on poles above the swampy ground.

8. Villages sometimes communicate ~~by the beat of drums~~.
9. Many ~~of the people~~ have little knowledge ~~of our civilization~~.
10. Some ~~of the tribes~~ never go ~~outside their own valleys~~.

EXERCISE 4

1. One ~~of the greatest magicians of all time~~ was Houdini.
2. ~~After his birth~~ in Budapest ~~in 1874~~, his family moved ~~to New York City~~.
3. ~~From the age of 14~~, he practiced magic tricks.
4. ~~At the age of 17~~, he became a professional magician.
5. One ~~of his tricks~~ was his Metamorphosis Trick.
6. The meaning ~~of *metamorphosis*~~ is "change."
7. ~~In this trick~~ he escaped, ~~with his hands bound~~, ~~from a locked trunk~~.
8. Then Houdini's brother, ~~with hands also bound~~, appeared ~~in the trunk~~.
9. ~~On another occasion~~ 40,000 people watched Houdini's daring hand-cuffed jump ~~from a Pittsburgh bridge~~.
10. ~~In about three minutes~~ he freed himself ~~under water~~.

EXERCISE 5

1. One ~~of the most scenic places in the United States~~ is the 49th state.
2. ~~At the beginning of last summer~~ I flew ~~to Anchorage in Alaska~~.
3. ~~From there~~ I took a number ~~of backpacking trips~~.
4. Alaska has 8,000 miles ~~of scenic highways~~.
5. ~~Within its vastness~~, everything is big.
6. ~~For example~~, the Malaspina Glacier is 1,700 square miles ~~in area~~.
7. And one ~~of the longest navigable rivers in the world~~ is the Yukon.
8. The 20,320-foot Mount McKinley is the tallest peak ~~in North America~~.
9. Snow perpetually covers the upper two-thirds ~~of the mountain~~.
10. Mount McKinley is ~~in Denali National Park~~.

EXERCISE 6

1. Tobogganing ~~over hard-packed snow~~ is an exciting sport.
2. The Indians were the first to use toboggans.
3. They probably transported things ~~on them~~.
4. A modern toboggan carries 12 people.
5. A steersman ~~in the rear~~ trails a foot ~~in the snow~~ to guide the toboggan.
6. ~~In the Far North~~ snowshoeing is popular.

7. <u>Snowshoes</u> ~~for traveling~~ ~~in the woods~~ <u>are</u> only two feet long.

8. But Alaskan <u>snowshoes</u> ~~for racing~~ <u>are</u> seven feet long.

9. The <u>first</u> to use snowshoes <u>were</u> the Indians.

10. <u>They</u> probably <u>tied</u> branches ~~of a fir tree~~ ~~to their feet~~.

EXERCISE 7

1. Plant cools
2. water flows
3. water keeps
4. geese discovered
5. geese arrive

6. Ten thousand spend
7. they are
8. some weigh
9. they come
10. they return

EXERCISE 8

1. road is
2. Canada completed
3. it goes
4. monument is
5. highway spans

6. road crosses
7. parks are
8. parks are
9. number are
10. highway comes

EXERCISE 9

1. I drove
2. Neither had
3. we did
4. both enjoyed
5. we hiked

6. we had
7. we explored
8. we walked
9. trip was
10. Both hope

EXERCISE 10

1. field is
2. workers are
3. Americans forget
4. workers are
5. They make

6. jobs require
7. applicants are
8. prestige lures
9. pay discourages
10. jobs rank

More about Verbs and Subjects (p. 67)

EXERCISE 1

1. I could concentrate
2. mind would wander
3. I began
4. I became, began
5. I was concentrating
6. I can sit, keep
7. mind wanders
8. I am finding
9. I should have been concentrating
10. Learning has been

EXERCISE 2

1. wind tore, scattered
2. sleet, snow obliterated
3. I shoveled, did tackle
4. woodpecker was hammering
5. Hugh went, cut
6. He removed, put
7. children unpacked, put
8. decorations had been used
9. Some had been made
10. Everyone was, had

EXERCISE 3

1. (You) browse
2. you will find
3. person weighed
4. (You) do be discouraged
5. record is
6. album is
7. race was
8. speed is
9. poem is
10. It has appeared

EXERCISE 4

1. Seals spend, are descended
2. They have, breathe, bear
3. seal can close, can hold
4. It uses, uses
5. Conservationists have fought, have succeeded
6. Conservationists are working
7. saying was
8. saying must be changed
9. exhausts, factories are pouring
10. lead is being absorbed

EXERCISE 5

1. Cities may look
2. skyscrapers are going
3. Building goes, is
4. floors have been excavated
5. equipment is
6. advantage is
7. climate varies, remains
8. Most is lighted
9. lenses beam
10. occupants find

EXERCISE 6

1. Lincoln was born
2. cabin was chinked, had
3. cabin has been placed
4. Lincoln moved, spent
5. He worked, studied
6. Lincoln was elected
7. New Salem has been reconstructed
8. Visitors can ramble
9. buildings have been reproduced, furnished
10. Visitors can take

EXERCISE 7

1. I have been learning
2. tongue may be
3. badgers can run
4. atoms are
5. span was
6. star is
7. words are
8. form was
9. Egyptians extracted, rubbed
10. jar was

EXERCISE 8

1. scientists have made
2. satellite sent
3. surfaces are
4. level drops
5. level reflects
6. surface is
7. Gravity causes
8. scientists could map
9. map shows
10. it reveals

EXERCISE 9

1. Shoes have had
2. people covered, held
3. Sandals have been found
4. people wore, tied
5. persons wore
6. shoes were
7. Edward II originated
8. ladies imitated, wore
9. shoes were made
10. shoes were made

EXERCISE 10

1. I have been reading
2. products were named
3. products were named
4. names have
5. Chevrolet was named
6. coffee was served, took
7. Teddy Roosevelt asked, called
8. buses were painted
9. owner likened
10. buses got

Correcting Run-together Sentences (p. 74)

EXERCISE 1
1. It takes, development is called
2. eggs are laid, caterpillars emerge
3. caterpillars eat, caterpillars may be eaten
4. caterpillar sheds, skin is
5. caterpillar is, it sheds
6. it has turned, chrysalis is
7. chrysalis is, Changes are occurring
8. it cracks, butterfly emerges
9. wings dry, harden; monarch flies
10. It goes

EXERCISE 2
1. math.
2. up.
3. professor,
4. chance.
5. work.
6. hours.
7.
8. grades. During
9. came,
10. mark.

EXERCISE 3
1. me. She
2. busy,
3. listen;
4. career. Then
5. time,
6. years. Then
7.
8. receiving;
9. work,
10. write,

EXERCISE 4
1. Uemura. He
2, world. Every
3. huskies. It
4. F.,
5. underwear,
6. dogs,
7.
8. supply. Then
9. bag,
10. returned,

EXERCISE 5
1. feast. It
2. wanderers,
3.
4.
5. fish,
6. midair;
7.
8. fat. A
9. pounds,
10. appetite,

EXERCISE 6
1. silent. No
2. chirp. No
3. silent. Researchers
4. corroded. Farmers
5. States.
6. blame. The
7. atmosphere. The
8. stand. They
9. emissions. The
10. expensive. Industries

EXERCISE 7

1. acquiring. Making
2. cartons. It
3. white,
4. striking. It
5. refinishing. It's

6. treatment,
7. piece,
8. cupboard,
9. varnish. Then . . . turpentine,
10. work,

EXERCISE 8

1. work. Work
2. one. Unstring
3. money. That . . . advice. Don't
   . . . nickel. Invest . . . yourself.
4. election;
5. experiences. It

6. career. None
7. duck. Keep . . . surface,
8. criticize,
9. thought-provoking;
10. Louvre. It

EXERCISE 9

1. people,
2. Korea. It
3. holes,
4. it,
5. waterfowl,

6. roam. Pheasants
7. herbicides. Thus
8.
9. cranes, . . . remain. Three
10.

Correcting Fragments (p. 81)

EXERCISE 1

1. You have to practice until using the rules of writing becomes automatic.

2. When you know a few rules, writing becomes easier.

3. The only difference between an independent and a dependent clause is that the dependent clause begins with a dependent word.

4. If you know the dependent words, you'll have no trouble.

5. If you don't, you may not punctuate your sentences correctly.

6. A comma is required when a dependent clause comes first in a sentence.

7. When a dependent clause comes first in a sentence, a comma often prevents misreading.

8. When you have done a few sentences, the rule becomes easy.

9. It will help you when you are punctuating your papers.

10. When you punctuate correctly, your reader can read with ease.

EXERCISE 2

1. that is working day and night
2. which amounts to about 3,000 pounds of dead plants and animals per acre every year
3. which may number ten billion in just 60 cubic inches of forest soil
4. until it can be eaten by earthworms and insects
5. As these creatures pass the debris through their digestive systems
6. which then nourish new plants and animals
7. that without earthworms all vegetation would perish
8. which involves billions of organisms
9. Although pine needles may take three or four years to be turned into soil
10. that recycles the forest floor

EXERCISE 3

1. which is the first "surround" music hall in the country
2. While most seats are within 65 feet of the stage
3. which opened in 1978 to raves from the public and from music and architecture critics
4. that have "surround" music halls
5. that has the most telephones per capita
6. than it has people
7. whereas the national average is 77 phones per 100 persons
8. that has opened my eyes to the universe
9. that the light from one galaxy started to come to us 100 million years ago when dinosaurs were on earth
10. that one teaspoonful of it would weigh as much as 200 million elephants

EXERCISE 4

1. Whenever you are ready to leave, we'll go.
2.
3.
4. Because I tried harder and harder and finally succeeded, I was elated.
5. I knew that she was a loving and trusting person.
6. If I would study more and spend more time writing my papers, I'd learn more.
7. After I had played tennis for two hours without stopping, I spent the evening on the sofa.
8. Although I had never been in Woodland Hills before, I soon felt at home.
9. Wherever I went on those streets, I found something of interest.
10. My son made a sketch while I enjoyed the view.

EXERCISE 5

1. That's the place where we camped last year.
2. I cooked the dinner while she sat in the shade and drank lemonade.
3.
4. I'll phone her because I know she will understand.
5. After I came home and took a long shower, I was ready to practice.
6. I'm staying away from the coffee maker because most of my nervousness is caused by drinking too much coffee.
7. As I become more and more sure of myself, I'm enjoying my speech course.
8.
9. Before I took this course and learned a few rules, my writing was impossible to read.
10.

EXERCISE 6

1. Yesterday we went to the zoo because I hadn't been there for ages.
2. We went first to the sea lion tank because I wanted to feed the sea lions.
3. They ignored the fish that we threw to them because they had been fed too many fish.
4. They were named sea lions long ago because someone thought they roared like lions.
5. Although they are really seals and are related to fur seals, they lack the valuable coats of the fur seals.
6. In another part of the zoo small whales performed tricks since they can be trained just like seals.
7. Next we saw a sable antelope who had a one-day-old baby.
8. She prodded the baby with her knee because she wanted to make it walk.
9. She was persistent until finally she made it take a couple of steps.
10. Since I always learn a lot at the zoo, I should go more often.

EXERCISE 7

1. Although I've often said "busy as a beaver," I really knew nothing about beavers.
2. Now I know a little because I've just read an article about them.
3. A beaver's four front teeth are constantly growing because the beaver wears them down by gnawing trees to make dams.
4. Since a beaver's teeth are sharp, a beaver can cut down a small willow in only a few minutes.
5. When the tree suddenly begins to totter, then the beaver dashes for safety.
6. When finally all is quiet again, the beaver then returns to work.
7. Because a family of beavers work hard, they can fell a thousand trees in a year.
8. A beaver has a flat tail that he uses in many ways.
9. When he stands up to gnaw a tree, his tail serves as a prop.
10. When he slaps his tail against the water, his tail sounds an alarm.

EXERCISE 8

1. One Christmas when I was about eleven, I got a new hockey stick.
2. Since I thought I could play better with a new stick, I was inspired.
3. Because we played with a tennis ball on the street, we called it street hockey.
4. The goalie wore a baseball glove on one hand while he wielded a hockey stick with the other.
5. As we hit that tennis ball hard, he tried to keep us from shooting it past him.
6. When it got really cold in the winter, then we flooded the backyard.
7. When the ice finally became solid, my brother and I put on our skates.

8. Since we played with a real puck, we pretended we were stars of the Maple Leafs.
9. Because the whole neighborhood gathered at our "rink," we felt like real pros.
10. Those were exciting games that left some great memories.

EXERCISE 9

1. Since most of the trash in the United States is burned or buried or dumped, only a fraction of it is recycled.
2. Because newsprint can be recycled many times, it's a billion dollar business.
3. At the World Trade Center in New York, where each day's waste-paper is sold to paper brokers, not even a memo is wasted.
4. Aluminum is the most treasured trash because reprocessing aluminum takes only 5 percent of the energy needed to smelt new metal.
5. The United States now recycles about 32 percent of its aluminum, which is twice as much as was recycled 12 years ago.
6. But since we don't recycle as much garbage as we should, we lag behind other countries in turning refuse into a resource.
7. It isn't surprising that Japan is a leader among nations in recycling when one Tokyo suburb recycles 90 perent of its garbage.
8. Since the rest of the suburb's garbage is burned for energy, the suburb managers sometimes complain that there isn't enough garbage.
9. The United States needs to catch up with the other countries because a valuable resource is being wasted.
10. Although individual communities can act, the national government also needs to pass laws to encourage recycling.

More about Fragments (p. 88)

EXERCISE 1

1. Thinking we had missed the turn several miles back, we turned around.
2. She left me standing there holding the bag.
3. Not just kids my own age but younger and older people were there too.
4. Never believing anyone would come to my rescue, I tried to swim ashore.
5. The important thing was not whether we won or lost.
6. I was tired of going to meetings that served no purpose.
7.
8. He did only the things that he wanted to do.
9. Her confidence was built up after each win.
10. If he were someone whom I could sit down and talk to, it would be easier.

EXERCISE 2

1.
2. Writing a clear thesis statement and backing it up with reasons is always important.
3.
4.
5. If you do things for others without being asked, you'll be appreciated.
6. That is something that will take years of experience to learn.
7.
8.
9.
10. I'm constantly striving to improve my writing.

EXERCISE 3

1. I decided to look up all the words I don't know.
2.
3. I did something that I had always wanted to do.
4. I'm going to start now while I still have time to finish my paper.
5.
6. That is what I should have done long ago.
7. I hear that the Mounties always get their man.
8. She was making the most of every opportunity.
9. I've just learned that the Nile is the longest river in the world.
10.

EXERCISE 4

Come to Canada where there is endless surprise. Around the corner, down the road, just over the hill, wherever you turn, your Canadian vacation is a medley of fascinating histories and colourful cultures. Here honoured customs live on amid the modern, and old-world customs live beside the cosmopolitan. And here your pleasure and comfort is always our first concern.

EXERCISE 5

Spring and summer are full of big events like graduations and picnics and maybe a June wedding. There's always a birthday to celebrate or the big . . . .

EXERCISE 6

Y is for you secretaries. We've spent the last 50 years making typing easier for you and our typewriters smarter and sturdier for you. And what about you? . . .

EXERCISE 7

. . . Who cares about smoggy skies and polluted lakes? Who cares about empty cans and trash littering our countryside? Who cares about plants and trees and animals dying in our forests? . . .

EXERCISE 8

. . . You are a blind student facing four years of college with about thirty-two textbooks to read plus fifty . . . .

You can manage with Recording for the Blind. Since 1951, we've helped over 53,000 blind, perceptually and physically handicapped students get through school by sending them free recordings . . . .

Review Exercises for Run-together Sentences and Fragments (p. 92)

1. Robert Frost is undoubtedly the most beloved American poet. People who are indifferent to most poetry can often quote "Birches" or "Stopping by Woods on a Snowy Evening." He . . . .
2. There's a place set deep in the woods of northern Minnesota that is very special to me. Every time I go there I'm surrounded with feelings of serenity. The quietness of the area is something that I don't find anywhere else. There's an occasional cry of a hawk circling up above, and sometimes I hear chipmunks scurrying around in the leaves on the ground. These noises always make me feel closer to nature. I . . . .
3. I began wrestling seriously in my freshman year. The wrestling coach was walking around and talking to the kids playing football. He was looking for recruits for the upcoming wrestling season. Several of my friends had decided that they would go out for the team. I decided wrestling would be a good way to keep busy through the winter. Looking back over my wrestling years, I feel it was good for me. I learned that through hard work I could accomplish my goals. My . . . .

"I Have a Dream . . ."
Martin Luther King, Jr.

Five score years ago, a great American, in whose symbolic shadow we stand, signed the Emancipation Proclamation. This momentous decree came as a great beacon light of hope to millions of Negro slaves who had been seared in the flames of withering injustice. It came as a joyous daybreak to end the long night of captivity.

But one hundred years later, we must face the tragic fact that the Negro is still not free. One hundred years later, the life of the Negro is still sadly crippled by the manacles of segregation and the chains of discrimination. One hundred years later, the Negro lives on a lonely island of poverty in the midst of a vast ocean of material prosperity. One hundred years later, the Negro is still languished in the corners of American society and finds himself an exile in his own land. So we have come here today to dramatize an appalling condition.

In a sense we have come to our nation's Capital to cash a check. When the architects of our republic wrote the magnificent words of the Constitution and the Declaration of Independence, they were signing a promissory note to which every American was to fall heir. This note was a promise that all men would be guaranteed the unalienable rights of life, liberty, and the pursuit of happiness.

It is obvious today that America has defaulted on this promissory note insofar as her citizens of color are concerned. Instead of honoring this sacred obligation, America has given the Negro people a bad check, a check which has come back marked "insufficient funds." But we refuse to believe that the bank of justice is bankrupt. We refuse to believe that there are insufficient funds in the great vaults of opportunity of this nation. So we have come to cash this check—a check that will give us upon demand the riches of freedom and the security of justice. We have also come to this hallowed spot to remind America of the fierce urgency of <u>now</u>. This is no time to engage in the luxury of cooling off or to take the tranquilizing drug of gradualism. <u>Now</u> is the time to make real the promises of Democracy. <u>Now</u> is the time to rise from the dark and desolate valley of segregation to the sunlit path of racial justice. <u>Now</u> is the time to open the doors of opportunity to all of God's children. <u>Now</u> is the time to lift our nation from the quicksands of racial injustice to the solid rock of brotherhood.

Using Standard English Verbs (p. 98)

EXERCISE 1

1. walked, happened
2. doesn't, wants
3. dropped, returned
4. does
5. asked
6. helped
7. finished, talked
8. discussed, helped
9. enjoyed
10. worked, work

EXERCISE 2

1. asked
2. pleased, asked
3. walked, ordered
4. likes, ordered
5. were
6. had, needed
7. do
8. have, want
9. did, watched
10. work, am

EXERCISE 3

1. happened
2. walked, asked
3. supposed
4. learned
5. asked
6. walked
7. had
8. was
9. am
10. learned

EXERCISE 4

1. jogged
2. were, arrived
3. like
4. wanted, was
5. is, hope
6. prefer
7. is
8. plan
9. intend
10. are, expect

EXERCISE 5

1. have
2. live, has
3. has, are
4. include
5. sells
6. draw
7. has, is
8. has, saves
9. has, provides
10. think

EXERCISE 6

1. attended
2. play, played
3. expect
4. worked, learned
5. was
6. practiced, like
7. enjoy
8. plan, want
9. hope
10. change, have

EXERCISE 7

1. think, give
2. are
3. destroy, sting, are
4. die
5. sleep
6. lay
7. is
8. use
9. pass
10. store, pass

Standard English Verbs (compound forms and irregular verbs) (p. 105)

EXERCISE 1

1. liked, met
2. met, builds
3. supposed
4. met, taught
5. devoted, taught

6. gives, given
7. became, designs
8. concerned
9. caught
10. supposed, surprised

EXERCISE 2

1. intends, is
2. plans, does
3. attend
4. has
5. wonder, does

6. says, does
7. intends, hopes
8. were, were
9. missed, were
10. was, have

EXERCISE 3

1. had
2. wish, had
3. knew, made
4. understood
5. offer, make

6. solve, talking
7. be
8. is
9. use
10. has, spend

EXERCISE 4

1. gone
2. did, appreciated
3. drank, drunk
4. asked, gave
5. was mad, said

6. filled
7. saw, saw
8. were, weren't
9. ran, run
10. knew, were

EXERCISE 5

1. haven't time
2. any
3. This book, anyway
4. friend did well
5. was hard

6. all those, were supposed
7. any
8. watched, any reading
9. decided
10. that test

EXERCISE 6

1. somewhere
2. haven't
3. brother wants
4. was never
5. anywhere, have been

6. Anyway
7. those atlases, are
8. isn't
9. have never been to any
10. himself

Proofreading Exercise (p. 110)

A DOLPHIN LESSON

The stuff I'm learning in college ~~doesnt~~ *doesn't* have much to do with life—or so I thought. I learn about the Napoleonic Wars. I study ~~Freuds~~ *Freud's* theory of the id. I learn to do statistical analysis. I read Sandburg's poems. But then I go out to have pizza with my friends, and we talk only about parties.

But last week something clicked.

Out at Marine World I saw some Atlantic bottle-nosed dolphins put on a show. With their sleek gray bodies, front flippers, and strong tails, they looked beautiful and friendly as they repeatedly surfaced and ~~than~~ *then* dived again into the water. Their performance was astounding. They "walked" on ~~there~~ *their* tails on the surface of the water, turned nose over tail in the air, jumped three times their body length in the air, spun in the air, jumped ~~threw~~ *through* hoops, and jumped over a rope stretched high across the pool. They performed faultlessly. Every minute was exciting.

But the best part came at the end when the trainer told how she trains them. It takes her six months to teach a dolphin to do an air spin and a year or more to get it ready for show business. She said she uses affection training and operant conditioning. Operant conditioning! I had just been reading in my psychology ~~coarse~~ *course* about B. F. Skinner's theory of operant conditioning—the theory that animals or children or adults can be trained by giving them rewards for good behavior.

And ~~hear~~ *here* I was seeing the theory in practice. The trainer said, "When they do something we like, we give them something they like." When a dolphin does what the trainer wants, she gives it an affectionate pat and a small fish. If it doesn't do what she wants, she ignores it or sometimes

even gives it a tiny bop on the snout.

So here was my psychology course being used in real life. Maybe more

of the things ~~Im~~ *I'm* learning in college relate to reality. I'll have to see.

Progress Test (p. 112)

1. B	6. B	11. A
2. B	7. A	12. A
3. B	8. B	13. A
4. A	9. A	14. B
5. A	10. B	15. B

Making Subjects, Verbs, and Pronouns Agree (p. 115)

EXERCISE 1

1. gets
2. are, miss
3. writes, hands
4. includes, are
5. sorts

6. gets her
7. get theirs
8. like
9. doesn't
10. gives

EXERCISE 2

1. is
2. were
3. were
4. gives
5. include

6. show
7. is
8. reveals
9. show
10. is

EXERCISE 3

1. is
2. take
3. wish
4. get
5. type

6. has
7. doesn't
8. take
9. finds his
10. wish

EXERCISE 4

1. has, her
2. is
3. drives
4. have
5. have

6. have
7. doesn't
8. helps
9. helps, is
10. is

EXERCISE 5

1. has
2. have
3. have, is
4. are
5. have, is

6. want
7. come
8. varies
9. is
10. comes

EXERCISE 6

1. wants
2. are
3. is
4. are
5. look

6. wants
7. are, grow
8. plan
9. has
10. intend

EXERCISE 7

1. are
2. lie
3. have
4. stand
5. cover

6. are
7. are
8. hope
9. suits
10. think

EXERCISE 8

1. is
2. wants
3. are
4. have
5. seems

6. has
7. doesn't
8. is
9. doesn't
10. is

Choosing the Right Pronoun (p. 120)

EXERCISE 1

1. me
2. him
3. He
4. me
5. me

6. I
7. us
8. We
9. I
10. I

EXERCISE 2

1. me
2. I
3. him
4. him
5. he

6. I
7. we
8. me
9. me
10. I

EXERCISE 3

1. I
2. her
3. I
4. me
5. I

6. me
7. me
8. me
9. Carol and I
10. We

EXERCISE 4

1. Jason and I
2. him, me
3. me
4. he and I
5. I

6. me
7. I
8. him, me
9. me
10. he, I

EXERCISE 5

1. My brother and I
2. I am
3. him and me
4. I
5. I

6. me
7. I
8. us
9. we
10. he and I

Making the Pronoun Refer to the Right Word (p. 123)

EXERCISE 1

1. When Curt showed his father the dented fender, his father . . . .
2. His father said, "You will . . . ."
3. She showed us a conch shell and explained how the molusk lives in it.
4. The parents take turns supervising the park playground, where the children . . . .
5. He said to his instructor, "I don't think you understand the novel."
6. His instructor said, "Maybe I haven't . . . ."
7. The clerk said to his boss, "I am . . . ."
8. When the professor talked with him, Roland was really worried.
9. She said to her girlfriend, "Your record collection needs . . . ."
10. She said to the job applicant, "Come back after you have . . . ."

EXERCISE 2

1. His motorcycle hit a parked car, but the car . . . .
2. As I went up to the baby's carriage, the baby . . . .
3. Rebecca said to her mother, "My wardrobe is . . . ."
4. As soon as the carburetor was adjusted, I drove my car home.
5. I couldn't find the catsup bottle, and I don't like hamburger without catsup.
6. His father was going to have . . . .
7. Susanne said to Cynthia, "I failed the exam."
8. Her shyness kept . . . .
9. He finished typing his paper and took it to class.
10. When we couldn't find the cake plate, we decided my husband must have eaten the cake.

EXERCISE 3

1. When the dentist pulled the tooth, the child screamed.
2. I finished my exam, put down my pen, and handed my paper in.
3.
4. My parents disapproved of my decision to take a different job.
5. When I opened the dog's carrying case at the airport, the dog ran away.
6. The cars streamed by, but no one paid . . . .
7. Darryl said to Max, "Your parakeet is loose in your room."
8. It wasn't easy, but I finally made up my mind to major in math.
9. When Debbie phoned, her mother was quite ill.
10. He said to the salesman, "Come back when I'm not so rushed."

EXERCISE 4

1. He said to his father, "Your car needs a . . . ."
2. After I read about Tom Dooley's career in medicine, I decided that I wanted to be a doctor.
3. After talking to the boss, Alfredo was . . . .

4. He loves to wrestle and spends most of his time wrestling.
5. The park commission established a hockey rink where people . . . .
6. The doctor said to the orderly, "You've . . . ."
7. She said to her sister, "Take my car."
8. My car hit a truck, but my car . . . .
9. She said, "Mother, you're . . . ."
10. As we approached the nest, the robin . . . .

EXERCISE 5

1. She said to her daughter, "I was always too shy."
2. Erica's mother said, "You may wear my . . . ."
3. He said, "Dad, I've made . . . ."
4. She slammed her cup into the saucer and broke the saucer.
5. I enjoy figure skating and would like to be a figure skater . . . .
6. The president said to the chief accountant, "I made an error in reporting my income."
7. Hawaii has June . . . .
8. She was excited when her . . . .
9. He said to his father, "You . . . ."
10. His father said, "I don't . . . ."

Correcting Misplaced or Dangling Modifiers (p. 127)

EXERCISE 1

1. He watched her strolling along garbed . . . .
2. My brother-in-law took me to the hospital after I broke . . . .
3. We watched hundreds of fireflies glowing . . . .
4. After I had finished . . . .
5. After I had cleaned the cage and put . . . .
6. I discovered my boyfriend sound . . . .
7.
8. When I was six, my mother . . . .
9. I gave to a charity that blue suit I didn't . . . .
10. While I was answering . . . .

EXERCISE 2

1. Cruising in the glass-bottom boat, we could see hundreds . . . .
2. While the baby was playing on the floor, I noticed that it . . . .
3. After I was wheeled . . . .
4. While Mark was watching the football game, his bike . . . .
5. The bank will make loans of any size to . . . .
6. Rounding a bend in the road, I was confronted by . . . .
7. Flying at an altitude of 5,000 feet, I could see . . . .
8. After I had finished mowing . . . .
9.
10. Because I had broken . . . .

EXERCISE 3

1. After I had done . . . .
2. I spotted a monarch butterfly flitting . . .
3. After I drank . . . .
4. We thought the cows looked contented standing . . . .
5. The Museum of Science and Industry is the most interesting museum that I have visited in the city.
6. She was going out with a man named Harold, who . . . .
7. We gave all the meat we didn't want to the cat.
8.
9. Determined to learn to write, I slowly mastered the textbook.
10. After we had a quick . . . .

EXERCISE 4

1. The little town where I was born is . . . .
2. From nine until five every day except Friday, you may visit . . . .
3.
4. She put the clothes she had not worn back . . . .
5. Although it is almost ten years old, he . . . .

6. I saw that my little car was smashed beyond repair.
7. I went to see what was the matter with my puppy, who was barking . . . .
8. Sitting there looking out over the water, she finally made . . . .
9. Because the child was crying pitifully, I tried to find his mother.
10. Because he is a . . . .

EXERCISE 5

1. A man sold me a secondhand car with generator trouble.
2. I read in the evening paper that . . . .
3. We gave the Boy Scouts all the newspapers that have been . . . .
4. She left on the table the meat . . . .
5. The police made a report about . . . .
6. I watched the wren building its nest and twittering . . . .
7. Because he was a conceited . . . .
8. After my dog had smelled up the whole house, I finally gave it . . . .
9. While I was . . . .
10. Because I was unsure . . . .

Using Parallel Construction (p. 132)

EXERCISE 1

1. or skiing without . . . .
2. and good plays . . . .
3. and even sail . . . .
4. and clear thinking.
5. or law.
6. and especially camping . . . .
7. but how you do it.
8.
9. to get our instruments tuned immediately . . . .
10. I need her.

EXERCISE 2

1. and how to think up . . . .
2. and lack of parallelism.
3. and having people come . . . .
4. how to organize my time . . . .
5. A good salary, pleasant working conditions . . . .
6.
7. and move . . . .
8. kitchen a soft blue.
9. and getting some exercise.
10. whatever your obligations . . . .

EXERCISE 3

1. and then help his . . . .
2. clean, to help with the dishes . . . .
3. and get up early . . . .
4. but to comprehend more . . . .
5. as to understand themselves . . . .
6. and indulgently handed . . . .
7. and a cool breeze coming . . . .
8. than in Long Beach.
9. and too costly.
10. and teach them to live . . . .

EXERCISE 4

1. and spend less money.
2. and with a view.
3. two hundred feet long.
4. and too expensive.
5. and to move . . . .
6. and wash the windows . . . .
7. and finding work . . . .
8. and often goes home . . . .
9. and a message.
10. and maybe also a bit of luck.

EXERCISE 5

1. and punctual.
2. and promote the firm.
3. and a summary of . . . .
4. and get a better . . . .
5. and of course the balmy . . . .
6.
7. and a host of . . . .
8.
9. and the degree of . . . .
10. seashores, national cemeteries , . . .

EXERCISE 6

1. Recycling cans and bottles **has** been worthwhile.
   1.
   2. It has prevented littering.
   3.

2. Air bags should be standard equipment on new cars.
     1.
     2.
     3. They are worth the cost.
3. My summer job on the playground for the handicapped was valuable.
     1.
     2.
     3. It gave me an opportunity to do something for society.
4. A camping trip in Estes Park gave me some new insights.
     1.
     2. I have a new interest in nature.
     3. I learned something about ecology.
5. Improving one's vocabulary is important.
     1.
     2. It will lead to a more successful career.
     3. It will give one personal satisfaction.

Correcting Shift in Time (p. 137)

EXERCISE 1

1. walked
2. decided
3. began
4. gave
5. decided

6. registered
7. came
8. learned
9. described
10. came

EXERCISE 2

1. explains
2. had oil

3. is told
4. says that it must be

EXERCISE 3

. . . One little girl was . . . . One boy was tapping . . . . One was trying to propel . . . . Another was walking . . . . Thus they were gaining . . . .

EXERCISE 4

. . . reached for my bearskin blanket . . . . I reached but couldn't find it. I checked the floor to see if it had . . . . My mind woke . . . . I paused and tried . . . . I couldn't see . . . .

I got up, groped for the light switch, and saw that my desk drawers were . . . . And there was . . . .

Now my mind raced as I scanned . . . . my TV was . . . . someone had been . . . . someone had been looking . . . .

. . . gave up . . . .

EXERCISE 5

. . . so I grabbed . . . .

. . . as we moved higher and saw . . . .

. . . It seemed so easy . . . . and I nervously tried . . . . we weren't going to suddenly fall . . . .

I learned . . . . I learned . . . . Then I was reminded . . . . my instructor asked me if I knew where we were. It had been . . . . I had no idea . . . .

Correcting Shift in Person (p. 143)

EXERCISE 1

1. I feel so good when I
2. anyone more than
3. makes me
4. as I grow older, I
5. I have to do a lot of memorizing if I
6. we have
7. Often people can find work if they are willing to take what they
8. It's wise for beginning drivers to stay out of heavy traffic until they
9. you really need
10. their gowns

EXERCISE 2

1. us to finish
2. Anyone who has done all the exercises in this book should
3. Iraq and also many other
4. we could see
5. we got tired
6. we could do
7. we could see
8. we could see
9. one isn't
10. I can talk

EXERCISE 3

1. My room was in a mess.
2. I was terrified.
3. Swimming is the best exercise.
4. Nonmembers can attend the Kiwanis Club breakfast.
5. Specific details always make a paper more interesting.
6. Her paper was excellent; obviously she had spent time on it.
7. A good vocabulary is necessary for success in college.
8. Wide reading will improve one's vocabulary.
9. I felt foolish after saying that.
10. I looked forward to that weekend.

EXERCISE 4

1. Watching television for an evening will show how much violence is on the programs.
2. One's a different person after taking that psychology course.
3. My two days in Williamsburg were not enough for me to see everything.
4. To keep fit, exercise every day.
5. Call this number for more information.
6. To prevent air pollution, have a tune-up twice a year.

7. The above facts show that many companies still discriminate in hiring.
8. I was frustrated because I couldn't get there on time.
9. She wore an elegant costume to the masquerade.
10. After such an escape, I felt lucky to be alive.

EXERCISE 5

. . . I could see the black mark or "whisker" on each side of the head and the black collar below the light throat. On a few of them I could even see . . . .

Correcting Wordiness (p. 148)

EXERCISE 1

1. An experienced player would have known what to do.
2. My college roommate was coming to see me.
3. Electronics is a good field to go into.
4. We have two May birthdays in our family.
5. My grandfather told me this story.
6. The government should speed up the judicial process.
7. Justice should be swift and sure.
8. I grew up in a small town.
9. I was too busy to accept their invitation.
10. I didn't know she was leaving.

EXERCISE 2

1. History interests me.
2. The professor makes his subject interesting.
3. No doubt he spends a great deal of time preparing each lecture.
4. This polish will make your shoes last twice as long.
5. A friend of mine has a unique invention.
6. The taxpayers objected.
7. We started at 5 A.M. and got there at 6 P.M.
8. In August most of our employees take a vacation.
9. I have not had time to prepare an agenda for this afternoon's meeting.
10. I want to repeat my conclusion.

EXERCISE 3

1. The purple martin circled the martin house for half an hour and then disappeared.
2. He was arrested for drunken driving.
3. Modern medicine has practically wiped out polio.
4. A number of spectators couldn't get seats.
5. The grandstand should be larger.
6. A fly has suction cups on its feet, enabling it to walk on the ceiling.
7. My hardest exam last semester was psychology.
8. The exam included things I had forgotten.
9. The magpie is a large bird with a black head, a long greenish tail, and white wing patches.
10. She will always do what she promises.

EXERCISE 4

1. Although I hadn't eaten since morning, I wasn't hungry.
2. I hope I'll find a job soon.
3. Since the meeting hadn't been announced, not many came.
4. Ten people were planning to come.
5. Within three months, six in the department have resigned.
6. I learned to identify three kinds of ivy on this morning's field trip.
7. I've gained ten pounds since I began this diet.
8. At the opening of the new store, everyone there received a gift.

9. I use too many words in my writing.
10. Many people do the same.

EXERCISE 5

1. What has been accomplished is a result of the cooperation of the administration, faculty, students, and library staff.
2. So that they will always be available, periodicals do not circulate. Many divisions have facilities for copying articles.
3. The Information Center gives assistance in using the card catalog and basic reference works. A library orientation program explains library procedures and the interlibrary loan service.
4. The Reserve Reading Room contains required reading for current courses.
5. The Music Division has ten listening stations, six of which are equipped with cassette recorders.
6. Much material essential to a new library is no longer available in printed form, but the library contains over one million items on microfilm, microcards, and microfiche, as well as microprint machines for making copies.

Avoiding Clichés (p. 153)

EXERCISE 1

1. We had planned to go to the lake, and I was up early.
2. But my wife and son were still asleep.
3. I started the breakfast, but I couldn't get the orange juice can open.
4. Finally I did get the breakfast on the table and called the others. I was determined to get started on our trip.
5. When they finally came downstairs, they were hungry but complained that the toast was cold.
6. I told them they should be grateful that breakfast was ready.
7. Eventually we started, but we had gone only a mile when it began to rain.
8. Finally the skies cleared, and we got to the lake.
9. Our son immediately jumped into the lake because he's a great swimmer.
10. My wife soon followed him, but I just sat on the beach and rested.

Review of Sentence Structure (p. 154)

1. A	6. B	11. B	16. B	21. B
2. B	7. A	12. B	17. A	22. B
3. B	8. A	13. A	18. B	23. A
4. A	9. B	14. A	19. B	24. A
5. A	10. A	15. B	20. B	25. B

Punctuation (p. 160)

EXERCISE 1

1.
2. these:
3. game;
4. country. It's
5. farmhouse;

6. remodeling. We'll
7. work. It
8. off. At
9. slowly. There's
10. surroundings. We

EXERCISE 2

1. snow?
2. ice?
3. children. It
4. sterile. Actually
5. snow. The

6.
7. crystals. They
8. shapes. Their
9. snowflake. The size
10. alike. Most

EXERCISE 3

1. cans? The
2. them;
3.
4. preserve. Another
5. mushrooms. Others

6. trombonist?
7. these:
8. records.
9. store.
10. summer.

EXERCISE 4

1. pests. Now
2. following:
3. world. They're
4. design;
5. thread. It

6. ways:
7. world. Some . . . pinhead;
8. difficulty. It
9. male. Sometimes
10. nature. They

EXERCISE 5

1. winters? Some
2. round. There
3. snow;
4. grow. A
5. age:

6. ice cap;
7. icebergs. They
8. tiny;
9. above the water. Also
10. water. The

EXERCISE 6

1. road?
2. highways. One
3. 1973. They
4. too. The
5. roads. Moreover

6. past:
7. changed. Plank
8. has. Visitors
9. commercialism:
10. roads:

EXERCISE 7

1. roots. It's
2. happen. They
3. roots:
4. "to believe." About
5. believable. Anything
6. beliefs. *Credentials*
7. "study of." It
8. "earth";
9. "ancient";
10. "star." *Astrology*

EXERCISE 8

1. PATH. It
2. "together";
3. "against";
4. words:
5. sounds. A
6. afar. A
7. apart;
8.
9. roots. They
10. me.

EXERCISE 9

1.
2. following:
3. people—
4. B.A. Then . . . M.A.
5. interests. He
6. cook. He
7. hymn:
8. children:
9. pain:
10. health. Generous

Commas (p. 166)

EXERCISE 1

1.
2. had,
3. college,
4. college,
5. work,
6. work,
7. grade,
8. learn,
9. learning,
10. future,

EXERCISE 2

1. errors,
2. hour, we . . . statement, a rough draft,
3. aloud,
4. Friday,
5. promptly,
6. class,
7. was,
8. sure,
9. paper,
10. statement,

EXERCISE 3

1. devastation,
2. Helens,
3. ash,
4. eruption,
5. later, tiny fir trees, pink fire-weed,
6. pocket gophers, elk,
7. ladybugs, black ants,
8. back,
9. timber,
10. years,

EXERCISE 4

1. things,
2. invention,
3. milk, honey,
4. 1777,
5. ice, and . . . cream, sugar, eggs,
6. crank,
7. freezer,
8. hour, the . . . frozen,
9. rapidly,
10. melt,

EXERCISE 5

1. birds,
2. ways,
3. example,
4. flight,
5. drink,
6. feat,
7. altitudes,
8, comparison,
9. hour,
10. record,

EXERCISE 6

1. freestanding poles,
2. Vancouver,
3. house,
4. house,
5, people,
6. legends, or . . . raven, bear, beaver, frog,
7. represented,
8. height,
9. uses,
10. trees,

EXERCISE 7

1. Galesburg, Illinois, on January 6,
2. wagon, porter in a barbershop, sceneshifter in a theater,
3. fields, washed dishes at hotels in Kansas City, Omaha, and Denver,
4. college, became a newspaper reporter,
5. "Chicago,"
6. things,
7. poems,
8. poetry,
9. airplanes, Polaroid cameras, food freezers, frozen vegetables, radar, V-8 engines, electric razors, electric typewriters, drive-in movie theaters, color television, the United Nations, the atomic bomb,
10. Canada, and . . . Mexico, and . . . continent,

EXERCISE 8

1. recycled,
2. Conservancy, the Wilderness Society, the Sierra Club,
3. Vostok, Antarctica, on August 24,
4. Yes,
5. Azizia, Libya, on September 13,
6. Mt. Waialeale, Hawaii. It . . . year,
7. Wales,
8. designed, built,
9. 17 pounds,
10. years,

EXERCISE 9

In the issue of *Saturday Review* that appeared on the newsstands the week before Robert Kennedy was killed, Richard L. Tobin gave the following report of an eight-hour monitoring of three TV networks and half a dozen local outlets: "We marked down ninety-three specific incidents involving sadistic brutality, murder, cold-blooded killing, sexual cruelty, and related sadism. . . . We encountered seven different kinds of pistols and revolvers, three varieties of rifle, three distinct brands of shotgun, half a dozen assorted daggers and stilettos, two types of machete, one butcher's cleaver, a broadax, rapiers galore, a posse of sabers, an electric prodder, and a guillotine. Men (and women and even children) were shot by gunpowder, burned at the stake, tortured over live coals, trussed and beaten in relays, dropped into molten sugar, cut to ribbons (in color), repeatedly kneed in the groin, beaten while being held defenseless by other hoodlums, forcibly drowned, whipped with a leather belt.

Commas (continued) (p. 174)

EXERCISE 1

1. Yes, Gregg,
2. evening, however,
3. wait, therefore,
4.
5. it,
6. wish, Filipe,
7. Surfing, however, won't . . . degree,
8. television,
9. Well, . . . do, I guess,
10. Yes,

EXERCISE 2

1. who, I understand,
2. Maturity, the lecturer explained,
3. is, as a rule,
4. person, on the other hand,
5. people, therefore,
6. said, furthermore,
7. disagreement, he said,
8. mature, he said,
9. unimportant, the lecturer continued,
10. relationships, it seems,

EXERCISE 3

1.
2. car, which . . . ago,
3. cottage,
4.
5. Stock, the . . . Symphony,
6. *Summer*, a novel . . . Heinlein,
7. games, which . . . civilization,
8. tug-of-war, which we think of as modern,
9. games, however,
10. ancients, moreover,

EXERCISE 4

1. Avalanches, I thought,
2. Now, however,
3.
4.
5. avalanches,
6. patrollers, who . . . jackets,
7.
8. today, undoubtedly,
9.
10. Switzerland, for example, in . . . 1950–51, which . . . times,

EXERCISE 5

1.
2. skin, however,
3. skin, on the other hand,
4. toad, which . . . land,
5. tongue, which . . . sticky,
6.
7. song, which . . . females,
8. eggs,
9. tadpoles,
10. toads,

EXERCISE 6

1. write, some people say,
2. should, some think,
3. us, however,
4. can, in fact,
5.
6. drill, we are told,
7. test, which . . . computer,
8. necessary, it seems clear,
9. more, undoubtedly,
10.

EXERCISE 7

1. cobbler, which . . . make,
2. pie, on the other hand,
3. prepare, I have found,
4. kitchen, as you can see,
5. homes, it seems to me,
6. lesson, I think, from the Japanese,
7. picture,
8. are, as a rule,
9. ways, however,
10. long, I fear,

EXERCISE 8

1. Leakey, wife . . . Leakey,
2. Laetoli, a remote . . . Tanzania,
3. Gorge, 25 miles . . . north,
4. Now, however,
5.
6. footprint, according . . . dating,
7. man,
8.
9. skeleton, which . . . song,
10.

EXERCISE 9

1. shocked, quite naturally,
2. frightening, according to the environmentalists,
3. waste, according . . . Agency,
4. companies, of course,
5. wastes, regardless . . . potency,
6. rest, which . . . fields,
7. are, according . . . Council,
8. these, it is estimated,
9.
10. years,

Review of the Comma (p. 179)

1. When it comes to eating,
2. The United States needs to add order to liberty,
3. She cried when she lost her contact lens,
4. Professor Gonzalez, whom I've known for four years,
5. The earliest parking meters ever installed were those put in the business district of Oklahoma City, Oklahoma, on July 19,
6. While I was watching a pretty face at the curb, the light turned green,
7. Yes, I'd like to go with you, Melanie,
8. After mending Julie's mitten, finding lunch money for Tim, and locating a lost workbook,
9.
10.
11. Some experiments have been conducted with chimpanzees,
12. A chimpanzee can aim a ball at a target almost as well as a person can,
13. If the first few shots are unsuccessful,
14. The chimpanzee, however,
15. If the aiming tests are made too difficult,

Quotation Marks (p. 181)

The italicized titles below would, of course, be underlined in writing or typing.

EXERCISE 1

1. "A college education is one of the few things a person is willing to pay for and not get," said William Lowe Bryan, former president of Indiana University.
2. "Americans have more timesaving devices and less time than any other group of people in the world," wrote Duncan Caldwell.
3. "If all misfortunes were laid in a common heap," said Socrates, "whence everyone must take an equal portion, most people would be content to take their own and depart."
4.
5. "I have been brought up to believe that how I see myself is more important than how others see me," said Anwar Sadat.
6. Speaking of his life of unceasing effort, the great pianist Paderewski said, "Before I was a master, I was a slave."
7. "An excellent plumber is infinitely more admirable than an incompetent philosopher," says John Gardner.
8.
9. "The secret of happiness is not in doing what one likes," said James M. Barrie, "but in liking what one has to do."
10.

EXERCISE 2

1. In an art gallery a man said to his wife, "I know what that artist is trying to say. He's trying to say he can't paint worth a damn!"
2. "The important thing in life is not the person one loves. It is the fact that one loves," said Marcel Proust in his novel *Remembrance of Things Past*.
3. "A diplomat is someone who remembers a lady's birthday but forgets her age," said the speaker.
4. "By working faithfully eight hours a day," said Robert Frost, "you may eventually get to be a boss and work twelve hours a day."
5.
6. Alexander Woollcott said, "All the things I really like to do are either immoral, illegal, or fattening."
7. "More and more I came to value charity and love of one's fellow beings above everything else," said Albert Einstein.
8. "A man who uses a great many words to express his meaning is like a bad marksman who, instead of aiming a single stone at an object, takes up a handful and throws at it in hopes he may hit," said Samuel Johnson.
9. A Sioux Indian prayer says, "Great Spirit, help me never to judge another until I have walked in his moccasins for two weeks."

10. In describing the Taj Mahal, Rufus Jones said, "Only a few times in one's earthly life is one given to see absolute perfection."

EXERCISE 3

1. "What's the most important thing you've learned in this class?" Brenda asked.
2. "Learning to write a complete thesis statement," Alex said, "because it's going to help me in my writing for other courses."
3. "I know that's important," Brenda replied, "but it's not most important for me."
4. "What's most important for you?" Alex asked.
5. "My biggest improvement has been learning to write concisely. My papers used to be so wordy."
6. "That never was my problem," he said. "My biggest achievement besides learning about thesis statements is that I finally decided to learn to spell."
7. "And have you improved?"
8. "Tremendously," he said. "Now I just spell every other word wrong. I used to spell every word wrong."
9. "Come on! You're not that bad. I read one of your papers, and there wasn't a single misspelled word."
10. "I'm getting there," Alex said.

EXERCISE 4

1. "Do commas and periods go inside the quotation marks?" Alex asked.
2. "Of course," Brenda replied. "They'd look lost on the outside."
3. "I guess they would," he said.
4. "Is there anything more you want to know about punctuation?" she asked.
5. "What do you do if you want to quote a whole paragraph from a book?" he asked.
6. "If the quotation is more than five lines long, then you punctuate it differently from ordinary quotations," she said.
7. "How?" he asked.
8. "You indent the whole quotation five spaces, single-space it, and forget about the quotation marks," she said.
9. "I suppose that makes it stand out clearly as quoted material."
10. "Exactly," she said.

EXERCISE 5

1. "And what have you been doing with yourself?" Kevin wanted to know.
2. "Oh, I've been doing a lot of reading for one thing," Natalie said.
3. "Still learning new words?" Kevin asked.
4. "Sure, I'm always learning new words," Natalie said. "Yesterday I learned what *energize* means."

5. "And what does it mean?"
6. "Well, the root *erg* means a unit of energy or work, and *energize* means to give energy to. For example, some people find cold showers energizing," Natalie said.
7. "I prefer to get my energy some other way," Kevin said. "I suppose that same root *erg* is in *energy* and *energetic.*"
8. "Right. And it's also in *metallurgy*, which means working with metals. Another interesting word is *George*. *Geo* means earth, and *erg* means work. Therefore *George* is an earth worker or farmer."
9. "I never knew that before," Kevin said. "It really helps to know word roots."
10. "It helps me," Natalie replied.

EXERCISE 6
1.
2. The moment I get in the door, the children shout, "Are you going to read to us?"
3. "Don't I always?" I say.
4. I often begin with one of their favorite poems like "Jabberwocky."
5. And then I may read a book like *Mr. Popper's Penguins.*
6. *Curious George* is another of their favorite books.
7. When I try to stop, they shout, "More. Read some more."
8. "You have to get to sleep," I say.
9. "Read just one more poem," they beg.
10. I read them "The Swing" from Robert Louis Stevenson's book *A Child's Garden of Verses*, and then I say, "That's absolutely all for tonight."

EXERCISE 7
1. "I had three chairs in my house: one for solitude, two for friendship, and three for society," wrote Henry David Thoreau in his book *Walden.*
2. "Sometimes," wrote Thoreau, "as I drift idly on Walden Pond, I cease to live and begin to be."
3. "If a man does not keep pace with his companions," Thoreau said, "perhaps it is because he hears a different drummer."
4. Victor Hugo wrote, "The greatest happiness of life is the conviction that we are loved, loved for ourselves, or rather loved in spite of ourselves."
5. "No matter what happens," said Marcus Aurelius, "you can control the situation by your attitude."
6. "It's very hard to take yourself too seriously when you look at the world from outer space," said Astronaut Thomas E. Mattingly II.
7. "If I could choose one degree for the people I hire, it would be English," says a senior vice president of the First Atlanta Corporation. "I want people who can read and speak in the language we're dealing with."

8. "It's hard," said Bill Vaughan, "for the modern generation to understand Thoreau, who lived beside a pond but didn't own water skis or a snorkel."

9. "Subsidies for growing and promoting tobacco are maintained, but school health programs are slashed. Social benefits are denounced as handouts, but it is proposed to open up vast areas of public lands to developers in what may be the greatest giveaway in our history," said Norman Cousins.

10. "Birds sing after a storm," said Rose Kennedy. "Why shouldn't we?"

Capital Letters (p. 187)

EXERCISE 1

1. *Time, Newsweek*
2. City College
3. College
4.
5. European, English

6. English, Chemistry, Hall
7.
8. Pacific College
9. English, Professor
10. *Age of Fable*

EXERCISE 2

1. East
2.
3. Fifth Avenue
4.
5. Community College

6. University
7. Elks Hall
8. Senator
9. Dad
10. Uncle

EXERCISE 3

1.
2. *Civilisation*
3. History
4. English
5. Professor, English

6.
7.
8. University
9. Community College
10.

EXERCISE 4

1. Community College
2.
3.
4. "My Candle Burns at Both Ends"
5. Mom

6. Mom's
7. Labor Day, River
8.
9. Duck Lake
10. Fourth

EXERCISE 5

1. Memorial Day
2. South, Northwest
3. *Rand McNally World Atlas*
4. Second Avenue
5.

6.
7. Area College
8.
9. Arctic, Church
10. *Saga of the North*

EXERCISE 6

1. Dean, Club
2. English, German, Spanish
3. Western Michigan University
4. President Johnson
5. Don't

6. Aunt Jayne
7. Midwest, West Coast
8.
9. Dad
10.

EXERCISE 7

1. Institute of Technology
2.
3. Rocky Mountain National Park
4. Main, Third Avenue
5. Building
6. This
7. English, French
8. Valley College
9. *Cosmos*
10. Dad

EXERCISE 8

1.
2. Junior College, Community College
3.
4.
5. *Extinction*
6. "Should We Mourn the Dinosaurs?"
7. "What Are We Doing and What Can We Do?"
8.
9.
10. Dad, Uncle

Review of Punctuation and Capital Letters (p. 190)

EXERCISE 1

1.
2. When a dependent clause comes first in a sentence,
3. The proper use of commas, I've found,
4. Stop! I'll go with you. Can you wait until 5 P.M.?
5. . . . Texas, Franklin Pollard says, "We had three rooms and a path."
6. . . . Community College
7. . . . "The Lake Isle of Innisfree."
8. . . . University of Wisconsin in Madison,
9. Heiden, an 18-year-old,
10. I think, Dad,
11. . . . walkers. An adult roadrunner, which is only nine inches tall,
12. "Life lived at its best is full of daily forgivin' and forgettin',"
13. . . . world. Only
14. . . . developed. Much
15. Commas are like pounds. You either have too many or too few,

EXERCISE 2

1. A study has shown that children whose TV viewing was cut back to no more than one hour a day improved their grades in school and seemed happier. They played more with other children and increased their concentration in school. One child changed from a passive loner into a friendly playmate. Then when the study was concluded, . . .
2. A hundred years ago when Edison was working on his first tin horn phonograph, he wasn't even thinking about music. He just wanted to make a dictating machine. In fact it took almost a whole generation for musicians to get interested in recordings. Fortunately . . . .
3. An Assyrian stone tablet of about 2800 B.C. makes the following statements: "Our earth is degenerate in these latter days; bribery and corruption are common; children no longer obey their parents; the end of the world is evidently approaching."

EXERCISE 3

1. Yesterday I had my first solo flight at the Flying Club. It's an amazing feeling when your instructor tells you to go flying alone. Then after you take off, you look around and find you really are alone. At that point it's too late to change your mind. You've got to land by yourself sooner or later. It's a great sensation. It's . . . .
2. The federal budget speaks in terms of billions, but how much *is* a billion dollars? If a man stood over a big hole in the ground and dropped in a $20 bill every minute day and night, it . . . .
3. There have been six basic changes in the tools people write with since the cavemen used sharp stones to scratch pictures on their stone walls. First came the quill pen. Then came the lead pencil. Next came the fountain pen. In about 1870 came the first typewriter. By 1960 the electric typewriter was taking over. And now it's the word processor.

Proofreading Exercise 1 (p. 193)

THE BIG GRIN ON MY FACE

One afternoon I was driving my car when I ~~notice~~ *noticed* a pinging noise in my engine. In a few days the pinging grew to a thumping and then to a loud clunking that couldn't be ignored.

My knowledgeable friends broke the news to me that it was undoubtedly my main engine bearings, and in the same breath they mentioned sums like four or five hundred dollars. Being a poor student, I had only two alternatives—walk or fix it myself.

Necessity ~~force~~ *forced* me to ~~chose~~ *choose* the latter alternative, and I found myself up to my elbows in grease and grime for the next few days. With the help of a lot of free advice from friends, who claimed to be undiscovered mechanical geniuses, and the guidance of a library book on engines, I removed and disassembled the whole thing.

An engine is something I take for granted as long as it goes, and only when it fails, do I really appreciate how intricate and complicated it is. ~~Their~~ *There* are all kinds of odd-shaped, highly polished parts, each one for some function. My taking the engine apart was like a little boy fixing an alarm clock. ~~each~~ *Each* new piece was so interesting and so completely unfathomable.

Then when it was all in pieces, the reassembly with new parts began, along with the job of trying to remember where each nut and bolt belonged. This work was a lot slower and required more help, but it was encouraging to watch the motor grow with each new piece.

Finally it was all connected in the car and ready to be tested. It had taken weeks of late evenings of work, but now it was ready at last. My friends stood around offering final advice and checking to make sure I had remembered everything. I held my breath and turned the key—the engine started and turned, a little rough at first, but soon it ran smoothly.

"Eureka! I've done it!" I shouted.

I was ~~overwhelm~~ *overwhelmed* with a great feeling of accomplishment, and . . .

Comprehensive Test on Entire Text (p. 197)

1. We girls made the ~~deserts~~ *desserts* for the party. ~~everyone like~~ *Everyone liked* them.

2. The altos carried the melody. ~~the~~ *The* sopranos ~~sung~~ *sang* the accompaniment.

3. Joe Namath was a talented quarterback in high school. ~~his~~ *His* team won

   lots of championships.

4. When we got to the end of the detour, we ~~turn~~ *turned* south and then ~~West~~ *west*.

5. ~~Which~~ *It* turned out to be the wrong thing to do.

6. Each of her trophies ~~are~~ *is* displayed in ~~it's~~ *its* proper place on the shelf.

7. Working hard that semester, ~~my grades improved~~ *I improved my grades.*

8. I enjoy math, social studies, and gym, but I find chemistry and ~~english~~ *English*

   difficult.

9. Making the most of every opportunity that came her way, *she succeeded.*

10. He spends most of his time, however, reading comic books, and ~~you~~ *one*
    ~~cant~~ *can't* do that and get satisfactory grades.

11. I ~~cant~~ *can't* decide whether to get a job, take a trip, or ~~whether I should~~ just

    loaf this summer.

12. Yes, ~~personally~~ I think ~~Amys~~ *Amy's* costume is more striking than ~~Beverlys~~ *Beverly's*.

13. She took ~~to~~ *too* many ~~cloths~~ *clothes* along on her trip; party dresses, beachwear,

    and half a dozen other outfits.

14. Her mother and father send her to ~~a~~ *an* exclusive school, but she ~~dont~~ *doesn't*

    appreciate it.

15. Leroy ~~told~~ *said to* his father, ~~he was~~ *"I am* embarrassed by ~~his~~ *my* old car.*"*

16. ~~Their quiet~~ *They're quite* pleased with ~~there~~ *their* new car although it was ~~to~~ *too* expensive.

17. Kurt, you ~~was~~ *were* driving ~~to~~ *too* fast when we ~~past~~ *passed* that cop.

18. We ~~didnt~~ *didn't* like the amendment**;** furthermore we ~~refuse~~ *refused* to vote for it.

19. ~~James~~ *James'* invitation to my girlfriend and me came as a surprise.

20. Each of the leaves ~~are quite~~ *is* unique in ~~their~~ *its* vein patterns.

21. ~~Ive~~ *I've* been wondering about you and hoping for a letter.

22. She memorized Masefield's poem **"**Sea Fever**"** from his book <u>Salt Water</u>

    <u>Ballads</u>.

23. John Masefield**,** who became poet laureate of England**,** was born on

    June 1**,** 1878**,** in Ledbury**,** Herefordshire**,** England.

24. **"**Life's always a struggle**.** *If* ~~if~~ anything's easy**,** it's not likely to be worth-

    while**," ,**said Hubert Humphrey.

25. **"**When you get to the end of your rope**,"** said Franklin D. Roosevelt**," ,**tie a

    knot and hang on.**"**

26. If I had known you ~~was~~ *were* coming**,** I would ~~of~~ *have* prepared a special meal.

27. Last week they ~~develop~~ *developed* a plan**,** and then they ~~proceed~~ *proceeded* to carry it out.

28. He decided to join Fritz and me on the golf course.

29. ~~There~~ *Their* house is in a better location than ~~our's~~ *ours*.

30. When you wind up a watch**,** you start it**;** when you wind up a speech**,**

    you end it.

Writing

EXERCISE 1 (p. 202)

1. Painting a room
Preparation for painting a room
New tools to help you paint a room
2. Baking is my hobby
Baking a birthday cake
Decorating a birthday cake
3. Buying a car
Buying a used car
Things to check in buying a used pickup
4. Camping out
Equipment for camping out
Buying the right sleeping bag
5. My trip to Washington, D.C.
The National Air and Space Museum
The Wright brothers' first plane
6. Growing your own vegetables
Growing tomatoes
Starting tomato plants
7. My German heritage
My German grandfather
My grandfather's famous expressions
8. Dancing for fun
Learning break dancing
Mastering the back spin
9. Saving our forests
Saying NO to developers in our county
Saying NO to developers near the state park in our county

EXERCISE 2 (p. 208)

1. topic	6. topic	11. thesis
2. thesis	7. thesis	12. thesis
3. fact	8. thesis	13. fact
4. topic	9. fact	14. thesis
5. topic	10. topic	

EXERCISE 3 (p. 208)

1. Choosing the right skates is important for figure skating.
3. The effects of the Alaska pipeline have not all been good.
4. The Rock and Mineral Show lets collectors gain knowledge and exchange specimens.
5. My summer vacation in Montana taught me three things about camping.
6. Teaching my six-year-old to ride a bike was a summer's job.
9. Insulating our house had many benefits.

10. It's easy to make a good pizza.
13. Practicing six hours a day enabled me to play in an orchestra.

EXERCISE 4 (p. 209)
I've decided to change my major to computer science.
1. There will probably be more jobs available in computer science.
2. A knowledge of computers is required in almost every field.
3. I'll be able to use my math skills.

Acid rain is harming the country in many ways.
1. It's killing evergreen trees in many areas.
2. It's killing the fish and amphibians in lakes.
3. It's hurting farm crops.
4. It's eroding buildings and monuments.
5. It's causing bad relations with Canada because half the acid rain falling in eastern Canada originates in the United States.

I'm doing three things to improve my study habits.
1. I'm listing each day the things I must do.
2. I'm studying in the library where it's quiet.
3. I'm not quitting until my work is finished each night.

EXERCISE 5 (p. 214)
These answers should be marked S: 1, 2, 3, 5, 6, 8, 9.

EXERCISE 6 (p. 221)
First of all,
Also, *or* Then too,
Also, *or* Then too,
Furthermore,
As for me,
Finally,

Summary of "The Jeaning of America— and the World" (p. 221)

An American symbol of equality now spreading throughout the world is a simple pair of pants called blue jeans. In 1850 Levi Strauss, a Bavarian-born Jew, made the first pair for a miner in San Francisco. Their popularity grew, but one miner complained that the pockets tore. As a joke, his pockets were riveted by a blacksmith, and jeans have had rivets ever since. They can be purchased preshrunk and prefaded for the proletarian look and are sold not only to working people but to all classes. Levi Strauss & Co., now in 35 countries, sells 83,000,000 jeans a year.

Index